POETRY MATTERS

CONTEMPORARY NORTH AMERICAN POETRY SERIES

Series Editors Alan Golding, Lynn Keller, and Adalaide Morris

Poetry Matters

Neoliberalism, Affect, and the Posthuman in Twenty-First-Century North American Feminist Poetics

BY HEATHER MILNE

University of Iowa Press, Iowa City

University of Iowa Press, Iowa City 52242
Copyright © 2018 by the University of Iowa Press
www.uipress.uiowa.edu
Printed in the United States of America

The University of Iowa Press is a member of Green Press
Initiative and is committed to preserving natural resources.

Printed on acid-free paper
Library of Congress Cataloging-in-Publication Data
Names: Milne, Heather, 1973– author.
Title: Poetry matters : neoliberalism, affect, and the posthuman in
twenty-first century North American feminist poetics / by Heather Milne.
Description: Iowa City : University of Iowa Press, [2018] | Series:
Contemporary North American poetry | Includes bibliographical references
and index.
Identifiers: LCCN 2017042815 (print) | ISBN 978-1-60938-577-4 (pbk) |
ISBN 978-1-60938-578-1 (ebk)
Subjects: LCSH: American poetry—Women authors—History and criticism. |
Canadian poetry—Women authors—History and criticism. | American
poetry—21st century—History and criticism. | Canadian poetry—
21st century—History and criticism. | Feminism in literature. |
Poetics—History—21st century. | Women and literature—United States. |
Women and literature—Canada. | BISAC: LITERARY CRITICISM / Poetry. |
LITERARY CRITICISM / Canadian. | LITERARY CRITICISM / Feminist.
Classification: LCC PS151 (ebook) | LCC PS151 .M49 2018 (print) |
DDC 811/.6099287—dc23
LC record available at https://lccn.loc.gov/2017042815

CONTENTS

ACKNOWLEDGMENTS

I WOULD LIKE TO THANK the poets whose work I discuss in this book: Jen Benka, Dionne Brand, Margaret Christakos, Marcella Durand, Larissa Lai, Yedda Morrison, Jena Osman, Claudia Rankine, Evelyn Reilly, Nikki Reimer, Jennifer Scappettone, Juliana Spahr, Rita Wong, and Rachel Zolf. It has been an honor and a privilege to work with your words. Thank you also to the small presses that publish this writing.

I am lucky to have wonderful colleagues at the University of Winnipeg both in the English Department and across the university who have supported this project both directly and indirectly. Thanks in particular to Andrew Burke, Brandon Christopher, Bruno Cornellier, Roewan Crowe, Paul DePasquale, Angela Failler, Fiona Green, Naomi Hamer, Catherine Hunter, Peter Ives, Peter Melville, Kathryn Ready, Candida Rifkind, Heather Snell, Margaret Sweatman, Catherine Taylor, Kathleen Venema, Jenny Wills, and Doris Wolf.

Thanks also to colleagues across the country and beyond whose insights have shaped this book: Jeff Derksen, Kit Dobson, Smaro Kamboureli, Susan Knutson, Sonnet L'Abbé, Tanis MacDonald, Anne Quéma, Susan Rudy, Trish Salah, and Erin Wunker. Some of the initial ideas in this book germinated from conversations with Elena Basile, Kate Eichhorn, and Christine Kim that took place many years ago when we were graduate students at York University; I am grateful to all three of them. Thanks also to Elena Basile for being a cherished friend and interlocutor and for providing helpful comments on an early draft of this manuscript. I am grateful to Melanie Dennis Unrau, Colin Smith, Erin Wunker, and Rachel Zolf for crucial conversations about poetics during the writing of this book. Thanks to Lauren Bosc for her careful attention in formatting the manuscript and to Paul Mendelson for his meticulous copy editing. Several research assistants offered crucial help at various states: Melanie Dennis Unrau, Devon Kerslake, Jessica Jacobson-Konefall, Nicole Necsefor, and Lindsay Brown. I am also grateful to Jaye Miles for helping me reach a place where I could believe in myself and in this project. The two anonymous readers of an earlier draft of this book engaged carefully and critically with this project and offered instrumental advice for reframing some of my arguments in ways that have considerably strengthened this book. Thanks to Dee Morris for her support throughout the writing and editing of this book. Thanks also to Lynn Keller and Alan Golding, as well as Jim McCoy at the University of Iowa Press. I would like to express my gratitude to the Social Sciences and Humanities Research Council of Canada and the University of Winnipeg for crucial research funding.

This book is dedicated to my mentor, the late Barbara Godard. There were many occasions during the writing of this book when I wished I could call up Barbara to ask a question or seek advice. Her knowledge of feminist poetics, literary theory, and Canadian literature was capacious. Barbara died in 2010 and she left an absence that can never be filled, but her legacy lives on in her writing, her translations, and in the work of the many students she inspired.

Thanks to my family, and especially my partner, Luanne Karn, for helping me realize (through much patience and persistence on her part) the value of downtime, and my daughter, Anna Milne-Karn, who is always up for a spontaneous dance party.

Feminist Poetics as Cultural Critique, or, Why Poetry Matters

THE EARLY YEARS OF THE twenty-first century have been marked by significant technological, scientific, economic, and geopolitical changes. Technological advancements have led to dramatic increases in the sheer volume of information available and the speed at which we can access that information and have radically transformed the ways in which we read, write, and communicate. Developments in scientific research involving genetic modification raise questions about the relationship between human animals, nonhuman animals, and machines, fundamentally challenging our understanding of what counts as human. These changes have occurred in conjunction with the development of an increasingly complex and precariously leveraged capitalist economic system, coupled with deregulation and privatization. The middle class has shrunk, youth unemployment is high, and disparities between rich and poor have grown in many parts of the world, including North America. At the same time, the national economies of countries like China, India, and Bangladesh have grown significantly as Western corporations have outsourced jobs to nations where wages are lower and where workers toil in unsafe conditions to manufacture goods and provide services for Western consumers. The events of 9/11 and, more recently, the emergence of terrorist organizations like ISIS have ushered in a new era of widespread anxiety over terrorism and security, military interventions in the Middle East by U.S. and allied forces, the suspension of civil liberties, and the intensification of biopolitical modes of surveillance and control. Meanwhile, environmental devastation brought about by oil spills, strip mining, hydraulic fracturing, and industrial runoff suggests that the activities of advanced capitalism are wreaking havoc on ecosystems.

These conditions form the social and political context in which the poetry I examine in this volume is written. This project explores poetry by women from the United States and Canada that documents the social and political turmoil of the early twenty-first century. This book also seeks to map the connections among gender, poetry, and contemporary politics by placing feminist poetics in dialogue with recent theoretical work on neoliberalism, new materialism, affect, and the posthuman.

In spite of references to the twenty-first century as a "post-feminist" era (Hall and Rodriguez 2003, 878) in which structural equality between the sexes has been achieved, women still earn less than men, gender-based forms of sexual violence against women continue to be commonplace around the world, and repeated attempts by conservative politicians to reopen debates regarding abortion suggest that the right to bodily self-determination for women remains tenuous and cannot be taken for granted. As Athena Athanasiou observes, the "current regimes of power," which she summarizes under the heading of "neoliberalism," function "not just as a mode of economic management and corporate governance" but as a

> matrix of intelligibility that . . . has everything to do with questions of racism, sexism, homophobia, heteronormativity, ableism, and familialism, all those questions that have been historically discounted as irrelevant to "real" politics. The capitalism of our times has everything to do with the biopolitics of social Darwinism—with all its implications of race, gender, sexuality, class, and ability—inherent in neoliberal governmentality. (Athanasiou and Butler 2013, 40–41)

Biopolitics, she goes on to argue is "at the heart of the logics, fantasies, and technologies that engender the political and moral economies of our late liberal times" (2013, 41). Those marginalized on the bases of sexuality, gender, ability, race, and class often find themselves especially vulnerable to the conditions of precarity that have emerged under neoliberalism.

Activists and cultural critics are striving to find vocabularies and effective modes of political resistance through which to make sense of the social and cultural impacts of these rapid and significant changes. Grassroots protest movements such as Black Lives Matter, the Indigenous-led Idle No More movement, protests in Canada and the United States in opposition to the construction of pipelines, the Occupy Movement, the Quebec student strike, protests in Europe in opposition to the austerity movement, the Arab Spring, the Toronto G20 protests, and the Gezi Park protests in Turkey suggest a widespread groundswell of unrest in recent years. These protests, while diverse in their aims, are unified by a shared opposition to precarity, neoliberalism, and biopolitical regimes of governance (Athanasiou and Butler 2013, 162–63); most are youth-led; and in most cases, these demonstrations have been countered by violent crackdowns by police, military, and other agents of state security. I evoke these protest movements not because I aim to analyze them in great detail, but because they comprise the political, social, and historical context in which my analysis of contemporary innovative feminist poetics will unfold.

Contemporary poets have been participating in and documenting protest movements as well as the political, social, environmental, and economic crises and conditions that have prompted people to gather in the streets in protest. In the early years of the twenty-first century, a poetics of dissent emerged in opposition to the military invasion and occupation of Iraq. In 2003, Sam Hammill formed a group called Poets Against the War in response to Laura Bush's decision to cancel a poetry event at the White House for fear that it might be political. Hammill issued a call for antiwar poems and received 13,000 responses, and as a direct response to Hammill's call, hundreds of poetry readings were held across the United States in opposition to the invasion of Iraq. As Nicky Marsh has argued, Poets Against the War "allowed poetry to appear a vital, democratic force at a moment when such possibilities appeared to be waning" (Marsh 2007a, 1). A flurry of antiwar poetry anthologies was published in the United States and Canada between 2003 and 2005 (Derksen 2009, 57). These movements position poetry as a dynamic space for dissent but also evoke the legacy of 1960s anti-Vietnam War poetry and "the faltering of this earlier movement's promise to radically renew democratic culture" (Marsh 2007a, 1). While the antiwar poetry of the 1960s and early 1970s may have faltered, the writers involved in Poets Against the War have not retreated from their engagement with public culture. Rather, a poetics of dissent has gathered momentum and expanded to address a wide range of pressing political and social issues. A group that called itself "Poets Occupy Wall Street" formed soon after the occupation of Zuccotti Park began in fall 2011. The culture of reading and writing was central to the Occupy movement; a lending library was soon established on the protest site, and the *Occupy Wall Street Poetry Anthology* was posted online and updated on a weekly basis as more contributors submitted poems for inclusion. The 887-page anthology is available for free as a PDF on the People's Library website.[1] Several poets involved with the Occupy movement have begun to publish collections that take up Occupy as a central focus. Betsy Fagin, the librarian for the People's Library of Occupy Wall Street, published a book of poetry that addresses the Occupy Movement called *All Is Not Yet Lost* (2015), and Juliana Spahr's *That Winter the Wolf Came* (2015b) is set against the backdrop of Occupy Oakland.

Activist poets have utilized the Internet as a strategic tool for publishing and disseminating poetry effectively and inexpensively and establishing communities of writers engaged in political activism. Amy King's Poets for Living Waters, a project created in response to the BP oil spill (2010), and the Enpipe Collective's *Enpipe Line: 70,000+ Kilometers of Poetry Written in Resistance to the Enbridge Northern Gateway Pipeline Proposal* (2012) are two recent examples of activist-driven, collaborative protest poetics. Poets are making use of social media to circulate poems written from the front lines of protests and demonstrations: Rita Wong's "#J28," a poem about participating in the Idle No More movement's practice of enacting round dances in public spaces as a form of anticolonial protest, was first published on Occupy Love's Facebook page. While the lasting effect of these poetic protest movements remains to be seen, their proliferation and energy make clear the fact that poetry has emerged in recent years as a dynamic space of political engagement. While most of the poetry I write about here has been published in print rather than digital form, it shares an oppositional energy and politics of dissent that I argue more broadly characterize contemporary activist poetry and poetics.

This study builds on Lynn Keller's assertion in *Thinking Poetry: Readings in Contemporary Women's Exploratory Poetics* that in the political context of the early twenty-first century, now more then ever, complex writing is important and its "opacities are not gratuitous" (2010, 2). I am wary of employing what Jeff Derksen refers to as "genre essentialism" to claim that poetry inhabits a privileged position as a "vehicle for national and transnational structures of feeling" (2009, 71). My point is not to claim that poetry holds the potential to facilitate a revolution or that it does a better job than other genres of raising social awareness and articulating critique. However, I do maintain that much innovative and avant-garde poetry is deeply engaged with the pressing social, economic, and geopolitical issues of our time and that its potential as a site of political engagement and protest warrants examination. As Juliana Spahr argues, poetry cannot necessarily reshape oppressive structures, but like the Greek riot dog that barked at the police during the anti-austerity protests in Athens, it can accompany you into the street. Politics, she argues, enters and reshapes literary practices in productive ways; the poem may not enter the street but the street might enter the poem, galvanizing it with a political energy or charge (Spahr 2015a). I read poetry as engaged in dialogue with theoretical discourses and activist modes of dissent, and I contend that poetry can advance complex forms of critique not just at the level of content, but also through its form and compositional strategy.

The title *Poetry Matters* makes a claim for poetry's continued relevance in the early twenty-first century; poetry does indeed matter, but "matter" in this case also refers to the materiality of language, of bodies, and of the physical world of objects, ecosystems, and geographies, themes that unify much of the poetry discussed in these pages. This poetry is characterized by an embracing of materialist poetics coupled with procedural and conceptual compositional methods, leading somewhat paradoxically to poems that are socially and materially situated yet not always referential in the way they convey meaning. Many of these writers work with found text, choosing to modify existing writing in addition to—and sometimes instead of—composing from scratch. They challenge the stability of the lyric "I" and the myth of the autonomous artist through their use of found material, fragmentation, procedure, constraints, and multivocality. While these political and aesthetic concerns are consistent with aspects of contemporary conceptual and innovative poetries in general and with the politics and aesthetics of language poetry, feminist writers have developed a poetics that advances and explores a politicized inquiry into the specific effects of contemporary politics on female subjectivity.

In *What Stirs* (2008), Margaret Christakos uses found language extracted from Google searches in order to build poems that use the breast-feeding latch as an overarching metaphor through which to explore the affective dynamics of attachment and alienation in the context of what Jodi Dean calls "communicative capitalism" (2011a, 2). Rachel Zolf relies on online search engines to compose the poems in *Human Resources* (2007), and builds these poems largely out of found material gleaned from websites, corporate communications, e-mails, PowerPoint presentations, literary and philosophical writings, and other found texts. Implicit in Zolf's strategy of recycling or redirecting language is a questioning of outworn notions of poetic genius and inspiration and the humanist and masculinist underpinnings of the lyric subject, while at the same time, this poetry also reflects a generalized anxiety regarding the unprecedented mass of information available in the context of the Internet and the 24-hour news channel. Brian Reed suggests that the turn toward "redirected language" in contemporary poetry tells us something "quite profound" about subjectivity in our historical moment, since the human subject cannot fully distinguish herself from the information she takes in (2011, 760). In a similar vein, Kenneth Goldsmith has named this kind of poetry "uncreative writing" (2011); faced with an unprecedented amount of available text in our contemporary moment, many writers negotiate this excess not by creating more text but by manipulating what already exists, doing so with both aesthetic and political intent. Much of the poetry written in opposition to the Iraq War uses found materials gathered from mainstream media reports. Dionne Brand's *Inventory* (2006) and Juliana Spahr's *This Connection of Everyone with Lungs* (2005) rely heavily on language taken directly from the media, enacting a poetics of resistance through recontextualization.

Recycling found discursive materials might also be read in relation to the strong environmental ethic underscoring much of this writing; many writers repurpose and recycle language as one might repurpose and recycle objects. Evelyn Reilly's *Styrofoam* (2009), a book of poems about a ubiquitous and virtually indestructible material that is sublime in its magnitude, draws on Google searches and websites devoted to the topic of recycling household waste into useable items; scientific discourses exploring thermoplastics, the molecular composition of Styrofoam, and carcinogens; and language gleaned from literature, philosophy, and film to create a politically, theoretically, poetically, and scientifically grounded meditation on the sheer volume of waste produced by humans in the anthropocene. Yedda Morrison's *Darkness* (2012a) erases all words related to human agency from Joseph Conrad's novel *Heart of Darkness* to create a sparse but powerful poetic commentary on imperialism and resource extraction. Morrison also explores the productive potential of displacing the human as a central frame of reference, a tactic also used by Rita Wong in *undercurrent* (2015) and Marcella Durand in "The Anatomy of Oil" (2008).

Redirecting and recycling found language functions not only to illuminate the complexities of the political present, but also as a means to excavate the past and explore ongoing legacies of violence, domination, and inequality. In *Janey's Arcadia* (2014), Rachel Zolf pillages several settler-colonial texts about the colonization of the Canadian Northwest, combining this material with police reports about missing and murdered Indigenous women in and around the city of Winnipeg and with contemporary news articles to develop a book of poems that excavates the gendered and colonial violence underscoring nation-building and considers the ongoing legacies of that violence. Jena Osman's *Corporate Relations* (2014) is written using language borrowed from U.S. Supreme Court rulings on corporate personhood; Osman uses poetic form to reflect critically on the legal status of personhood and to ask ethical and philosophical questions about who or what is entitled to protection under the law in the contemporary capitalist state.

Some of this work could be classified as conceptual writing on account of its appropriation of found material and its reliance on procedural and constraint-based compositional strategies. Indeed, many of the writers examined in this study are included in the recent anthology *I'll Drown My Book: Conceptual Writing by Women,* although several are ambivalent about being aligned with conceptualism. In her poetic statement in *I'll Drown My Book,* Zolf explains her reluctant and partial affiliation with conceptual writing: "Normally I'd never want to be part of a group that would have me as a member, but on reflection . . . I do see resonances with my practice. . . . So, while I haven't been attracted to the structuralist statements of a certain spokesman for the Conceptual Writing Phenomenon . . . one could say ragpicker Zolf thinks in excessive correspondences and practices an impure post-conceptualism" (2012, 440). The poets discussed in *Poetry Matters* are conceptually oriented—to borrow and modify Megan Simpson's characterizing of a slightly earlier generation of innovative feminist poets as "language-oriented" (2000, ix)—but they have varying degrees of affiliation with the conceptual poetry movement, and some do not identify with it at all.

Conceptual poetry has come under criticism in recent years due to its perceived racism, a fact that has made many politicized writers reluctant to identify with conceptual poetry as an aesthetic or poetic movement or school. A group called the "Mongrel Coalition Against Gringpo" ("Gringpo" is a hybridization of "poetics" and "gringo") has taken to social media to launch a very vocal and visible critique of conceptual poetry. In particular, the Mongrel Coalition objects to Kenneth Goldsmith's controversial performance in which he appropriated Michael Brown's autopsy report and read it aloud as a piece of conceptual writing at a conference at Brown University, and to Vanessa Place's "Miss Scarlett," which is comprised of lines spoken by the character Prissy in Margaret Mitchell's *Gone with the Wind,* as well as Place's related conceptual project of tweeting *Gone with the Wind* in its entirety. Goldsmith and Place's projects have prompted important critiques of the whiteness of conceptual poetry and measured reflections on the ethical and political responsibilities, as well as the problematic limitations, of appropriative and redirected writing. Joey De Jesus calls Goldsmith's performance "an appropriation of black suffering under the waving standard of 'conceptualism'" (2015). Elena Gomez states that conceptual poetry is not inherently racist, but that "insofar as it is a movement and genre with apparent gatekeepers, it is racist" and that the practices of conceptual poets "should be the blank terrain upon which any interested poet is free to play and experiment. Non-white writers such as Cecilia Vicuña or Kamau Brathwaite would possibly be far more widely known if not for those structurally white spaces" (2015). Following Gomez, I assert that while the conceptual projects of Goldsmith and Place point to a troubling inattention to political and ethical responsibility and an institutionalized racism that warrants serious critique, the *techniques* employed by these writers are not necessarily problematic. In fact, techniques of appropriation, constraint, and documentation are at the heart of some of the most politicized and ethical (what Joan Retallack calls "poethical" [2003]) texts of the twenty-first century. It is possible, as writers like Yedda Morrison, Harryette Mullen, Jena Osman, M. NourbeSe Philip,[2] Rita Wong, and Rachel Zolf demonstrate in their work, to deploy proceduralism and constraint-based techniques to create powerfully poethical poetry.[3]

I frame this body of writing as "feminist" even though gender is not, in most cases, its sole or even primary referent. While the themes of women's oppression and the struggle for autonomy are present in most of the writing explored here, contemporary innovative writing by both American and Canadian women exemplifies what Rosi Braidotti refers to as "an opening outwards of the process of redefining female subjectivity . . . that calls for a broadening of the traditional feminist political agenda to include, as well as the issue of women's social rights, a larger spectrum of options which range from cultural concerns related to writing and creativity, to issues which at first sight seem to have nothing to do specifically with women" (2002, 83). Such concerns include, but are not limited to, the environment, globalization, war, neoliberalism, advanced capitalism and precarity, as well as concerns more specifically related to the politics of gender such as queerness, bodily autonomy, and gender-based oppression. As Chandra Talpade Mohanty argues, "imperialism, militarization, and globalization all traffic in women's bodies, women's labor, and ideologies of masculinity/femininity, heteronormativity, racism, and nationalism to consolidate and reproduce power and domination" (2006, 9).

At least a third of the poets discussed in this book are queer-identified,[4] and I draw on queer theory as well as feminist theory in my reading of innovative poetics. Theorists like Sara Ahmed and Lauren Berlant, both of whom work at the interstices of queer studies and feminist studies, are vital to my thinking on feminist poetics, particularly in the later chapters of this book. Feminist and queer thinkers share an awareness of the ways in which language can challenge heteronormative and heteropatriarchal structures, and are especially attuned to issues like biopolitics and bodily self-determination, the importance of collective oppositional forms of struggle, and the fact that the personal cannot be separated from the political. These are concepts central to feminism as well as to struggles for queer rights and trans rights.

One of the central goals of this study is to set feminist poetics in dialogue with recent strands of feminist theory and philosophy. I read feminist poetics in relation to writings on neoliberalism and capitalism by Wendy Brown, Jodi Dean, and Nancy Fraser. I also draw extensively on new materialist and posthumanist theoretical frameworks developed by Stacy Alaimo, Karen Barad, Jane Bennett, and Rosi Braidotti; these frameworks offer vital models for challenging the colonialist, masculinist, and anthropocentric legacies of humanism and conceptualizing subjectivity, biopolitics, and political action at a time when science and technology are not only altering our environments but also changing the very notion of the human. The "affective turn" that has come to characterize much recent work in feminist and queer studies offers a productive framework for thinking about what Sara Ahmed calls the "cultural politics of emotion" (2004). Ahmed's work on emotion, along with Sianne Ngai's theorizing on "ugly feelings" (2005), Lauren Berlant's concept of "cruel optimism" (2011), and Ann Cvetkovich's understanding of depression as a "public feeling" (2012) offer useful frameworks for forging links between the domains of affect and cultural politics. Finally, Judith Butler's work on precarious lives and grievability in the aftermath of 9/11 (2004) provides a vital framework for reading post-9/11 poetics.

While these theorists frequently turn to film, news media, art, popular culture, fiction, and philosophy for examples through which to make sense of the shifts that have come to characterize the political landscape of the early twenty-first century, they rarely turn to poetry. One of the central claims of this book is that contemporary feminist experimental and innovative poetry constitutes an active and critical yet underexamined site of engagement with many of the defining economic, political, and ecological factors of the early twenty-first century. While poetry scholars like Jeff Derksen have explored how "poetry and art have driven a critique of neoliberalism" (Derksen 2009, 14), they have yet to explore the rich and complex critical engagements of contemporary innovative feminist poetics with the neoliberal and post-human economies of the twenty-first century.

My conviction that poetry functions as a site of theorizing intersects with Megan Simpson's understanding of poetry as a mode of knowing. In *Poetic Epistemologies*, Simpson argues that "language oriented" writing by women foregrounds the processes of language in order to "explore the relations among knowledge, language and gender, thus (re)writing art with philosophy, and both with social critique" (2000, ix). Innovative poetry, she argues, can make thinking visible, and by extension, can make social and political engagement visible. Like Simpson, I aim to posit "writing as a mode of knowing that continually interrogates its own methods and processes rather than a means to arrive at final conclusions" (Simpson 2000, 8). While Simpson is careful to present innovative feminist writing as wary of truth claims and as reluctant to distinguish between real and false knowledge, arguing that it "posits all knowledge as socially situated and discursively constructed" (10), my own thinking on the relationship between poetry and truth diverges from Simpson's because the current political circumstances in which notions of truth do or do not circulate is different now than it was at the turn of the millennium. In the years following 9/11, the American government made the false claim that the Iraqi government possessed weapons of mass destruction in order to justify its military invasion of Iraq. The government of former Canadian Prime Minister Stephen Harper drastically reduced the budgets for national archives and libraries, reducing public access to national records and making it virtually impossible for archives and libraries to retain their holdings; his government also muzzled scientists conducting research on climate change. More recently, Donald Trump seemed willing to say almost anything in his bid for the presidency, and his political campaign was buoyed by social media platforms that propagated hoaxes and misinformation; Trump's senior advisor Kellyanne Conway has reframed misinformation coming from the White House as "alternative facts." Many media pundits are now claiming that we live in an era of post-truth, and Oxford Dictionaries named "post-truth" their word of the year for 2016. In such a climate, the desire to locate the "truth" is arguably more urgent than it was at the end of the twentieth century. When Juliana Spahr ruminates on the fact that the warships fueling up in Hawaii on their way to the Persian Gulf are not mentioned in the media in *This Connection of Everyone with Lungs* (2005), or when Rachel Zolf seeks to wake people up from the foreclosures of their knowledge with regard to settler colonialism (2016), they seek the truth in a context where truths are often deliberately obscured, misrepresented, or ignored by those in positions of social and legislative power.

In its engagement with theory and politics, the poetry I explore inherits elements of language poetry, but while language poetry was primarily in dialogue with Marxist and post-structuralist frameworks (Greer 1989, 244), the poetry examined in this volume is primarily in dialogue with affect theory, critiques of neoliberalism, and articulations of posthuman feminist subjectivity. Rather than using theory to illuminate poetry, I seek to place poetry and theory in dialogue, a move that reveals what Sianne Ngai calls their "parallel and concurrent trajectories" and shared conceptual attunement (2005, 307). In a discussion of the connections between language poetry and post-structuralist theory, Ngai notes:

> Both practices share a basic commitment to the idea of "textual politics" and to the critique of liberal humanism; both emphasize and privilege difference over self-sameness and internal consistency, multiplicity over univocality, flux over stability, and ambiguity and slippage over rigid correspondences between words and meanings. Each would *seem* to be the other's "uniquely proper object." (Ngai 2005, 308)

Ngai goes on to caution, however, that placing these two practices in dialogue risks redundancy because their fit is "too close" (309). The belatedness becomes most acute when critics in the present read language writing from the 1970s and 1980s through the lens of post-structuralist theory that was written contemporaneously. Redundancy, Ngai implies, is not located in the poetry itself, but in the temporal lag that makes the poetry seem redundant in retrospect in spite of the fact that language poetry's exploration of polysemy and slippage occurred in tandem with post-structuralist theory, not as an offshoot, imitation, or application of post-structuralism. I seek to avoid, as much as possible, a lag between production and critical reception, and I look instead at how poetry and theory, placed in dialogue, ask crucial ethical and political questions that help us make sense of current geopolitics, economics, and environmental destruction and their effects on gendered, raced, and sexualized subjects. While the poets discussed in these pages are not language writers, they have inherited some of the formal, conceptual, and theoretical legacies of language writing, and many have strong affinities with language writing even if their theoretical and political investments move beyond Marxist-inflected engagements with historical agency and post-stucturalist engagements with the construction of subjectivity. I am most interested in how this body of poetry intervenes in and extends discussions about specific features of twenty-first-century cultural politics and geopolitics. The fit between contemporary innovative feminist poetics and contemporary theorizing is indeed close, but the breadth afforded by the range of political and theoretical issues with which the work engages negates tautology and redundancy and opens multiple productive conversations.

Although the work explored in *Poetry Matters* shares much in common with language poetry, it inherits most of its political and aesthetic energy from the innovative feminist poets who began publishing in Canada and the United States in the 1970s, 1980s, and 1990s, including Di Brandt, Nicole Brossard, Kathleen Fraser, Lyn Hejinian, Susan Howe, Daphne Marlatt, Erín Moure, Harryette Mullen, Leslie Scalapino, France Théoret, Lola Lemire Tostevin, and Betsy Warland. These women engaged and experimented with language in order to foreground and address the complexity and diversity of women's social, cultural, political, and embodied experiences, and indeed the vast majority of these writers continue to produce vital and challenging feminist poetry and poetics. While most of the male language poets engaged with Marxist and post-structuralist theoretical frameworks in their writing, and explored the "crisis in public meaning caused by the Vietnam War" (Derksen 2003, 54), their female counterparts often engaged with theories of gender and representation, a focus that inadvertently, though misleadingly, aligned their work with the personal and characterized it as outside the concerns of the public sphere that dominated language poetry. Women tended to be somewhat sidelined in anthologies, journals, and other publishing venues as well as in the critical academic discussions that defined language poetry, and many feminist poets had an ambivalent relationship to language poetry.[5]

The work of innovative and experimental women poets was also marginalized within feminist writing communities, particularly in the United States. Feminist poetry and poetry criticism emerged in the United States in the 1970s and 1980s with the goal of developing "a systemic framework and vocabulary for varieties of poetic practice, past and present, that insistently probed relations of gender and power and that specified the materiality of women's lives" (Kinnahan 2004, 3). This poetry was largely dependent upon a "coherent, accessible idea of voice and authenticity derived from the lyric tradition" (3) exemplified in the writings of Marilyn Hacker, Audre Lorde, Adrienne Rich, and Alice Walker. More innovative and experimental forms of writing were met with resistance as "many second-wave feminists sought to bring poetic language closer to common usage in order to 'make it more accessible to ordinary women'" (Vickery 2000, 8). Experimental and theoretical writing was seen by some as inaccessible and incompatible with the goals of feminism.

Lynn Keller and Linda Kinnahan have both persuasively argued that feminist poetics does not fit neatly or easily into the debates regarding lyric and language poetry that seemed to divide poetry, particularly in the United States, in the 1980s and into the 1990s. As Keller notes, the division between "mainstream" and "language" poetry reduces poetry to "inevitably simplifying monoliths" that "have been a particularly uneasy fit for many feminist poetries" (2010, 47). The poets I examine here are attentive to radical experimentation, but building on Keller's argument, I read them as drawing on the overlapping but distinct lineages of feminist poetry, lyric poetry, and language poetry.

Although poets of all genders have turned their attention to current social, political and economic concerns and make use of procedural and conceptual compositional strategies, I restrict my analysis to work by female-identified poets in part because of my interest in countering critical readings of poetry by women as aligned with the private sphere, looking instead to how poetry by women participates in shaping discussions about contemporary geopolitics. As Nicky Marsh argues, the critical emphasis on the "interiority of the poet" that dominated feminist poetry criticism throughout the 1970s and into the 1980s "could do little but affirm a politicization of the private rather than seek a reconstitution of the public" (2007a, 21). Following Marsh, I consider feminist poetry's engagement with the public sphere.

Moreover, I am committed to framing my inquiry through a feminist lens because women writers are still underrepresented in discussions of innovative poetry and poetics in spite of claims of gender parity in publishing. As the now-infamous "Numbers Trouble" debate has shown, women are not anthologized at the same rate as men, books by women are not reviewed with the same frequency as books by men, and female writers are often occluded from critical studies of innovative poetry. The backlash against Juliana Spahr and Stephanie Young's numerical tabulation of gender representation in various writing, publishing, and teaching venues has also shown that drawing attention to these inequalities evokes hostility. Spahr and Young note:

> We are somewhat exhausted from wondering why what we call the experimental/postmodern/avant-garde/innovative poetry scene that so defines our lives continues—despite forty years of explicit feminist discourse in the US; despite endless examples of smart, powerful books written by women; despite endless discussion and essays about the intersection between feminism and postmodern/avant-garde/innovative poetry—to feel at moments weirdly aggressive towards anything that even suggests the possibility of a contemporary feminism, or the need for feminist activism now, or the possibility of a feminism that isn't only historical. (Spahr and Young 2011, 12)

Spahr and Young's tabulation of the ratio of publications, prizes, and creative writing jobs awarded to women has sparked subsequent "counts" in both the United States and Canada. In the United States,

Vida: Women in Literary Arts, an organization devoted to fostering support and critical reception among women writers, has instituted a broad-based tabulation of the ratio of books by women reviewed in major print venues.[6] Their numbers reveal a persistent underrepresentation of books by women in most review periodicals. In Canada, CWILA (Canadian Women in the Literary Arts) established a similar "count" in 2013 (and has conducted annual counts ever since) that reveals similar inequalities existing north of the Canada-United States border.[7] Also similar was the hostile and patronizing dismissal of CWILA's numbers-based analysis of gender inequality in publishing, reviewing, and the granting of literary awards.[8] The paucity of critical engagement with writing by women, combined with the hostile reactions to queries about this ongoing lack of engagement with women's writing, suggests a continuing need for feminist scholarly engagement with women poets and their work.

This study builds on existing scholarship on feminist poetics, including Elizabeth Frost's *The Feminist Avant-Garde in American Poetry* (2003), Barbara Godard's *Collaboration in the Feminine* (1994), Lynn Keller's *Thinking Poetry: Readings in Contemporary Women's Exploratory Poetics* (2010), Linda Kinnahan's *Lyric Interventions: Feminism, Experimental Poetry, and Contemporary Discourse* (2004), Susan Knutson's *Narrative in the Feminine: Daphne Marlatt and Nicole Brossard* (2000), Deborah Mix's *A Vocabulary of Thinking: Gertrude Stein and Contemporary North American Women's Innovative Writing* (2007), Megan Simpson's *Poetic Epistemologies: Gender and Knowing in Women's Language-Oriented Writing* (2000), and Ann Vickery's *Leaving Lines of Gender: A Feminist Genealogy of Language Writing* (2000). These books develop crucial critical frameworks and genealogies through which to make sense of the relationship between gendered subjectivity, politics, and literary experimentation. Most of these studies focus primarily on twentieth-century writing. *Poetry Matters* builds on these projects, but extends their political and aesthetic lines of inquiry to develop an analytical vocabulary that is relevant to the social and political contexts of the first fifteen years of the twenty-first century and its attendant geopolitical and economic specificities. I focus on work published after 2001 by writers who mostly began writing after the feminist writing movements of the 1980s, but who have inherited and built upon their political, creative, and aesthetic strategies. All of the books discussed in this volume were published prior to the election of Donald Trump and the Brexit vote of 2016, events that signal a troubling shift in geopolitics that will undoubtedly be reflected in the politicized poetry of the near future.

Since this book focuses on English-language poetries, I do not take up works written in French or Spanish by Quebecoise, Chicana, or Latinx poets, nor do I take up works in translation. My decision to focus only on English-language writing is a practical one made mainly in the interests of reining in an already large project. To theorize the aesthetics and politics of translation or to analyze works in French would take me far beyond the scope of this project,[9] as would a consideration of the rich traditions of Chicana and Latinx feminist poetics.[10] My focus on English-language poetry also reflects my interest in looking at sites of exchange and overlap between Canadian and American poetry, and most of this overlap occurs in English.

Tessera and *HOW(ever)*: A Case Study in the Development of Feminist Poetics in North America

Although my focus is on twenty-first-century feminist poetics, it is crucial at the outset of this study to briefly draw attention to the work of a previous generation of poets and scholars who created spaces in which innovative writing by women was published, read, and discussed. It is also necessary to highlight some of the distinct historical and cultural differences, as well as the points of convergence, between Canadian and American feminist poetics and my reasons for reading American and Canadian texts together, a decision that goes against the grain of much Canadian scholarship, which has tacitly discouraged cross-border lines of inquiry. It also goes against the grain of much American scholarship, which more readily incorporates Canadian poetry but tends to locate it within a broader American context that places aspects of its national specificity under erasure. I will illustrate these claims over the next few pages through an analysis of two journals that were both key to the development of feminist poetics in the 1980s: the Canadian journal *Tessera* and the American journal *HOW(ever)*.

Canadian feminist poetics developed in the 1980s largely in relation to an aesthetics and politics of translation facilitated by the journal *Tessera*. In the late 1970s and early 1980s francophone feminist writers in Quebec were producing remarkably experimental and theoretically sophisticated writing that was largely unread and unknown in English-speaking Canada. Barbara Godard, a bilingual feminist professor and translator, organized the Dialogue Conference at York University in 1981 in order to bring together Quebecoise and English Canadian women writers. The plans for *Tessera* were first articulated at the Dialogue Conference and concretized two years later at the Women and Words Conference in Vancouver (Godard and Kamboureli 2008, 35).

The first issue of *Tessera* was published in 1984 as a special issue of the feminist journal *Room of One's Own* by a collective consisting of Barbara Godard, Daphne Marlatt, Gail Scott, and Kathy Mezei. It was conceived as a cross-cultural project that sought to forge creative and critical connections between writing in Quebec and English Canada, and as a project that actively pursued a feminist theory of translation. As Daphne Marlatt explains,

> Several thematic concerns recur through different issues. . . . Translation was one such abiding concern, both as literal process and as metaphor for how women are situated vis-à-vis the dominant culture. Yet again, reading back, what strikes me as ground-breaking over and over again is not so much the content as the form, the innovative structure of much of the writing. Fiction/theory, originating in Québécoise feminist writing, began to move over into English, modulated by an English sensibility. (Cotnoir et al. 1994, 13)

Tessera sought to break down the boundaries between theory and practice and to "encourage new modes of writing both 'creative' and 'critical' texts" (Basile 2013, 123). Godard notes that much of the feminist writing from Quebec that she sought to bring to English Canada "embraced a new critical posture, a writing with the text rather than a meta-discourse, or magisterial critique on the text" (Godard and Kamboureli 2008, 35). For the editors, contributors, and readers of *Tessera*, translation was not simply the act of taking a text written in one language and finding the equivalent words to express the ideas in another language; instead, translation was seen as an occasion for critical thought, disruption, connection, and politicization. *Tessera's* approach "had no equivalent south of the border" (Basile 2013, 50) as the journal channeled debates on the value of post-structuralist theory in an intra-national rather than international context through its focus on translational exchange (50). *Tessera's* focus on making innovative francophone writing accessible to an English audience cannot simply be understood as a smaller version of the debates that were happening at the same time in the United States around the importation of (mostly French) post-structuralist theory into American scholarship because Canada as a nation is "founded on the unequal colonizing fictions of its French and English settler societies.... The peculiarities of Canada's uneven post-colonial history deeply inflected the particular intensity of the feminist debates pursued [in *Tessera*]" (61). The writers who published in *Tessera's* early issues were some of the key figures in innovative feminist poetics in Canada: Nicole Brossard, Louise Cotnoir, Louse Dupre, Gail Scott, France Théoret, Lola Lemire Tostevin, Betsy Warland, Louky Bersianik, jam ismail, and Erín Moure. *Tessera* also published visual art and essays by feminist academics.

Tessera and *HOW(ever)* are comparable journals in terms of the vital role each played in providing a context for experimental writing; they share a symbolic currency as publications that shaped the lines of inquiry, issues, and debates that came to characterize innovative feminist writing in each country. Both journals were created to address the lack of attention paid to experimental and innovative work within the context of feminist scholarship and literary journals. For *Tessera*, this frustration stemmed from the fact that English Canadian feminist periodicals were not receptive to the innovative fiction theory coming out of Quebec. Godard has noted that the innovative work she was soliciting from Quebec and trying to publish in English Canada had "no appeal at the time in Toronto" (Godard and Kamboureli 2008, 35), where most feminist literary journals were hesitant to embrace theoretical and experimental writing. In the United States, a similar elision of experimental writing within feminist journals was framed as, in the words of Rachel Blau DuPlessis, "the occlusion of work that did not participate in a realist or apparently realist aesthetic" (2001) in feminist periodicals in the early 1980s. In *Translating the Unspeakable: Poetry and the Innovative Necessity*, Fraser recalls her own experience of marginalization in feminist poetry journals in the 1970s and 1980s:

> I'd long since been compelled by the linguistic innovations of Gertrude Stein and by Virginia Woolf's complex interior monologues—the resistance and playfulness of dictions peculiarly odd, particularly at odds with standard "accessible" modes of expression in poems and prose works. I recognized a structural order of fragmentation and a linguistic resistance to law-abiding traditional models that confirmed my perspective. I wanted this difference in my own work. Yet, ironically, this fascination with the innovative works of modernist women writers marginalized me even further. I continued to write, but I very seldom sent work out to journals. (Fraser 2000, 32)

Published between 1983 and 1992, *HOW(ever)* was initiated by a collective consisting of Kathleen Fraser, Frances Jaffer, and Beverly Dahlen. It was a journal of innovative and experimental feminist writing that provided a crucial venue for exploring the history, aesthetics, and politics of innovative and experimental writing by women. *HOW(ever)* was a vital space for female experimentalists who were marginalized from both the women's poetry community and the language poetry scene.

HOW(ever) was designed as a "modest-size publication that adventurous readers—otherwise besieged by dense work commitments and familial obligations—would feel compelled to read almost immediately" (Fraser 1994). Articles in *HOW(ever)* tended to be shorter than standard academic articles, and emphasized process rather than polished finished product. The only requirement of the editorial collective was that contributors provide a "working note" intended to offer insight into their creative process. *HOW(ever)* also included an "alerts" section that provided a critical context for previously neglected writers and introduced readers to new work, and a "postcards" section in which readers could publish brief notes and letters. *HOW(ever)*'s mandate was broader than *Tessera*'s. While *Tessera* organized each issue in relation to a specific topic, *HOW(ever)* solicited work for each issue on a range of topics related to feminist poetics, politics, and cultural production.

In spite of shared engagements with gender and language and a shared frustration with the lack of space afforded to discussions of experimental writing in feminist journals, distinct differences in the lines of inquiry informing *Tessera* and *HOW(ever)* underscore the extent to which feminist poetics developed in each country in accordance with a somewhat specific set of aesthetic and political concerns. *Tessera*'s particular focus meant that discussions of feminist poetics in Canada were overtly framed through a Quebec-Canada axis and away from a discussion of feminist poetics in a North American context. *HOW(ever)* framed its lines of inquiry more broadly through the lens of feminism.

HOW(ever) primarily published American poets, although it also published Canadian and British poets. Ann Vickery describes *HOW(ever)* as "set[ting] out to show that American and Canadian women writers participate in a common tradition" (2000, 92) and argues that "for the first time, working projects by both Canadian writers of the feminine (écriture au féminin) and Language writers could be presented in the same forum" (96). *HOW(ever)* did provide significant opportunities for exchange between American and Canadian writers and served as an important source of inspiration, information, and companionship north of the border, as Daphne Marlatt points out in a letter she wrote in 1989 lamenting the journal's impending termination:

> Quite simply, it's been a wonderful companion, giving me not only a surprising vista of the range of avant-garde work being written by women in the States, but also a very much appreciated sense of our shared tradition. . . . And i want to add that that sense of companionship, both vertical & horizontal, is all the more appreciated as, at least here, the work of those of us who are writing, for lack of a better term, feminist post-modernism continues to struggle against mis-reading, ignorance, disinterest—even from other women writers. As you know, *(HOW)ever* has been a model for *(f.) Lip*, which Betsy [Warland] continues putting out with Angela Hryniuk & several other women. It has also been a companion for us at *tessera*, which is expanding and stabilizing. (Marlatt 1989)

As Marlatt suggests, *HOW(ever)* served as an important resource and model for Canadian feminist writing and editorial projects. *HOW(ever)* and its later online reincarnation as *How2* were dynamic sites of engagement with poetics and politics, and both journals were intent on publishing poets from outside of the United States alongside American poets.

Nevertheless, it is important to note that when Canadian writers appeared in *HOW(ever)*, their work was often recontexualized to fit into a shared tradition of literary experimentation that often occluded this work's ties to a politics and aesthetics of translation and exchange between French and English Canada. An excerpt from Nicole Brossard's *These Our Mothers* is featured in an issue of the journal alongside the work of three American writers and one British writer, in a section titled "Five Poets in Prose" (vol. 2, no. 2). While the excerpt is an English translation of Brossard's text, the name of the translator (Barbara Godard) is not noted, suggesting that the issues of translation that were so pressing for *Tessera* did not register south of the border.

In vol. 6, no. 2, Daphne Marlatt published a short piece titled "Re-Belle at the Writing Table" (1990), which is an excerpt of a talk she gave at Le Discourse Feminine dans la Littérature Post-Modern de Québec, a conference held at the University of Western Ontario in November 1989. The portion of the talk extracted for publication in *HOW(ever)* focuses solely on Susanne de Lotbinière Harwood's coining of the term "re-belle," a feminization of "rebel," which Marlatt sees as a productive reclamation that offers great potential for her own attempt to develop a lesbian theory of writing. Although it is difficult to determine whether Marlatt herself or the editors of the journal extracted this particular excerpt from her longer conference presentation, it is important to note that any direct reference to Quebecoise writing (other than de Lotbinière Harwood's name) has been removed from the text for its publication in *HOW(ever)*. This recontextualization was not wholly problematic; it likely made sense given the readership and spatial constraints of the journal. Nevertheless, the ways in which Brossard and Marlatt's texts are framed for publication in *HOW(ever)* underscores the substantially *different* mandates of *HOW(ever)* and *Tessera* and the distinct questions and concerns that were brought to bear on the writing in each country. When Canadian writers published in *HOW(ever)*, their work often underwent a shift in context in order that it might fit more seamlessly within a North American frame of reference, but in so doing, its specific Canadian context was effaced.

While Canadian writers published regularly in *HOW(ever)*, *Tessera* generally did not publish American writers at all. Prior to 1989, the journal had an informal policy of limiting the acceptance of non-Canadian submissions to 20 percent, preferably "on theoretical topics, or on French-English translation, i.e. not translations from German or Spanish."[11] In 1989, the collective further restricted its editorial policy to accept only Canadian material. The decision to restrict submissions in this manner may have been linked to the fact that the journal received funding from the Canada Council for the Arts, an organization that has a mandate to fund Canadian cultural production and that has relatively strict Canadian content rules.[12] While the Canada Council's strict Canadian content regulations are arguably necessary for the preservation of Canadian culture, they have actively discouraged the publication of American writing in Canadian journals and the publication of translations of works in languages other than French and English.

In its tendency to privilege works that reflect upon or illuminate the nation in some way, the Canada Council has tended to favor more conventional literary forms over avant-garde writing (Dobson 2013, 13).[13] Jeff Derksen claims that nonrepresentational and experimental writing occupies a marginal position within Canadian literature:

> Politicized texts that contest normative representation within language and within a politics of recognition, or texts that look for effects outside a subscribed agency, are reconfigured as "difficult"—which shifts them into being language puzzles to be decoded by an individual reader. Or such texts are designated "experimental," leaving them within an aesthetic realm unaffected by social determinants. This depoliticizing of texts enacts a national boundary of intelligibility by failing to engage with the material determinations of these texts. (Derksen 2003, 57)

To some degree, feminist poetics has fared better than other dimensions of experimental writing in Canada because the bicultural exchange that fueled this work was recognizable in the 1980s and early 1990s under the sign of a nation divided and preoccupied by the tangible possibility of a sovereign Québec.[14]

Tessera seems to have retracted its "Canadian only" rule in 1993, when the journal published a segment of Lyn Hejinian and Carla Harryman's *The Wide Road*. The appearance of this piece of writing in the journal coincided with the inauguration of a new editorial collective comprised of Katherine Binhammer, Jennifer Henderson, and Lianne Moyes. Ironically, the journal published Harryman and Hejinian at the precise moment it broadened its mandate to incorporate other modes of feminist writing and inquiry. By 1993, the founding vision of the journal had waned as its original editorial collective departed, and the new editorial collective shifted the emphasis of the journal toward a cultural studies focus, a move that reflects both the shifting academic trends in the early 1990s and the editorial collective's strategic response to political and economic shifts in Canada that made arts funding increasingly scarce and grants increasingly competitive (Basile 2013, 203–4).

Tessera was not the only site of feminist publishing in Canada at the time, and it is important to note that other periodicals had different mandates and foci. The feminist broadside *F.(lip)*, which more closely resembled *HOW(ever)* than *Tessera* in its scope and format, and the Kootenay School of Writing's *Raddle Moon* published a great deal of innovative writing by women and placed this writing in contexts distinctly different from those offered by *Tessera*. However, their reach was not as broad as *Tessera*'s, nor were they as influential in terms of establishing a critical legacy for feminist poetics in Canada.

The Kootenay School of Writing (KSW), which is located on the west coast and therefore lies at a geographic and cultural distance from Toronto and Montreal, was more amenable to pursuing cross-border lines of inquiry and functioned as a vital site of exchange for innovative writers from the United States and Canada. The KSW exists in tension with the more established channels of Canadian literature, and while this is in part a function of geography (Vancouver has always had a cultural affinity with other west coast cities such as Seattle and San Francisco), it is also a function of KSW's political and aesthetic *openness* to American poetics. Jeff Derksen, a longtime member of KSW, argues that this connection "still draws criticism from more established Canadian writers and networks, as poetic output is offset by suggestions of American colonialism" (Vickery 2000, 133). In 1985 the KSW hosted the New Poetics Colloquium, a conference that drew several key figures from both Canada and the United States, including Nicole Brossard, Susan Howe, Carla Harryman, Gail Scott, Lyn Hejinian, Daphne Marlatt, Bruce Andrews, Steve McCaffery, Barrett Watten, and Ron Silliman (Vickery 2000, 128–30). The colloquium was instrumental in introducing language poetry to Canada, but it also had the unintended effect of alienating many Canadian feminists from language poetry. Paulette Jiles objected to what she viewed as the depoliticizing effect of much of the theoretically inflected talk at the colloquium, and observed that the female participants were somewhat silenced (quoted in Vickery 2000, 130). Janice Williamson wrote a response, an excerpt of which was published in *HOW(ever)* in 1986, that was critical of the privileging of masculine voices at the gathering: "This was literary history in the making . . . and like other feminists in the listening audience, I could feel my public discursive space shrinking towards either hysteria or silence" (quoted in Vickery 2000, 131). Some of the Canadian feminist participants were also troubled by the aggressive sexual imagery in the poetry of Bruce Andrews and Ron Silliman (132). As Vickery argues, "For a number of Canadian women, such imagery—interacting with and no doubt influencing the social rhetoric of the colloquium—did much to damage the early reception of Language writing in Canada" (132–33). Many of these women directed their energy into the kinds of poetic, aesthetic, and political affinities explored in *Tessera*, which were at a remove from American language poetry and American feminist poetics. The New Poetics Colloquium, occurring two years after the Women and Words conference and coinciding with the formation of *Tessera*, may have had the unintended effect of discouraging cross-border alliances and lines of inquiry among Canadian feminist poets. The American women who participated in the New Poetics Colloquium seemed to take less issue with the gendered dynamics of the conference and "approached the colloquium with enthusiasm and little sense of the heightened, radically feminist atmosphere they were entering" (Vickery 2000, 130).[15]

Where Are We Now? An Argument for Reading American and Canadian Feminist Poetics Together

While Canadian feminist poetics emerged in the 1980s through implicitly national frames of reference that rendered this writing intelligible within the context of Canadian literary criticism, these frames tacitly discouraged cross-border inquiry. These frameworks linger somewhat, but feminist innovative writing in Canada has changed significantly, leading to a disjunction between the critical frameworks through which feminist poetics has been read in Canada and the writing that is being produced today. As Kate Eichhorn notes in the introduction to the special issue of *Open Letter* she coedited with Barbara Godard in 2009 called "Beyond Stasis: Poetics and Feminism Today," "there are now at least two generations of innovative Canadian women writers who have been largely overlooked by critics" (8). Contemporary Canadian feminist poetics embodies rhizomatic lines of connection between multiple discursive, linguistic, cultural, economic, technological, and affective forces, most of which transcend the borders of the nation or reject the nation as a colonial construct, reflecting instead the realities of global capitalism and its attendant patterns of migration and consumption as well as the role of cyberspace in creating new affinities and alliances. Critical frameworks for situating this poetry within the context of Canadian literary criticism are just beginning to catch up with this complex and exciting body of work. It is helpful at this critical juncture to think about Canadian and American feminist poetics within transnational and global contexts while still being attentive, when necessary, to national and regional contexts.

Several editorial and curatorial projects have emerged in recent years that have been instrumental in facilitating new frameworks that build on the vital and important legacies of *HOW(ever)* and *Tessera* but extend them in necessary ways. We might look to the work of Belladonna* in New York City. From its inception in 1999, Belladonna* has been interested in and attuned to Canadian feminist poetics as a particularly vital space of literary experimentation. Rachel Levitsky, one of the founders of Belladonna*, cites the Montreal feminist poetry scene of the 1980s and 1990s as a direct inspiration for Belladonna*. Belladonna* has curated reading series, held a conference on feminist poetics and activism, and published numerous books and chapbooks and has always included Canadian writers as well as writers from numerous other countries in its initiatives and has been instrumental in facilitating key sites of exchange among feminist poets from many nations. In 2013 Belladonna* republished *Theory: A Sunday,* a key, collaboratively authored feminist text originally written in French and published in Quebec in 1988 by Louky Bersianik, Nicole Brossard, Louise Cotnoir, Louise Dupré, Gail Scott, and France Théoret. Belladonna*'s republication of this text as the inaugural book in its "Germinal Texts" series not only suggests that the legacy of *Tessera* and the kind of writing explored in its pages lives on, but also that it has transcended a Canadian context and has had an influence in a broader, North American context even if the founders of *Tessera* conceived of their project as firmly Canadian and Quebecoise.

Other recent editorial projects suggest that innovative feminist poetics in Canada and the United States increasingly circulate and function transnationally. Toronto-based Jay MillAr, founder and editor of the small press BookThug, publishes American and international authors alongside Canadian authors and has a strong commitment to publishing works by women, LGBTQ writers, and writers of color. The Toronto New School of Writing, founded by Jay MillAr and Jenny Samprisi, regularly brings in writers from outside Canada to facilitate writing workshops, as does the Vancouver-based Kootenay School of Writing. The Brooklyn-based Litmus Press, with its keen interest in translation and its commitment to publishing the work of queer writers, has been instrumental in the development of multilingual poetics. *Aufgabe,* the poetry journal published by Litmus Press, published works from around the world in translation, forging crucial links between American poetry and other national literatures. We might also look to the role of web-based publications and resources like PennSound, *How2* (a web-based offspring of *HOW(ever)*), *Lemon Hound, Delirious Hem, Harriet,* and *Jacket2* which have played a key role in the facilitation of poetic exchange beyond national borders in recent years. We might also look to Juliana Spahr and Stephanie Young's "Tell U.S. Feminists" project, which surveyed women poets from around the world to find out more about the conditions in which they write and live (2011, 20–21). These projects indicate an increasing appetite for a transnational poetics rather than one articulated along national lines.

For many contemporary Canadian and American poets, the nation proves to be not only a site of contestation but also one of radical destabilization and interrogation to the degree that their writing is not easily readable within existing national critical models. Much of this work is marked by the disappearance of national spaces and the emergence of global spaces, movement, exile, and travel, as well as an investigation into the geopolitics of warfare and global markets. If this work has a setting or location, it is often the non-geographically determined locales of cyberspace, the genome, the television screen, and the global financial market.

When nation is invoked, it is usually done in order to challenge discourses of nationalism and mourn the victims of colonialism, slavery, and other acts of racialized violence that lie at the origins of settler-invader nations like Canada and the United States, or to challenge state-sanctioned forms of biopolitical surveillance and military force. In recent years, a body of post-9/11 American poetry has emerged in an ambivalent relationship to the nation and in which poets speak as what Jeff Derksen calls "transnational national" citizens asking the nation that is representative of them to be responsive to their calls for accountability (2009, 83–84). This work complicates "containments of literature to a national scale . . . but nonetheless investigates the role of the nation within globalization" (97). This kind of critical engagement with the nation has roots in language poetry. As Marjorie Perloff explains, "Both in San Francisco and New York, the language movement arose as an essentially Marxist critique of contemporary American capitalist society on behalf of young poets who came of age in the wake of the Vietnam War and Watergate" (1996, 233).

Aspects of language writing live on in the work of many of the poets examined in this volume, but as already stated, not all of these writers identify with its legacy, nor do theories of language writing offer a full and satisfying account of the politics and aesthetics of this work. In addition to the fact that feminist poets have always had a somewhat conflicted relationship to language writing (Vickery 2000, 31), the political and theoretical contexts in which language writing circulated are no longer as relevant as they once were. Cold War politics has given way to neoliberal politics and counterterrorism discourses, and the theoretical terrain has shifted from a focus on Marxism and post-structuralism to a different set of political and theoretical contexts and approaches. New technologies have changed the compositional strategies that procedural writers employ. New poetry movements such as conceptualism and flarf have emerged as labels under which some—but by no means all—of this poetry might fit.

In many respects, as I have been suggesting, the nation matters less now than it did two decades ago. In recent years, poetics in North America has been characterized by an increasing degree of cross-border exchange facilitated in large part by the Internet. However, in other respects, the nation *does* continue to matter for poets in both countries. On a very basic level, poets apply for national grants and publish their work with presses that are also funded in part by national grants. Furthermore, the nation *does* matter for Canadian writers because they are still writing and publishing in a national literary context in which America looms large as a dominant cultural presence. And the nation *does* matter for both American and Canadian poets because many of them write about their respective nations' participation in violent acts of nation-building and imperialism. From Rachel Zolf's engagement with Canadian settler-colonialism and genocide in *Janey's Arcadia* (2014) to Claudia Rankine's rendering of America as a toxic organ poisoned by the overuse of prescription drugs, rampant consumerism, racism, and problematic foreign policy in *Don't Let Me Be Lonely* (2004), the nation looms large as a target of critique and a site of ambivalent identification. The tension between the nation mattering and not mattering is both irresolvable and productive, and this tension informs my analysis of contemporary feminist poetics and my tendency to both invoke and override national specificity in my analysis of contemporary Canadian and U.S. poetry.

Poetry Matters places feminist poetics in dialogue with recent currents of feminist theory, including new materialism, affect theory, the posthuman, and feminist engagements with neoliberalism and capitalism. The book is divided into three parts, each of which is subdivided into two chapters. Parts 1 and 2 read innovative feminist poetics through strands of feminist theory that argue for a return to a consideration of matter and materiality as a dimension of a posthuman, affective politics that poses an alternative to neoliberalism. Part 1, "Economies of Flesh and Word: Biopolitics and Writing the (Posthuman) Body in Late Capitalism," examines how feminist poets deploy what Jennifer Scappettone calls "strategic embodiment" as a mode of feminist critique (2007). The first chapter in this section considers Jennifer Scappettone's *From Dame Quickly* (2009b), Margaret Christakos's *What Stirs* (2008), and Larissa Lai and Rita Wong's *sybil unrest* (2013). I argue that these three poets foreground an active resistance to the ways in which the female body is both marked and marketed (L'Abbé, 2011) in the context of biopolitics and global capitalism. Scappettone engages critically in her poetry with a history of Western thought that links the materiality of the body to the feminine and casts that body as passive. Christakos enacts a procedural poetics that addresses the affective vectors of what Jodi Dean calls communicative capitalism through an extended poetic engagement with the breast-feeding latch and digital communications (2010). Lai and Wong enact a posthuman, hybrid poetics of dispersal and deferral that locates the queer, racialized body as a site of resistance to capitalism and biopolitics. The second chapter in this section draws on recent cultural theories of disgust to posit corporeal disgust as a poetic and political strategy for critiquing capitalism in Nikki Reimer's *[sic]* (2010) and Rachel Zolf's *Human Resources* (2007).

Part 2, "Poetic Matterings: New Materialist and Posthuman Feminist Ecopoetics," examines recent works that displace or call into question the humanist subject and reevaluate the relationship between humans and the material world. Through readings of Yedda Morrison's *Darkness* (2012a) and Marcella Durand's "The Anatomy of Oil" (2008), I explore the tendency of these poets to decouple language from the human and decenter the humanist subject that is so central to conventional nature poetry. I argue that these writers enact a politicized posthumanism by decentering the human from the frames of reference through which resource extraction is typically understood. I then read Rita Wong's (2015) *undercurrent* (a poetic attempt to think with water) and Evelyn Reilly's (2009) *Styrofoam* (a poetic meditation on plastic and Styrofoam) through recent critical and theoretical work that challenges engrained understandings of humans as separate from their environment. Together, these chapters argue that contemporary feminist ecopoetics enacts the very "displacement of our world-view away from the human epicenter" and "establishes a continuum with the animal, mineral, vegetable, extra-terrestrial, and technological worlds" that Rosi Braidotti articulates (2013, 183) in her call for a posthuman feminist mode of inquiry.

Part 3, "Geopolitics, Nationhood, Poetry," consists of two chapters, each of which examines the relationship between contemporary feminist poetics and geopolitics. The first of these chapters reads Juliana Spahr's *This Connection of Everyone with Lungs* (2005), Claudia Rankine's *Don't Let Me Be Lonely: An American Lyric* (2004), and Dionne Brand's *Inventory* (2006) as antiwar poems written in the aftermath of 9/11 and during the lead-up to the U.S. invasion of Iraq. I examine the tendencies of these writers to draw directly on news media as raw material in the construction of their poetry and to foreground the poet as a mediatized witness located in the domestic sphere but connected to world events through technology. I consider how this writing develops a poetics of political dissent that moves strategically between the intimate and the global, and I anchor my reading of these texts in relation to theorizing on the political dimensions of affect (Ahmed 2004, 2010; Berlant 2011; Cvetkovich 2012), recent feminist work on global intimacy (Pratt and Rosner 2012), and theories of witnessing (Felman and Laub 1992; Forché 1993). The final chapter investigates poetry that is critically engaged in the implicit and explicit forms of violence and precarity upon which nations and national imaginaries are founded and maintained. Rachel Zolf's *Janey's Arcadia* (2014), Jena Osman's *Corporate Relations* (2014), and Jen Benka's *A Box of Longing with Fifty Drawers* (2005) draw on texts that are closely aligned with ideologies of nation-building and the state. Rachel Zolf engages with early Canadian settler and missionary texts to explore Canada's ongoing history of colonial violence and the crisis of missing and murdered Indigenous women. Jena Osman works with the transcripts of Supreme Court decisions in which judges drew on U.S. constitutional amendments to grant constitutional rights to corporations; Osman shows how corporate personhood has become progressively embedded in the American legal system since the Civil War. Jen Benka writes fifty-two poems inspired by the fifty-two–word preamble to the U.S. Constitution to illustrate the failure of the United States to live up to the goals and principles outlined in the Constitution. All three writers engage with foundational texts that are central to their country's national imaginaries; in the process, they enact critiques of national institutions and values. For all three, poetic form and process are integral to the articulation of political critique.

This book does not aim to offer a complete survey of the field of contemporary feminist poetics and political dissent. Rather, my goal is to start a conversation focused on the intersections between contemporary feminist poetics, geopolitics, and recent currents of feminist theoretical inquiry. The archive of texts on which I draw in this volume is admittedly incomplete, and I have mapped only one of many potential paths through this rich and complex body of writing. There are many writers who could and should be included here but, due to the constraints of time and space, have been left out. Ana Božičević, Angela Carr, Amy Sarah Carroll, Jen Currin, Erica Doyle, kari edwards, Laura Elrick, Betsy Fagin, Liz Howard, Julie Joosten, Amy King, Rachel Levitsky, Shannon Maguire, Carol Mirakove, Erín Moure, Sachiko Murakami, Akilah Oliver, M NourbeSe Philip, Sarah Pinder, Kristin Prevallet, Sina Queyras, a. rawlings, Lisa Roberson, Trish Salah, Nancy Shaw, Catriona Strang, Nathalie Stephens/Nathanaël, and Stacy Szymaszek, among many other writers, are not given the attention they deserve in these pages. I name them here so that readers can pursue their writing and extend the conversation I hope to start here.

PART ONE

Economies of Flesh and Word: Biopolitics and Writing the (Posthuman) Body in Late Capitalism

IN 2007, JENNIFER ASHTON PUBLISHED an article called "Our Bodies, Our Poems" in which she dismissed recent critical, editorial, and curatorial projects related to women's experimental writing as manifestations of critical obsolescence and essentialism. The article generated several responses, many of which countered Ashton's claim by arguing for the continued need for and relevance of such projects. Among these responses was Jennifer Scappettone's "Bachelorettes, Even: Strategic Embodiment in Contemporary Experimentalism by Women," in which Scappettone identifies a praxis of "strategic embodiment" operational in contemporary feminist poetics (2007, 178).[1] Scappettone argues that, contrary to Ashton's claim that a poetics focused on embodied female subjectivity is by definition essentialist, the body functions in many poetic texts by women not as a passive surface or "naturalized prop" but as an instrument to be politically, critically, and strategically deployed (181). For Scappettone, this corporeal poetics is "no unmediated return to a body proper" but rather a "provocative feature of poetry riotously opposing a culture that continues to cast women as certain kinds—peculiarities—of subjects" (181). The body is not, in other words, an essentialized object located outside of language and culture; rather, the body and bodily production are "a function of the social world's inscriptions" (182). Moreover, in a political, social, and economic climate in which the subject is increasingly implicated in and by neoliberalism, global capitalism, and technology, poetic articulations of bodily materiality deploy tactics that necessarily differ from those of earlier decades. As Scappettone argues, many "younger experimentalists expose and take aim against forms of social embedding—not only gender but race, class, and nationhood—that weigh persistently upon the subject. . . . Now emerging from a climate repoliticized by right-wing ascendancy, these acts necessarily deploy tactics deviating from those of the eighties or the nineties" (2007, 179–80). To be clear, Scappettone is not intent on dismissing feminist body-based poetry from the 1980s and 1990s as essentialist. Rather, she is arguing that the techniques, tactics, and political stakes of writing the body in the twenty-first century are informed by political urgencies, environmental catastrophes, economic situations, and technological factors that are specific to the twenty-first century. Rather than applying critiques of essentialism drawn from feminist theoretical discussions dating from earlier decades,[2] readings of body-based poetics in the early twenty-first century need to consider how this work engages the intensification of biopolitics and technocapitalism under neoliberalism. The body in this instance could be said to be posthuman since, as Rosi Braidotti argues, contemporary capitalism deploys biopiracy to exploit "the generative powers of women, animals, plants, genes and cells" (2013, 95), placing humans on a continuum with non-anthropomorphic, animal, and earth others.

The poets I discuss in the following two chapters deploy strategic embodiment to enact feminist critiques of neoliberal capitalism. Chapter 1 builds on Scappettone's claims in "Bachelorettes, Even: Strategic Embodiment in Contemporary Experimentalism by Women" by examining the role of strategic embodiment in three recent poetry texts: Jennifer Scappettone's own collection of poems *From Dame Quickly,* Margaret Christakos's *What Stirs,* and Larissa Lai and Rita Wong's collaborative long poem *sybil unrest.* I explore how these poets use language to engage the materiality of the body through and against the vectors of capitalism. These writers do not just "write the body," they "write the body politic," using "language pillaged from social and political realms" to "call into question the way meaning is inscribed through dominant discourses onto our bodies and minds" (Prevallet 2012).[3] For Scappettone, this entails an extended poetic challenge to the conflation of matter with the feminine in Western thought; for Christakos, it entails the deployment of the breast-feeding latch as a metaphor through which to reflect upon the affective implications of attachment and alienation in the context of online communication; for

Lai and Wong it requires foregrounding the ways in which the racialized, posthuman, queer female body becomes caught up in networks of capitalism and biopower. In all three books, the body is strategically deployed in order to critically engage the social and material forces that mediate cultural understandings of female embodiment. These texts actively resist essentialist understandings of corporeality while simultaneously foregrounding the material relationship between gender, embodiment, and capitalism. Chapter 2 reads Nikki Reimer's *[sic]* and Rachel Zolf's *Human Resources* as articulating an affective poetics of bodily disgust as a form of capitalist critique that refuses neoliberal appropriation. Both poets make a point of dwelling in a poetics of dirt and disgust where linguistic signs become sticky with the affective, corporeal, and industrial residues of late capitalism. I situate this poetic deployment of disgust as a form of strategic embodiment related to those discussed in the previous chapter but distinct in its recourse to disgust rather than desire and its attendant features of *jouissance*, dispersal, and hybridity.

This writing builds on the embodied feminist poetics of a previous generation of writers like Lyn Hejinian, Beverly Dahlen, Nicole Brossard, and Daphne Marlatt. It also draws on feminist theoretical frameworks that explore the relationship between self-expression and the female body, such as those developed by French feminist theorists like Hélène Cixous and Julia Kristeva. As Megan Simpson has argued, *écriture feminine* "has helped suggest new possibilities for women writers, possibilities that many language oriented women writers in the United States have been exploring" (2000, 1). In Canada, theories of embodied translation that drew from French feminism became a strong thread within feminist poetics, and the Canadian writers discussed in this section engage with this legacy in direct and indirect ways. However, the poets discussed in these two chapters also draw on theories of affect and the posthuman in order to address the complexities that factors such as neoliberalism, technology, and global capitalism have brought to bear on subjectivity and embodiment in recent years. What sets this work apart from that of a previous generation of writers is not so much an ideological or aesthetic split or schism—indeed, this work shares much in common aesthetically and politically with earlier iterations of feminist poetics—but rather a growing urgency to address the slipperiness and the ubiquity of neoliberal capitalism and a response to the ways in which technology and capitalism impact gender and sexuality. These poets each grapple with the contradictions of neoliberalism and are acutely aware of the specific effects of capitalism on the lives and bodies of women. Read together, they articulate a materialist and affective poetics of writing the posthuman body.

Strategic Embodiment: Materiality, Proceduralism, and Biopolitics in Jennifer Scappettone's *From Dame Quickly*, Margaret Christakos's *What Stirs*, and Larissa Lai and Rita Wong's *sybil unrest*

Neither Fish nor Flesh: Jennifer Scappettone's Materialist Poetics

From Dame Quickly (Scappettone 2009b) is striking as a material object. Its pages are eight and a half inches tall by eleven inches wide, making it much larger than most books of poetry; the wide pages accommodate Scappettone's often extremely long lines, and in some cases, allow for more than one column of poetry to be printed on a single page. One section of the book is comprised of vibrant collages of texts and images printed in full color on glossy paper. The care and attention paid to the form and design of this book reflect an appreciation of the book as an object or material "thing" and can be read as a manifestation of Scappettone's overarching interest in the reclamation of matter and materiality and the ways that matter can function not only as a container for content, but also as an active site of meaning-making.

From Dame Quickly was published in 2009, two years after Scappettone's essay on strategic embodiment, suggesting that she may have worked on the projects simultaneously and they likely informed each other. *From Dame Quickly* can be read as a manifestation of Scappettone's argument in favor of strategic embodiment; she describes *From Dame Quickly* as "an attempt at a new materialism" (2009a) and articulates her poetic process as a setting down of "dumb matter which has not yet been inscribed, the matter/mater of the feminine, the earth" against poetic forms that have been "emptied of material" (2009a). She develops a poetics that challenges the gendered relationship between form and matter, and more specifically, the ways in which the female body has traditionally been associated with matter, passivity, and silence. Scappettone reclaims matter, framing it not as "dumb" but as an active site of signification, disruption, and agency.

The disruptive logic of the feminine is introduced in Scappettone's book most directly through the figure of Dame Quickly, who is invoked in the book's title and also in an epigraph derived from Karl Marx's *Capital* that reads: "The objectivity of commodities as values differs from Dame Quickly in the sense that 'a man knows not where to have it'" (2009b). By placing this quotation at the beginning of her book, Scappettone locates her project as materialist and grounds it in relation to a female character that Marx borrows from Shakespeare. Dame Quickly is a minor character in several of Shakespeare's plays, including *Henry IV*, where she is a bawdy tavern keeper who, as the pun contained in her surname implies (Quickly/Quick-lay), is associated with sexual availability and promiscuity. In *Henry IV*, part 1, Falstaff refers to Dame Quickly as an otter, "neither fish nor flesh," and suggestively contends that "a man knows not where to have her." Dame Quickly replies by amplifying the sexual innuendo contained in Falstaff's accusation, "Thou art an unjust man in saying so: thou or any man knows where to have me" (*Henry IV*, part 1, act 3, scene 3). For Marx, Dame Quickly signifies the collapse of the boundaries between public and private entailed in prostitution; sex in this context goes from being a private exchange to a commodity that circulates in the marketplace, but one that makes men uncertain as to "where" they should "have" her. This ambiguity is amplified by the collapse of the sex act and the body of the prostitute under the sign of the commodity. Passing entirely over the disorienting effects this conflation might have on the sex worker's understanding of selfhood, Marx focuses on its destabilizing effects on her customer, thereby erasing her subjectivity and turning her solely into a commodity, a material object ascribed a value in a capitalist marketplace. Scappettone's sustained engagement with Dame Quickly in this text challenges the sexism that underscores both Shakespeare and Marx's representations of this figure, and relishes the ambiguity and instability of signification that seemed to confound both Falstaff and Marx.

The preposition "from" in the book's title might suggest that the poems are told from Dame Quickly's perspective, although the poems are too fragmentary and elusive to be traced to a single speaker. Scappettone layers fragment upon fragment to construct multivocal, refracted, nonreferential poems. Michael Cross identifies a tendency in Scappettone's writing to bend language through "a multitude of registers, so that as the poem unfolds, the thing is turned and turned before us, and with each revolution, it is not what it was moments before." Her long sentences "refract into any number of clauses, spinning out and shifting under our feet" so that, like Falstaff or Marx, the reader is left somewhat disoriented (2014). However, as Scappettone explains, one of the underlying motivations for this project is a desire to reclaim matter, including the materiality of language. A focus on language as matter entails a focus not on logical sematic progression so much as on fragments of language and utterances as objects unmoored from context and set in striking and unanticipated relation to one another.

"Thing Ode" (Scappettone 2009b, 24) is arguably the poem in this collection that most clearly illustrates Scappettone's attempt to develop a new materialism in her poetry. "Thing Ode" evokes the female body and matter through fragmentary strands of text that are combined and recombined to generate meaning through juxtaposition and shifting contexts. As an "ode," the poem pays tribute to "thingness," or to the objective existence of material objects, yet "things" in this poem are not concrete and finite objects as much as they are abstract concepts and functions. "Ode" subtly references its homophonic twin "owed," creating a productive conflation between praise and debt, surplus and lack; "thing" is both the object of admiration and that which is "owed" to another in a capitalist system of exchange.

The opening lines of the poem read:

Say, what thing—Darling—what thing keeps you
up at night?—security collaboration,
innovation, client satisfaction,
productivity, the new black
global pipeline of sharing,
(Scappettone 2009b, 24)

It is unclear who the speaker is or what her relationship is to the person she is addressing, although the word "darling" could indicate a degree of intimacy. What is clear, however, is that the implied sources of the addressee's anxiety, the "things" that keep her up at night, seem to be linked to contemporary geopolitics and capitalism: "security collaboration," "client satisfaction," "global pipeline[s]." Scappettone then goes on to evoke the feminine through an oblique reference to Dame Quickly:

> a garrison'd ecosystem
> waxing margins of the sure thing
> now neither fish nor flesh
> nor a damn of Mater
> equipping itself to torque and spin
> this leak of social substance?
> (24)

Here the "torque and spin" of the feminine, the "damn of Mater," and "leak of social substance" rupture the stability and containment of the "garrison'd ecosystem" and the "margins of the sure thing." Neither fish nor flesh, both producer and commodity, the feminine signals a productive collapse of conventional meaning. "Mater" is the etymological root of both "mother" and "matter," a connection central to the poem's interest in the relationship between the feminine and materiality.

Through references to Dame Quickly and the sex trade, the poem gestures to the connections between women, sex, and commodities: "the genitive case / of a narrow home, / horum, harem; darling at your side, / I became again, I learned to taste the good soldier" (Scappettone 2009b, 25). "Horum" and "harum" are both the Latin genitive plural forms of *hic* (here). Scappettone changes the spelling of "harum" to "harem": this shift in spelling signifies an important shift in meaning as well. Historically, harems have functioned as female-only spaces in Muslim cultures, but within the context of a popular culture informed by Orientalism, harems have a long association with sexuality and prostitution. "Horum," when placed next to "harem," implicitly evokes "whore-um," a double meaning that is rendered particularly apparent when the poem is read aloud. Scappettone is obliquely referencing Shakespeare's *The Merry Wives of Windsor*, and more specifically, a scene in which Dame Quickly hears Sir Hugh Evans quizzing

William Page on his Latin grammar and, upon hearing the boy recite the genitive case of this verb, assumes he is uttering vulgar slang. The line becomes a source of comedy in the play, and serves to emphasize Dame Quickly's lack of formal education and predilection for hearing and conveying sexual innuendo. Several of the phrases in "Thing Ode" are actual lines spoken by Dame Quickly in Shakespeare's plays. These lines are decontextualized, disassembled, and join a polyphonic chorus of other poetic fragments. The poem continues:

> the clients wanting sober ceremonies, with sighs,
> I became so lost in lexicography as to forget
> that things are the sons of earth,
>
> manly characters
> whose speeches give us
> voices between human beings whose barriers have fallen
> (Scappettone 2009b, 25)

The speaker has become so caught up in her study of language that she must be reminded of the importance of materiality or "things." "Things" here is explicitly masculinized as the "sons of earth" and "manly characters." Scappettone problematizes the conflation of matter/mater with the feminine, and opens up new ways to understand matter as other than passive. However, several lines later she invokes the feminine through reference to the "servile and effeminate / age we devoutly embrace / the rare branding of / bodies in motion" (26). Whether the "we" in this context embraces the "servile and effeminate age" or the "rare branding of bodies in motion" is unclear. In any case, the bodies here are branded, insofar as they are both "marked" and "marketed" (L'Abbé), but they are also in motion, suggesting a refutation of passivity and stasis, qualities typically associated with the feminine.

Scappettone posits matter/mater as "that which has not been inscribed" (2009a). In so doing, her poetry might be read at first glance as presenting bodily materiality as what Judith Butler calls a sign of irreducibility, as that which bears cultural construction but is not itself a construction (1993, 28). However, Scappettone's exploration of matter, like Butler's, ultimately challenges this irreducibility. Butler problematizes understandings of matter as prior to or outside of discursive systems. In tracing matter back to its etymological roots, Butler also explores its relation to mater (mother) and matrix (womb), noting the same long-standing associations between women and matter that Scappettone explores in her poetry. However, Butler also demonstrates that for the ancient Greeks and Romans, matter was not a blank surface awaiting inscription. On the contrary, she argues, classical understandings of materiality and signification understand them as indissoluble (1993, 31).

> Insofar as matter appears in these cases to be invested with a certain capacity to originate and to compose that for which it also supplies the principle of intelligibility, then matter is clearly defined by a certain power of creation and rationality that is for the most part divested from the more modern empirical deployments of the term. To speak within these classical contexts of *bodies that matter* is not an idle pun, for to be material means to materialize, where the principle of that materialization is precisely what "matters" about the body, its very intelligibility. (Butler 1993, 32)

Like Butler, Scappettone explores matter's generative capacities. The body in "Thing Ode" is conceptualized *through* rather than *outside* its relationship with language; matter generates language and language itself is understood as material, as illustrated in the following passages:

> the introjecting suck
> of speech's bust (25)
>
> . . .
>
> I pray thee, go the casement,
> find any body in the house,
>
> kick heels against the alphabeted mass,
>
> stance to make Chranachian stomach of us
> to master
> being a first plié toward bodilessness— (26)
>
> . . .

antigonal charm at the mouth—
open avowal—
whirled in a tangle. . .
(Scapettone 2009b, 28)

For Scappettone, matter is not inert and passive. Kicking "heels against
the alphabeted mass" indicates an agential body rather than a pas-
sive one, and configures language as material. Verbs like "open" and
"whirled" suggest activity rather than passivity, and a "first plié to-
ward bodilessness" suggests, perhaps somewhat paradoxically, the
possibility of escape from embodiment and materiality through the
embodied act of dancing. Scappettone develops a materially and cor-
poreally grounded feminist poetics that problematizes the distinction
between body and text, matter and language and shows how a poet-
ics of "strategic embodiment" can "strip bare the essentializing acts of
determination and domination that buttress a regressive social world"
(Scappettone 2007, 184).

"Thing Ode" is prefaced with two epigraphs that, taken together,
link the project of analyzing the relationship between form and matter
to feminist procedural poetics and "strategic embodiment." The first of
these quotations, from Bruce Mau and the Institute without Bound-
aries' "Massive Change" exhibit, reads: "We will build intelligence
into materials and liberate form from matter. . . . Instead of designing
a thing, we design a designing thing. In the process, we have created
superhero materials and collapsed the age-old boundary between the
image and the object, rendering mutable the object itself" (2004, 24).
Mau is a Canadian designer whose book and touring exhibition "Mas-
sive Change" (originally curated by the Vancouver Art Gallery in the
early 2000s) explores the ways in which design might be used to ad-
dress major social, cultural, economic, and environmental problems.
For Mau, design holds the potential to become an active, or even an
activist, agent of social change, a "superhero" material. The object that
is designed—the "thing"—is the site where that social change takes
place. Such an object would, like Dame Quickly, fulfill the roles of both
commodity and producer; it is not just a "thing designed" but a "de-
signing thing." Mau's claim to "liberate form from matter" and design

not simply a "thing" but a "designing thing" informs Scappettone's project, where meaning and significance are located less in relation to the poem as finished product than they are in relation to process and the questions that inform its production. Process and form become scriptive agents in her poetry.

However, Scappettone is not so much interested in "liberating form from matter" as she is in querying the distinction between form and matter and asking questions about how the distinction between form and matter is imbued with gendered assumptions. How might "matter," the physical matter of the gendered body, become a "designing thing," or a scriptive agent in its own right? How does this relate to poetry? The second epigraph, borrowed from Juliana Spahr and Stephanie Young's "Foulipo" essay (2011), provides a possible answer to these questions; the quotation reads: ". . . and yet caught in the cultural anybody of the momentanity that said we had to be thingal and younghede. . ." (2011, 24). Scappettone draws extensively on Spahr and Young's "Foulipo" essay/performance in her essay on strategic embodiment. "Foulipo" emerges as a critical response to the male-dominated Oulipo (*Ouvroir de littérature potentielle*) tradition of constraint-based writing. In composing "Foulipo," Spahr and Young deploy strategies derived from Oulipo, including the N+7 technique of replacing each noun with the seventh noun following it in the dictionary. They also "slenderized" their text by removing all of the "r"s in portions of the essay. They explain the intent behind these procedures using the aforementioned slenderizing technique to great effect:

> What we wanted fom foulipo was a numbe of geneative and estictive, numbe based pocesses and constraints that helped us undestand the messy body. One that did not pesent a beautiful, complete and obviously gendeed naked body but one that still lets us deal with the I AM HEE, one that lets us get dessed and undessed, one that lets us constain and expand. (Spahr and Young 2011, 42)

When these sections are read aloud, the reader's voice acquires a lisping and infantile tone that undermines her authority. This lisping voice becomes one of several performative aspects of the talk. Spahr and Young took turns reading out the non-italicized parts of the talk. The italicized portions were read over a loudspeaker, while Spahr and Young repeatedly undressed and dressed (Spahr and Young 2011, 15). Meaning is conveyed as much through bodily performance in this essay as it is through the actual words on the page. The dressing and undressing and the lisping voice remind the reader/listener that bodies *do* matter, that far from being inert and passive, the body can function as a productive site of meaning-making. Furthermore, their "Foulipo" essay/ performance demonstrates the political potential of procedural techniques where the subversive and political force of the text lies less in the content of the words and more in the material form of the text and the procedures enacted on the text. In the case of Spahr and Young's "Foulipo" essay, these procedures, developed out of careful and considered political analysis, are inextricably linked to the material, gendered bodies of the authors/performers of the text *and* to the arguments they advance in their essay. In other words, the essay's arguments are in large part made *through* the material presence of the body.

For Scappettone, Spahr and Young powerfully demonstrate that "bodily experience and production are a function of the social world's inscriptions" (Scappettone 2007, 182) and express a "commitment to unveiling the redundant forms of entrapment into which an essentialized subject is cast" (2007, 183). In invoking "Foulipo" in the epigraph to "Thing Ode," Scappettone orients the poem in relation to a recent history of feminist constraint-based experimental writing and performance that focuses on the social and political implications of female embodiment. The female body is absolutely central to *From Dame Quickly* as Scappettone, like Spahr and Young, deploys the body strategically as a productive site of politically engaged feminist poetics.

Although Scappettone's poems do not deploy strictly Oulipean or even "foulipean" strategies, the final section of "Thing Ode" is partially comprised of recombined words and phrases from the earlier sections of the poem, suggesting that the poem was composed using procedural techniques that allow it to become a kind of self-generating mechanism akin to Bruce Mau's "designing thing." Language in the poem functions like building blocks whereby content may be secondary to material form; meaning accrues through the structural repetition, recombination, and dispersal of these building blocks. The interplay of form and content here reflects Scappettone's overarching interest in the gendered history of the relationship between form and matter, since, as Judith Butler argues, "to invoke matter is to invoke a sedimented history of sexual hierarchy and sexual erasures" (1993, 49).

In contrast to the short, fragmented lines of the first five pages of the poem, the final section recombines language from the earlier sections into longer but still fragmented lines:

I became again, I learned to taste the good soldier   now neither fish nor   fleisch
        of my scream life, the yellow dress   emptied of our

little old men, the suck   equipping itself to torque   and spin selection,
        the feebler and passive characters   bringing thee to manly stains,

bodies in motion to be   repulsed   lining the walls of a room hammering   enemy
        positions, some john with his comma   at the daily hog facility

        hunted   spikes of speech's bust   breathless and tawdry.   Behold a
Thing with supersoaker   in the public zones of a house breathing shadows

of a servile and effeminate rule   of endings we fancy   belong to us, uniform
of   ascesis,   of the austere pubic woman   infectious
(Scappettone 2009b, 29)

Scappettone invokes the language of sexual exchange, and specifically prostitution, but infuses this with references to speech and punctuation; the "john with his comma" implicitly compares a john's penis with a punctuation mark, a comparison that effectively emasculates the john. References to "manly stains" and "little old men" foreground the materiality of men's bodies more than women's, and subvert the association of matter with the feminine. In fact, the "public woman" in this poem is associated with "ascesis" (extreme bodily control and self-discipline) rather than bodily excess. The speaker of the poem goes on to explain that she "became so lost in lexicography as to forget the / clients   wanting sober ceremonies, with sighs" (Scappettone 2009b, 29); she would rather study language than participate in a sexual exchange for money. If this speaker is Dame Quickly, she is a far cry from the Dame Quickly of Shakespeare's plays or from Marx's analysis of prostitution, and perhaps this is precisely the point.

As Scappettone argues, a poetics of strategic embodiment is a vital component of a "riotously opposing" poetics of the early twenty-first century (2007, 181). Scappettone's poetic reclamation of "thingness" articulated in "Thing Ode" is part of her "riotously opposing" poetics and implicitly informs her engagement with geopolitics throughout *From Dame Quickly*. References to Dame Quickly and female embodiment are present throughout the book, and often occur in the context of poetic engagements with current events. *From Dame Quickly* was written in the historical context of the U.S. invasion of Iraq, an event addressed in several of the poems in the collection that juxtapose media coverage of the Iraq War with obituaries of the French philosopher Jacques Derrida to provide a critical poetic commentary on the media's inability to address complexity and ambiguity (Scappettone 2009a). The book offers a poetic engagement with early twenty-first-century geopolitics and the discourses used by the U.S. government and media to justify the invasion of Iraq.

Scappettone's enigmatic poetry is difficult to read; it refutes the position of easily consumable commodity, yet remains persistently attuned to the materiality of language and bodies as it leads the reader on a quest for meaning. As I have been suggesting, meaning resides less in what the words say and more in their juxtaposition, combination, and recombination, and in the procedural techniques that Scappettone enacts to compose some of these poems. Like Scappettone, Margaret Christakos refuses to present the reader with easily consumable or readable poems. Through a poetics of strategic embodiment, Christakos's *What Stirs* (2008) explores the relationship among bodies, affective attachments, and commodification in the context of late capitalism. I turn now to an analysis of *What Stirs*.

Communicative Capitalism and Affective Vectors: Margaret Christakos's Maternal Poetics

Rosi Braidotti argues that the maternal body is fetishized in the context of the "cyber-teratological imaginary" of late capitalism because it represents and reproduces the future; the maternal body carries the burden of inscribing futurity within "the regime of high-tech commodification which runs today's market economy" (2002, 207–8). Braidotti sees this fetishization as problematic insofar as it reduces women to maternal power and then displaces that power onto corporately owned technologies, and she suggests that the "turbulence" created by this double bind exacts a toll on "empirical females" in the form of "discontent, pathology and disease" (208). In her 2008 collection of poems *What Stirs*, Margaret Christakos critically engages the fetishized maternal body through a poetics of a "cyber-teratological imaginary," but rather than seeing the maternal as reductive, she understands the maternal as expansive and as broadly informing the affective dimensions of techocapitalism. While discontent and alienation figure prominently in these poems, Christakos also writes about the persistence of affective attachments in the face of (and sometimes as a function of) technology and capitalism. She engages the cultural expectations and burdens projected onto the maternal body and traces the ways in which these burdens become transferred onto other forms of attachment in the context of capitalism and commodity culture. Christakos presents the maternal as caught up in, but never fully contained by, the market economy and as a primary relation or precondition that informs patterns of consumption and commodification.

Like Scappettone, Christakos develops a poetics of strategic embodiment. The maternal body and the breast-feeding latch function as central metaphors in *What Stirs*. Christakos uses the latch to explore dynamics of affective attachment, gratification, frustration, and alienation, but she extends the metaphor of the latch beyond the maternal body and the mother-child dyad to consider how these dynamics undergird neoliberal technocapitalism, specifically in the context of online environments. Christakos employs procedural strategies to generate patterns and repetition out of which meaning emerges; individual words and blocks of language migrate from poem to poem as she plays with the resonance and dissonance of the familiar and the strange. Meaning develops not so much through the content of words, but rather through their recirculation as previously read phrases are encountered again and again in new and unexpected configurations. Through recombination, fragmentation, and substitution, words "latch on" to other words while other connections are displaced and deferred. Her focus on the latch gives the book a thematic cohesiveness and situates it in relation to the maternal. However, she broadens her scope by using the latch to ask questions about the intensities of affects and attachments: What do we latch onto? What do we recoil from? How do we establish and maintain meaningful human connection through the vectors of technocapitalism, and, as the book's title suggests, what stirs us?[1] Like Scappettone, she uses language as building blocks that represent the materiality of the female body but do not reduce that body to a primordial essence.

Much of the actual text in *What Stirs* comes from Internet searches; this language is reproduced in Christakos's poems as fragmentary strands of text that mimic the rhizomatic and disjunctive structure of the Internet. These strands of text can be read as a manifestation of what Jodi Dean identifies as "communicative capitalism"; in fact, *What Stirs* is, in large part, a poetic commentary on the affective vectors of communicative capitalism. Dean defines communicative capitalism as a paradox specific to online communication whereby readers encounter a surplus of text but a deficit of content:

> The astronomical increases in information that our searching, commenting, and participating generate entrap us in a setting of communication without communicability. As contributions to circuits of information and affect, our utterances are communicatively equivalent; their content, their meaning is unimportant. On a blog, for example, gibberish written by an automated bot is as much a comment as any thoughtful reflection. The specific contribution has no symbolic efficiency; rather, it marks only the fact of its having been made. This decline in a capacity to transmit meaning, to symbolize beyond a limited discourse or immediate, local context, characterizes communication's reconfiguration into a primarily economic form. (Dean 2011b, 127)

Dean sees much online communication as essentially empty of meaning, but she identifies a strong affective impulse and desire for connection, attachment, and affirmation that fuels participation in online activities. Blogging and social media "produce and circulate affect as a binding technique" (Dean 2011a, 95). The circulation of communication for its own sake produces affect out of the

> endless circular movement of commenting, adding notes and links, bringing in new friends and followers, layering and interconnecting myriad

communications platforms and devices. Every little tweet or comment, every forwarded message or petition, accrues a tiny affective nugget, a little surprise enjoyment, a smidgen of attention that attaches to it, making it stand out from the larger flow before it blends back in. (Dean 2011a, 95)

Dean's description of the affective dimensions of communicative capitalism resonate strongly with Christakos's compositional method in *What Stirs*. Christakos circulates language for the sake of circulating it, but the affective dynamics of attachment that motivate the entire project are located precisely in the combination, recombination, and circulation of these strands of text. Jodi Dean calls this the "open, distributed, recombinant, chaotic feedback loops of affective networks" through which communicative capitalism operates (2011a, 103).

In its persistent interest in dynamics of attachment and connection, *What Stirs* challenges Fredric Jameson's claim that fragmented, paratactic poetry, which he reads as a symptom of late capitalism, contributes to the depthlessness and "waning of affect" (2001, 567) that he understands as a defining element of postmodernism. *What Stirs* does enact a "breakdown of the signifying chain" that on the surface might appear to produce "a series of pure unrelated presents in time" (568), but Christakos utilizes a highly disjunctive, paratactic poetic form as a vehicle for the exploration of affect, connection, and attachment in the context of technocapitalist postmodern culture. In so doing, her poetry reflects an optimistic belief in the persistence of affective bonds and their ability to survive the disorienting and often alienating effects of communicative capitalism.

Christakos writes extensively about the maternal body. A suite of procedural poems about a pregnant woman named Sherry Mary culminates in the birth of Sherry Mary's baby. This poem is composed by alphabetizing the words in each of the previous poems; these lines are interspersed with numbers that increase and then diminish in volume, reflecting a climaxing and receding contraction. "News Now" describes a baby being breast-fed:

Almost a backward swoon.
Little yawn.
Coming up soon on your

local nipple.

A gain.

A gain.

A gain.

(Christakos 2008, 18)

The poem perfectly captures a small intimate moment between mother and baby, an infant yawning just before latching. However, the key to Christakos's poetics of strategic embodiment lies in her linking of the maternal body and the attachment and alienation that underscores the mother-child dyad to the attachment and alienation of communicative capitalism.

Christakos's use of the breast-feeding latch as a metaphor for attachment is clear in "Turret Door," a poem composed of fragments of texts gleaned from the Internet. The fragments in this poem are unified through the fact that they each, in their original forms, contained the word "latch," sometimes in reference to breast-feeding and sometimes in relation to latches on doors, purses, and other objects. Christakos systematically replaces the word "latch" with the words "hyphen dash" (usually in direct succession, although sometimes she uses either "hyphen" or "dash"), resulting in a playful poem in which the latch is absent but constantly invoked:

> The fixed door is usually held closed using a hyphen dash on the edge of the
> door that slides upward into the jamb at the top.
>> There's a hyphen dash you pry open with your finger to release the chip.
>> Yep.
>> I had a red patent leather one, with a hyphen dash that clicked.
>> Was a hyphen dash key kid.
>> Photos show baby dash on with 'asymmetric' dash.
>> The hyphen dash is stuck and there's no way Kim can get it unstuck so Kim
> has to cut her out of it!
>> Handles, straps and a hyphen dash.
> (Christakos 2008, 27)

Her use of substitution and displacement begs the question of the relationship between what we latch onto as adults and primary infantile forms of attachment; how does the latch manifest in new contexts as we progress beyond infancy, and can we trace all of our attachments and desires back to the latch? The fact that she replaces "latch" with two words that are, in effect, marks of punctuation suggests an additional connection between language and the latch. Latches have a dual function: they can open something or they can hold something in place. Similarly, hyphens and dashes both function grammatically to join and separate. "Turret Door" uses a simple act of word substitution to ask complex questions about connection and displacement. Using language gleaned from websites to build poems about latches, Christakos's poems directly address the ways in which communicative capitalism "produce[s] and circulate[s] affect as a binding technique" (Dean 2011a, 95).

The relationship between language and the maternal body is also evident in the poem "My Attaché Case" when Christakos writes: "My breasts have held milk / and expressed milk and / held language by the tit / so to speak attachment" (2008, 41) and "My breasts have held / milk to a new / stanza code held language / by the tit effect / like visual splendour coupons" (42). These words find an echo in a poem titled "Visual Splendour Coupons" in which Christakos writes, "My idle eyes beheld milk / and milk's surrogate: tears of disbelief, fatigue" (15), and also in "Attouché" where she writes: "Our breasts have held pleased nonslip perfect milk to / pleased new stanza code held language / We concede its cup its plastic by touched tit effect" (46). Christakos is clearly influenced by French feminist conceptualizations of *écriture feminine* in her exploration of the relationship between writing and the female body. However, her work departs from that of the French feminists in her reliance on procedural compositional methods, her use of the vernacular, her reliance on popular culture rather than the texts of high modernism, and her use of irony, factors that distinguish her work as materially grounded in relation to lived experiences and the everyday. In this regard, Christakos's work diverges from a sort of idealized and metaphoric maternal explored in Julia Kristeva's "Stabat Mater" (1977) or Hélène Cixous's "Laugh of the Medusa" (1976). Christakos's invocation of the maternal breast is marked by absence rather than presence; her reference to "milk's surrogate" and the "tit effect" suggests a displacement by which it is only possible to access surrogates and effects rather than originals. The "tit effect" is further likened to "visual splendour coupons"; once again she invokes displacement rather than presence, deferral rather than satisfaction. Coupons are items of exchange in the context of commodity culture, assigned a value equivalent to an absent but desired item. The coupon invokes the "visual splendour" of commodity culture—toys, food, gadgets, and sex—without rendering these things actually present. Christakos invokes an economy of exchange in which the most sought-after items are virtual rather than actual; this is an erotics of absence rather than presence. This theme of exchange is anticipated and established in the book's opening dedication: "for you*" which is qualified by a footnote that reads "*fully redeemable." Although there is some degree of ambiguity regarding what, exactly, is fully redeemable (the book? the dedication? the reader? the writer?), the dedication raises the closely related notions of value and exchange. If the dedication represents a kind of attachment, it is one that we may trade in for another or return for a refund if we are not satisfied; the reader is overtly cast as a consumer. The redeemability of this dedication can be read as undermining the very concept of attachment. It can also be read as a critical commentary on the neoliberal tendency to reduce everything to market value.[2]

Christakos extends her exploration of attachment to an examination of the relationship between reader and writer: on what basis do we form an attachment to a piece of writing or an authorial or lyric voice? What happens to the attachment when the stability of that voice is undermined? She works in a variety of vernacular registers to create lyric voices and personae onto which the reader can "latch." She also challenges the reader's connection to the lyric "I" by undermining the stability of the speaker through fragmentation and shifting registers. She explains:

> As a reader you have to figure out, who's this? Is this Margaret or is this some character she's producing or is this manipulated text where there is some kind of trace of her voice or some sense of the source. It's really very much about what does stir us to the surface and why we want this aesthetic experience of attachment, whether it is to each other or to texts or art in general. (Christakos 2009, 115)

Because it is often impossible for the reader to determine whether the voice in a given poem is a character, the poet herself, or manipulated text generated from procedural experiments, the reader's affective bond (real or perceived) to the lyric subject is constantly called into question. For example, Christakos creates a series of poems called "The Hoity-Toity Supplements" that center on a pregnant character named Sherry Mary. In addition to poems written from the perspectives of Sherry Mary, her therapist, and her boyfriend Billy Bob that explore the emotional and personal ties among these characters, this section also contains cryptic list poems out of which the more lyrical poems are created. The list poems become, in Christakos's words, "the armature" for the lyric poems (2009, 114), and the reader can actually trace the migration of words from list poem to lyric poem. The opening lines of "The Chronic Files of One Sherry Mary," which read: "Surreptitious breasts as in / Reptilian lights, UV as in / Petalled heights as in / Leapable bells as in" (2008, 59), become part of the following lines from "Ash, as in Ashen, Sherry Mary Feels": "Surreptitious breasts of the brain's inside, crammed with / reptilian lights, UV or incandescent, zoom lens for the purpose of / petalled heights. Sherry Mary saw him hunkered and hiding, grasping / leapable bells in his greasy palms. Smarmy knots" (67). Christakos builds a more narratively driven poem using the list poem as a kind of scaffolding. The primacy of the lyric voice is undermined because the procedurally generated poems exist prior to the lyric poems, and the reader is invited to question the privileging of the lyric as more authentic or affectively charged than procedural poetry.

The poem "(I Really Don't Think You're) Strong Enough" plays with the conventions of confessional poetry and the expectations some readers bring to bear on poetry as a genre that expresses the poet's most intimate thoughts. The phrase "something inside me" is repeated 110 times in this ten-page poem and each time, the phrase is followed by a somewhat random phrase generated through poetic procedure. Here are the opening lines of the poem:

Something inside me was screaming Write
you fool! Tell the whole damned
world how you

feel! Something inside
says there's somewhere
better than this
Holy one I have something inside me
something nameless I started thinking about
    Yes
Poland and something inside me wanted
to come back Listen to Something
    Inside Me by
    Elmore James for free
    on Rhapsody Something
    inside me wishes
this was photoshopped
(Christakos 2008, 90)

The "something inside me" is never revealed to be a deeply personal or emotional expression. Instead, it is fleeting, fractured, multiple, and random. The poem can be read as a commentary on the paradox of living in a confessional culture in the context of communicative capitalism; subjects are prompted to reveal their feelings excessively and those feelings circulate as excess, empty speech in online environments.

Closely connected to Christakos's persistent interest in attachment and alienation is her curiosity about the attachments we form to texts, and by extension, to commodities. In this regard, her work continues in the tradition of the language poets who resisted the commodification of language and the supposed attachment the reader forms to texts through identification and projection.[3] The title poem of the book, "What Stirs?" addresses the reader directly to interrogate the implicit expectations that readers place on narrators and speakers and the attachments they form to them: "You will care about me as your narrator, not as your buddy or tour guide. I / can't be your laundress and I won't suck you off. You are a shallow / consumer if your palm is starting to perspire, already, before your arse / is even warm" (Christakos 2008, 82). She further identifies and questions the conventional relationship between reader and writer: "Perhaps I am a selfish brat but so are you if you have a book / in your hand. I'll tell you what it is to be a writer so you let / yourself off the hook of longing that any reader winches tighter one / lung at a time" (82), and a few lines later: "You want what it's worth as if ideas / could be money. It is time to reveal something about being a writer" (84). While Christakos refuses to act as tour guide to the "shallow consumer" or complacent reader, she does encourage readers to take an active role in the process of meaning-making and to reflect upon the dynamics of attachment and alienation as these apply to the relationship between writers and readers.

The personae in the poems in *What Stirs* form attachments to Internet pornography, pharmaceuticals, lovers, and other subjects and objects, both tangible and intangible, that get placed in their metaphorical "attaché cases," a symbol Christakos deploys in order to think about the social dynamics of attachment: "And in my attaché case / I put all the things / that have stood in for / me Stand up for me— / Stood guard" (2008, 43). The attaché case functions as an extension of the self and a symbol for attachment, but Christakos suggests that attachment does not necessarily equal ownership:

> I mean the person thinks
> they can own something
> and then there must also
> be things not owned
> nor carried around for another
> effect like visual splendour
> weight rebalancing mood alteration transfer
> to a new stanza.
> (2008, 41)

"Visual splendour," a phrase repeated several times in different poems, underscores the relationship between aesthetics, commodity fetishism, and the desire for connection. On the next page, Christakos repeats and recontextualizes several phrases from the previous page, this time linking ownership to the complexities of bodily autonomy experienced by the breast-feeding mother:

> . . . I mean
> the person thinks they

can own something timeshare
and then there must
also by who owns
it convincingly nor carried
around for another so
to speak attachment cabaret
weight rebalancing mood alternation
transfer and expressed milk
(2008, 42)

Here Christakos presents the maternal body as a site of contested ownership and compromised agency. The lactating mother inhabits her body as a kind of "timeshare"; when nursing, one's degree of bodily autonomy is compromised insofar as one's body is placed in the service of another, is partially given over to another. The "timeshare" metaphor presents the mother's body as a commodity or property to be owned, shared, exchanged, or bartered in the context of maternal relations. By transferring and expressing milk, the mother encourages the infant to take a bottle, thus asserting a degree of bodily separation and freedom, although this separation can be experienced as loss.

"My Attaché Case" explores notions of displacement, barter, and exchange, suggesting that the objects to which one is attached usually stand in for some other more primary form of attachment: "You know that what you / carried in it was / not the important object it / was the surrogate of / what could not be carried / at all but bartered" (Christakos 2008, 41). Cumulatively, the poems in *What Stirs* suggest that the subject's primary attachment to the mother's breast, an attachment characterized by a dialectic of gratification and frustration, goes on to fuel our subsequent libidinal and destructive impulses and comes to characterize the insatiable drives of commodity culture and communicative capitalism.

In its exploration of the perpetual search for connection and intimacy in the context of networked environments, *What Stirs* inevitably engages with the world of online pornography. In a poem called "Compared to Poetry," pornography is described as "impaired by poetry," but also "impaired, compared to poetry's precision" (Christakos

2008, 77). Pornography and poetry may be viewed as starkly divergent modes of expression, yet consumers of each genre often come to the material with an expectation that they will gain something from it, whether that "something" comes in the form of arousal, knowledge, reflection, release, or some other experience. How, Christakos seems to ask, is the affective experience that readers seek from poetry similar to or different from the affective experience they seek from pornography? She offers fragmentary descriptions of Internet pornography, moving quickly from image to image as if clicking from web page to web page:

> Pillow like opal compared to poetry aglow in the silent bedroom. Sexy as recording of homemade intercourse on Internet, blond chick with dildo moaning. Impaired as French geek solving Rubik's cube with chimpanzee toes— he's faking it, reverses video—grunts arousal. If you can see yourself in this playback mirror, clap your soles. Purgatory like jouissance—jouissance like a population purged of the intimate
> (2008, 77)

Jouissance in a psychoanalytic context is understood as a kind of pleasure that borders on the uncomfortable or unbearable. The intolerable aspect of *jouissance* is crucial to the ways in which desire and sexual pleasure function in the poem; this is *jouissance*-as-purgatory. *Jouissance* is, more broadly, also integral to the reader's experience of the poems in this book, where meaning is not always apparent and the reader has to dwell in the somewhat alienating pleasure of "not getting it."[4] *Jouissance* is also central to Jodi Dean's theory of the affective networks of communicative capitalism and is thus directly relevant to the disorienting effects that networked environments have on the subject. Drawing on Lacan, Dean argues that *jouissance* is associated with surplus enjoyment, and by extension, anxiety that is facilitated by communicative capitalism (2011a, 91–92). What is stirred to the surface in Christakos's poems is a kind of anxiety-ridden *jouissance*, a disorienting and disconcerting yet oddly pleasurable and immediately identifiable exploration of affect and embodiment in the context of communicative capitalism. Christakos uses Internet pornography as a metaphor for this alienating *jouissance*:

Botox botany in megasuperstore. Jade leaves inflated, about to orgasm. We are all inches from a precipice expecting ecstasy. So depressed another coffee feels marvellous. I rub your shoulder blade, you bleeping spasm! Messy as poetry compared to itself, a slurped orgy of impaired hearts flickering and melamine-spiked minnow feed.

(2008, 77)

Linking sexual pleasure to purgatory and a lack of intimacy, invoking bodies made unreal by plastic surgery, Christakos suggests that the world of online pornography seems to be populated by solitary voyeurs, seeking but not finding connection. If, as Stephen Maddison argues, pornography can be seen as a "barometer of the changing conditions of sex in cultural politics" (2013, 102), then the kind of sex represented online reflects broader social and cultural shifts. Maddison links Internet porn to neoliberalism, positing Internet porn as a

> function of the post-Fordist working experiences of porn consumers seeking pleasure in terms that replicate and facilitate work patterns or that offer compensations for the privations of neoliberalism. Here porn consumption offsets the impossibility of the sexual standards it installs: impossible to achieve because we don't have enough time for an elaborate recreational sex life, or at least one that patterns the affective capacity of the sexualized society; impossible to achieve because we are unable to autonomously realize our libidinous capacity, because we're too tired, alienated, socially inept, or domestically and socially compromised, or because our sensory and affective responses might relate more to mediated, networked interactions than to "meat" intimate bodily ones. (Maddison 2013, 107)

Porn, then, becomes a kind of fantasy projection that tries to compensate for what is ultimately unobtainable. For Christakos, Internet porn gestures to the limitations of this post-Fordist world insofar as it manifests, through sheer falsity, the gulf between lived reality and projected fantasy, a fantasy that is "purged of the intimate," leaving us "inches from a precipice expecting ecstasy," and "depressed" (2008, 77). In the poem's concluding verse, the speaker concedes "Everything's sort of ugly ... / All desire so / gaseous even perfection's impaired, compared to poetry" (77). Although this comparison seems to favor poetry over pornography, Christakos's poems, in their refusal of closure and their tendency to vacillate between the registers of the readable and the unreadable, can be said to mimic the fragmented, fleeting, and explicit world of online pornography; both offer the promise of attachment and connection but both also withhold, frustrate, and alienate.

Central to Christakos's poetic and political project, not just in *What Stirs* but in her entire poetic oeuvre, is a determination to frame the maternal subject as both a sexual and desiring subject (2009, 114). Furthermore, Christakos seeks to articulate the complexity of maternal subjectivity beyond the reductive stereotypes of the selfless, nurturing mother and the selfish, narcissistic mother. The body in this text is inseparable from the affective, economic, and technological networks of communicative capitalism. By forging connections between online communication, attachment, desire, and the maternal body, *What Stirs* embraces what Jennifer Scappettone calls "strategic embodiment" in an attempt to understand the affective dimensions of communicative capitalism in the Internet age. *What Stirs*, as its title suggests, is ultimately about the things that hold the power to "stir" us in the context of networked environments and consumer culture, the connections we yearn for, and the ways in which those connections, while sometimes deferred and frustrated, also show up in places so surprising and unexpected that they lead not only to new affective bonds but to also to new ways of seeing and reading.

Larissa Lai and Rita Wong's Hybrid Poetics of Resistance

Written in the wake of the SARS crisis and in the months following the U.S. invasion of Iraq, Larissa Lai and Rita Wong's long poem *sybil unrest* ([2008] 2013) offers a strategically embodied poetics that critically engages neoliberalism, globalization, and technocapitalism. In contrast to Christakos, who develops a poetics premised on attachment, Wong and Lai enact a poetics of dispersal, deferral, and hybridity. Dispersal, deferral, and hybridity occur on at least three levels in the text: through collective authorship; through an understanding of the body not as a discrete entity but as implicated in networks of biopower; and through the mobilization of puns that disperse meaning and allow language to signify in multiple ways.

sybil unrest strategically unsettles the stability of the lyric I, producing instead a "range of i's emerging and fading back as instances that unsettle the (capitalist) time and space we occupy" (Lai and Wong, 127). The posthuman speaker of the poem is "imaginatively dispersed across two authorial bodies, a strategy that raises the question of where boundaries of voice, identity and authorship lie" (L'Abbé 2011). *sybil unrest* incorporates Lai's persistent interest in posthuman, plural subjectivities and genetic modification as explored in her novel *Salt Fish Girl* (2002) and her collection of poems *Automaton Biographies* (2009), and Wong's use of poetic form to trace the connections between biopiracy, capitalism, and colonialism and to decenter the humanist subject as part of a strong environmental and anticolonial ethic as explored in her collections of poetry *monkeypuzzle* (1999), *forage* (2007), and *undercurrent* (2015). Although *sybil unrest* bears the unmistakable influence of both of these poets, it is impossible to trace specific lines, images, and metaphors to either Wong or Lai because the work is truly collaborative and coauthored.[5]

sybil unrest enacts a posthuman poetics that resonates with Rosi Braidotti's claim that posthumanism is an effective "navigational tool" for "engaging affirmatively with the present" (2013, 5). Identifying a disciplinary division between theoretical studies of science and technology on the one hand, and political analyses of capitalism on the other, Braidotti identifies a "need to review this segregation of discursive fields and work towards a reintegrated posthuman theory that includes both scientific and technological complexity and its implications of political subjectivity, political economy, and forms of governance" (43). *sybil unrest* works precisely across these fields. As Sonnet L'Abbé argues, Wong and Lai "destabilize the frame of the 'human' as containing a single self, or single organic unit. They ask how the human organism survives despite being relentlessly organized into capitalist systems of language and other media in a race-class-and-gender-inflected late capitalist geopolitical landscape" (2011).

The book's title positions the collective narrator/speaker of these poems as a "sybil" or prophetess engaged in an extended, restless critique of civic and social issues. Like the sybils of classical myth, the speaker of this poem couches her truths in riddles and word games. The poem's title, an obvious play on the term "civil unrest," is a socially and politically engaged call to rise up against the master narratives of capitalism, nationalism, colonialism, and patriarchy.

Like Scappettone and Christakos, Wong and Lai strategically foreground the body in their work. One of the book's central preoccupations is with the ways in which the queer, Asian, female body becomes implicated in networks of biopower that are fueled by heteropatriarchal capitalism. The body is exoticized and eroticized by these networks but it also functions as a site of agency, resistance, and subversion. The poem's opening lines foreground a subversive, queer sexuality:

shrinkwrapped pushy
condemns on sale
dill pickle harmless
let her strap on
law's garters
lend me your tears
cunt remand
loved fist
loose brigand
safe sects
nimble clamps
over and over
just a mother
hole in the wall
tribade's revelations
wet pinch of salt
on the stroke of midknife
(Lai and Wong 2013, 3)

Through the deployment of puns that obliquely conjure dental dams, condoms, dildo harnesses, fisting, and nipple clamps, Lai and Wong enact a poetics located squarely in the realm of queer desire. The fact that the revelations are the property of a "tribade" can be read as positioning the speaker, the restless "sybil," as a queer female subject, situated in opposition to the phallic "skyscrapers spent, flaccid" referenced two pages later (2013, 5) or the "corporate mounties . . . / batons erect" (11), although perhaps not immune to the "sadomarketism" (7) that commodifies even the queerest of sexualities and the "mammary lands / of milk and money" (86) in which "fifteen famous porn stars stimulate / economy" (22). Transposing the intimate realm of the body into the very public and global contexts of economy, technology, manufacturing, colonialism, and imperialism, Wong and Lai explore the ways in which biopower mediates and structures public and private relations, exposing the "patterns that recur when sex, gender, and the global imaginary combine" (Pratt and Rosner 2012, 2).

Puns and wordplay become key strategies through which Lai and Wong articulate dispersal and hybridity. They deploy homonyms and words that sound similar enough to other words that they evoke multidimensional associations. Through the extensive use of puns, many of which are created by modifying familiar advertising slogans, song lyrics, poems, and clichés, the language of *sybil unrest* is "double mortgaged in one reading; in another, they accrue additional value to themselves. Words, like genes, have become something that can be owned; everyone knows who the 'swoosh belongs to. They are traded on an exchange, but puns subvert their fixed value" (Mayer 2009b). In this regard, Lai and Wong share much in common with Harryette Mullen, whose poetic wordplay and strategic punning in texts like *Trimmings* (1991) and *S*PeRM**K*T* (1992) critically examine the ways in which "commodification, desire, and identity are rigidly interpolated" (Mix 2007, 51) especially with regard to racialized bodies. Mullen can be read as an influence on Lai and Wong and an important precursor to the kind of embodied poetics they develop in *sibyl unrest*.

Bob Dylan's famous song "Knock Knock Knocking on Heaven's Door" mutates in *sybil unrest* into "knock knock knocking on chevron's door" (2013, 78), and "Swing Low Sweet Chariot" becomes "swing low sweet patriot / . . . coming for to carry me / to the land of social insecurity" (75–76). Lai and Wong's rewriting of the famous lines spoken by the three witches in the opening scene of Shakespeare's *Macbeth* invokes the exploitation of the environment in the interests of capital, but also draws attention to the impact of this activity on the individual subject whose domestic water supply has become contaminated by environmental pollutants:

crumble crumble oil and bumble
liars churn and exxon valdez tumbles
roadkill carcasses pile higher, mired, find
reboot won't do
as tons of sewage carry pesticides,
estrogen, prozac, pcbs into
the kitchen stinks
(Lai and Wong 2013, 78)

They reimagine Descartes's famous line "I think therefore I am" as "i think therefore i ham" (2013, 79) By modifying a statement that is closely linked to the development of the mind/body split and the rise of the humanist subject in Western philosophy, Lai and Wong pose a playful but pointed challenge to Western philosophical traditions by calling into question the boundaries and divisions upon which the subject of humanism is founded, a subject that is, as Braidotti argues, "modeled upon ideals of white masculinity, normality, youth, and health" (2013, 67–68).

"i think therefore i ham" can also be read in relation to the numerous references to pigs that occur throughout the poem, mostly in the context of discussions of factory farming and genetic modification. The following passage illustrates the prevalence of this concern in the text:

leap hog factory farm
industrial replication
love's lepers lost
mimicry introduces mutation
charmed I'm sure
autocorrect capitalizes the subject
the pig pisses next to the pig pissing next to the pig
passing the cellular difference
stalled on the hill
clutching the genome's
correction mutation
in time with the tao
of the piglet disney bought
(Lai and Wong 2013, 10)

Through puns and wordplay, Lai and Wong explore issues ranging from factory farming to genetic modification to Disney's purchasing of the rights to A. A. Milne's famous anthropomorphized animals. These topics are united not only through the passage's (and indeed much of the book's) overriding porcine imagery, but also through the connection between each of these themes and global capitalism.

Genetic modification is a central concern in Wong's single-authored collection, *forage*, published shortly before *sybil unrest*. In *forage*, Wong splices words like a scientist splices genes, creating a poetic language that reflects genetic modification at the levels of both form and process. Lai and Wong employ a similar method of splicing in *sybil unrest*, where they speak of "robocrop[s]" (2013, 23) and describe scenes in which "stuck pig grunts / pumped full of antibiotics / psychotic bacon / beckons / know thy enzyme / transgenic estrogenic / effluvium transfers / into your porcine gut / glow-in-the-dark hashbrowns / come with the order" (19). Their critique of genetic modification resonates strongly with Timothy Morton's observation that genetic engineering "turns life forms into private property to enrich huge corporations. . . . Capitalism has always restricted gene pools and amassed large quantities of property, with accompanying stability and power" (2010, 86). Morton observes that the "capitalist language of deregulation, flow, and circulation masks the static, repetitive, 'molar' qualities of capitalist forms. But processes of privatization and ownership contradict the liquid, queer, multigenetic, shadowy, and ungraspable qualities of life forms" (86–87). Through the use of puns, Lai and Wong create a poetics that mimics, reflects, and subverts the capitalist discourses of flow, deregulation, and circulation. However, unlike capitalism, Wong and Lai's intent is rhizomatic rather than molar; they dislodge and question hierarchies, and embrace queer, pluralized forms in their poetics.

Lai and Wong's interest in genetic modification and biopiracy is closely linked to their feminist and antiracist convictions. In this regard, their poetics resonates strongly with recent feminist critiques that forge critical connections between biopolitics, capitalism, and the environment. For example, Rosi Braidotti, building on Felix Guattari's emphasis on the importance of creating transversal lines between environment, social context, and subjectivity, argues for the need to see the multiple interconnections among misogyny, racism, capitalism, and industrial pollution (2013, 93). As Vandana Shiva (1997) argues, biopiracy is an extension of colonialism and a manifestation of capitalism, and although it places all living beings in peril, those most at risk include women, citizens of developing nations, and nonhuman animals. Lai and Wong write from a similar political position, and the fragmented and polyvocal structure of *sybil unrest* allows them to move precisely across this terrain. One of the challenges of writing about *sybil unrest* lies in the fact that Lai and Wong's critical engagement with issues as diverse as genetic modification, industrial pollution, the violent history of nation-building, globalization, neoliberalism, misogyny, racism, and homophobia intersect to such a degree that it is nearly impossible to isolate one or two political themes about which to write. But this is precisely the point they are trying to make; *sybil unrest* is a rhizomatic text insofar as it strives to create a multitude of "connections between semiotic chains, organizations of power, and circumstances relative to the arts, sciences, and social struggles" (Deleuze and Guattari 1987, 7).

Lai and Wong also utilize poetic form to explore the relationship between the rise of the Canadian nation-state, the reliance on exploited Asian workers for nation-building projects such as the Canadian Pacific Railroad, and the ongoing exploitation of these workers in a free-market global economy when they write:

> few men chew
> chew choose the train
> whether they built the tracks
> or drove the last spike
> or bought containers
> that make up the train
> that goes on the tracks
> that made up the railway that cn built
> (Lai and Wong 2013, 12)

They begin with a reference to Fu Man Chu, the "outlandish turn-of-the-century creation figured by tropes of the Yellow Peril" (Chen 2012, 115).[6] By changing the spelling to "few man chew" they invoke a secondary meaning; "few men chew" could refer to a shortage of food or money, and by extension to the economic conditions that led many Chinese men to "chew choose train," or in other words, to participate in the difficult and dangerous work of constructing the Canadian Pacific Railroad, a project of nation-building that was directly linked to the colonization of the Canadian West. In naming the "containers / that make up the train," they allude to the long freight trains that traverse Canada and which carry containers that have come off ships (mostly from China) full of goods manufactured in Asia that are destined for distribution warehouses and, eventually, for big-box stores in towns and cities across the country. Like the workers who built the railroad, sweatshop laborers toil in unsafe conditions for meager pay, but due to a lack of better opportunities, choose to carry out this work upon which the consumer-driven cultures of Europe and North America depend. By overlaying examples from two distinct historical periods, both of which underscore the global economy's reliance on exploited Chinese laborers, Lai and Wong comment wryly that there is "no point reinventing the deal / that worked so well the first time" (2013, 12). They not only underscore the continued reliance of Canada on Chinese labor, but also imply a continuity between racist discourses that cast Chinese workers as a "yellow peril" in the late nineteenth century, and modern-day treatment of Chinese immigrants and labourers in Canada, "illegal until proven guilty / want the labour without the body" (16). This history of marginalization is manifested in the bodies and voices of twenty-first-century Asian Canadians:

last century's logic said
we'd never learn
ghost our bodies through
proper pronunciation slips distance
racialized lunge for glottal stops
exchange intimate vernaculars
choice body and body only or
language and language only
quick fix labour's assembly line
(Lai and Wong 2013, 36)

Rather than "ghosting" the Asian body by adhering to Anglo-Canadian linguistic and cultural norms, Lai and Wong foreground the Asian body, and specifically the Asian, female, and frequently queered body as a site that is both subject to biopolitical surveillance and control *and* a potential site of agency and disruption. As Sonnet L'Abbé argues, "In *sybil unrest*, easy alignments of racialization with identification, or marginalization, are knotted and tangled as articulations of racialized and gendered experience inform declarations of power and engagement—as well as disaffection—within a global economy." Race, nation, gender, and sexuality are "commodities of shifting value, marketable and wearable as signs of moment-to-moment big brand affiliation" (2011). Lai and Wong describe a "glossy crotchshot / in a hongkong subway" that "sells jeans / sheen of commerce / . . . arched breath unzips / her marketed anatomy" (2013, 39). The Asian female body is, as L'Abbé notes, both marked and marketed, and Lai and Wong's "attention to both the circulation of images of Asian women and of labour in a global economy and in the Western imaginary demonstrates their awareness of inhabiting simultaneous positions of social privilege and dislocation." They utilize wordplay, puns, and homophones in order to address complex aspects of subjectivity, identity, and politics through their poetry: "try sector, trimester, perpetual scrutiny, / slowly bound with china / adopt garment labour / filament lesbos to / polyglot postwhore girls" (62). Through a poetics of dispersal, deferral, and hybridity manifested through collective authorship, language play, and an understanding of the body as implicated in biopolitics, they address the relationship between women's bodies and surveillance, the working conditions of garment workers, queer desire, capitalism, war, and the sex trade in these five short lines. Puns and wordplay allow an economy and efficiency of meaning; indeed, "economy" and "efficiency" are put to use in this poetry in ways that run deliberately counter to their deployment in neoliberal and capitalist discourses.

Through a constellation of interlinked references, Lai and Wong show the Asian female body as subjected to biopolitical forms of control and racialized forms of violence in the context of warfare and global capitalism and further reveal our (often unintentional) complicity in these practices. They reference Nick Ut's famous photo of a naked Vietnamese girl (Phan Ti Kim Phuc) running from a napalm attack during the Vietnam War, noting she is "napalm naked" (Lai and Wong 2013, 120). On the next page, we learn that the Dow corporation sold the napalm: "bring that dow to market / to court / before thousands of unseen bodies / who lived in the earth" (121). Redress for this action "remains to be seen" (121). Their expansive poetics excavates the layers of global capitalism and urges readers to face their own complicity; Dow plastics and chemicals are nearly ubiquitous since we use their products daily in our homes and workplaces. We are indirectly implicated as consumers in supporting a company responsible for this and other atrocities.

In spite of their insistence on foregrounding the ways in which queer, Asian female bodies are "marked" and "marketed" (L'Abbé 2011) in the context of late capitalist global culture, Wong and Lai do not present these bodies as lacking in agency but rather as sites of resistance and pleasure: "defiant vulvas venture / through patriarchal corridors / their ragged magma / turns convention to convection" (2013, 52). Theirs is a "vengeance / of the dispossessed / flash angry breasts / fossil fuels erotic offer / venous on the half shell" (88). The restless sybil in Lai and Wong's poem fuses organic and inorganic, animal and machine in a cautionary yet playful critique of advanced capitalist technoculture, which, while impossible to escape, is there to be fucked with in every sense:

> we clock our overdraft
> in times new roman
> loose mysteries
> twist forked laughter
> as goddesses sign in triplicate
> "the pleasures of being multiple"
> (Lai and Wong 2013, 53)

This restless sybil enacts "spiral dance or viral pranks / who can spill the difference?" (2013, 117). The spiral dance, a participatory ritualized dance commonly performed at pagan gatherings as a way of invoking creative and activist energies, is certainly reflective of the political and spiritual undertones of *sybil unrest*. However, viral pranks, with their connotations not just of the speed of online networked environments where things can "go viral" and where computer viruses can take down networks, but also of a world where viruses like SARS may pass quickly from person to person, or from animal to person, underscore the fact that vulernability and interconnectivity are equally central to the activist strategies explored here. The posthumanist speaker of *sybil unrest* echoes elements of Donna Haraway's cyborg: she is "committed to partiality, irony, intimacy, and perversity. . . oppositional, utopian, and completely without innocence" (Haraway 1991, 151). And, as Haraway reminds us, "writing is pre-eminintly the technology of cyborgs" (176).

Like Jennifer Scappettone and Margaret Christakos, Larissa Lai and Rita Wong enact a strategic embodiment in their poetry that is crucial to their engagement with capitalism. Lai and Wong deploy puns that actively contribute to the multiplication and hybridity of meaning in the text; puns ensure that meaning is always in flux and operating simultaneously in different registers. Embodiment becomes a primary factor in their critique of biopolitics, advanced capitalism, and the racism and heterosexism that underscore narratives of nationalism and nation-building. The body also operates in the text as a site of agency, pleasure, and resistance. The poem's dual authorship and collaborative compositional structure actively undermine any attempt to trace the body in this text to a single author; instead, both body and speaker become caught up in posthumanist networks of resistance to biopolitics. I turn in the next chapter to a feminist poetics of strategic embodiment that enacts its politics not through the multiplicity of hybridity and dispersal, but rather through the singularity of disgust.

CHAPTER TWO

The Affective Politics of Disgust

Nikki Reimer's *[sic]* and Rachel Zolf's *Human Resources*

Meet Me at the Intersection between Art and Commerce: The Body as Subversive Commodity in Nikki Reimer's *[sic]*

Nikki Reimer's *[sic]* (2010) was written in Vancouver at a time when the city was undergoing widespread and rapid gentrification that has made it extremely difficult for writers, artists, students, and other creative and cultural workers to live and thrive there.[1] Like the work of other writers affiliated with the Vancouver-based Kootenay School of Writing such as Jeff Derksen and Stephen Collis, Reimer's poetry is driven in part by a critique of neoliberalism. Her writing is distinct, however, in its persistent concern with the impact of neoliberalism on women and, more specifically, in its exploration of the ways in which the female body is disciplined under capitalism, yet also subverts and exceeds capitalist logic. Reimer's exploration of the female body as a commodity in the context of late capitalism is most evident in the section of the book titled "corporate whores," a suite of poems devoted to exploring the connections between capitalism, the body, gender, and urban spaces. In the first poem in this suite Reimer writes:

> please respond to the social imperative to martyr oneself;
> clutch thorns to chest and march down hastings street
> work the job to job the work to job the work to
>   work the job to job to work to job
> we all go to work in the panopticon but some of us are
> frillier than others corporate whore says why can't i wear
> pink boots and fishnet stockings to work?
> (2010, 19)

Reimer questions the ethic that governs increasingly precarious forms of work and specifically draws attention to the panoptic surveillance and regulation of women through the imposition of sartorial regulations that limit their agency and enforce social norms. The repetition of "work" and "job" has a numbing effect and draws attention to the repetition and monotony of most paid work. Through the deployment of Catholic imagery (a trope that recurs throughout [sic]), she draws parallels between Catholicism and capitalism; both demand faith from their participants: martyring oneself for the sake of a job holds the promise of greater material gains, while martyring oneself for the sake of religion holds the promise of greater spiritual gains. Women occupy an equally contradictory role in relation to Catholicism and capitalism. In the context of Catholicism, the feminine is both celebrated through the exaltation of the Virgin Mary and marginalized, since women are barred from occupying positions of power within the church; moreover, female sexuality is tightly regulated and women are denied control of their bodies through prohibitions on birth control and abortion. In the context of capitalism, women's bodies are central to commodity culture, where they are used to sell everything from cars to alcohol, but in spite of this, women reap far fewer economic benefits and hold far less economic power than men.

Reimer explores the contradictory rhetoric of female liberation in the context of late capitalism, where women's empowerment is linked to their sexual desirability and their role as consumers. In a poem titled "epistemologically speaking, i've had it," she writes: "consumerism makes me feel so good like yesterday i / bought a blush called *Orgasm*, and i thought, / naomi wolf would be proud" (2010, 24). Under neoliberalism, freedom is linked to purchasing power, but this kind of liberation is ultimately circumscribed by its focus on individual gratification. "That the height of supposed female emancipation coincides so perfectly with consumerism is a miserable index of a politically desolate time," writes Nina Power in *One Dimensional Woman* (2009), her scathing critique of neoliberalism's co-optation of feminism. Contemporary feminism, Power argues, is marketed to women as a movement of individual rather than collective action, of self-esteem and consumption. "Almost anything turns out to be feminist," Power argues, "shopping, pole dancing, even eating chocolate" (27). Neoliberal feminism strips feminism of political struggle and rebrands it so that the desire for emancipation becomes coterminous with the desire to buy (28). As Rosi Braidotti states, "Post-feminist neoliberalism is pro-capitalist and hence it considers financial success as the sole indicator of the status of women" (2006, 45). In a similar vein, Angela McRobbie argues that while women are encouraged to participate as consumers and workers in a culture she identifies as "postfeminist," the "rhetoric of the confident female consumer forecloses on the re-emergence of feminism in favour of apathy and de-politicization" (2009, 43). Through "tropes of freedom and choice" which are linked to young women, "feminism is decisively aged and made to seem redundant" (11) even as it becomes "for young women, in rather indiscernible ways, an object of loss and melancholia" (94).

Sianne Ngai notes that under postmodernism, discourses of desire have proliferated while discourses of disgust have remained comparatively underdeveloped. In a "public sphere [that] has become increasingly coextensive with the marketplace" (2005, 338), she argues, theoretical discourses of desire offer a broader context for the subject's relationship to art. While disgust is urgent, specific, and singular in its aim, desire is closely aligned with theories of polysemy, multiplicity, slippage, and indeterminacy, concepts central to postmodern and post-structuralist frameworks as well as central to much feminist poetry. In this context, desire, with its attendant strategies of proliferation and multiplicity, has become shorthand for "virtually any perceived transgression of the symbolic status quo" (2005, 337–38). For Ngai, desire's "tropes of semantic multiplicity" make it "concordant, ideologically as well as aesthetically" with the paradigms that have come to define the postmodern, including capitalism (344). Like desire, postmodern cultures are pluralistic and operate in accordance with principles of tolerance; art is tolerated in late capitalist culture because it is ultimately deemed to be ineffectual and nonthreatening. In contrast to desire, Ngai argues, the "centrifugality, agonism, urgency, and above all refusal of the indifferently tolerable" that characterize disgust "offers an entirely different set of aesthetic and critical possibilities than the ones offered by desire" (345). To be clear, Ngai is not aligning postmodernist and post-structuralist theories of desire and multiplicity with a capitalist agenda, but she is suggesting that this kind of writing is easily appropriated by neoliberalism.

If, as Sianne Ngai infers, the slipperiness of desire as a signifier makes it conducive to appropriation by neoliberal capitalism, it is perhaps only logical that rhetorics of female sexual liberation have been co-opted and transformed to conflate sexual desirability and empowerment with consumerism. Reimer's poetry displays an acute awareness of this conflation: "abandon sexual politics it's all scripted commercialism," she states in a poem called "officious" (2010, 38). Reimer's "script for a blue movie" directly addresses the implications of post-feminism:

> you seem not to understand that to inhabit
> a female body *is* a kind of hybridity
> skin the love you're in temper this liminal space
> with a throw pillow or two; perhaps a doily feminism is, like, so
> over "can you angle your pussy a bit more towards the camera?"
> fixated-retentive doesn't understand what's so funny
> about the word "beaver"
> (Reimer 2010, 23)

Reimer invokes the familiar postmodern language of multiplicity and liminality in relation to the female body before gesturing sarcastically to its symbolic domestication through references to doilies and throw pillows, and then perhaps more seriously, to its domination through pornography and sexual objectification in a world where "feminism is, like, so / over" (2010, 23). The theme of sexual objectification and commodification continues throughout the poem. The final two verse paragraphs of "script for a blue movie" read:

> "being disingenuous" vs. "late for pole-dancing class"
> look, if all those women didn't want to disappear,
> they shouldn't have been there ~~(drug-addicted prostitutes)~~
> in the first place march furiously past the library,
> check out the books gone wild!
>
> if we put a pussy on the other side of the nickel i think kids
> would really start to understand the value of a dollar
> (Reimer 2010, 23)

Through a constellation of references, Reimer explores the link between sexual objectification, exploitation, and the economy. Here pole-dancing class evokes the kind of neoliberal post-feminist rhetoric discussed above, a sentiment echoed in the oblique reference—via the delightfully bibliophilic image of books gone wild—to the popular 1990s Girls Gone Wild video franchise in which young college-age women dance, make out, and expose their breasts for the camera. Reimer also makes reference to the sex workers who "disappeared" from the Downtown Eastside of Vancouver, many of whose DNA was found on Robert William Pickton's pig farm in an outlying suburb of the city.[2] By crossing out the words "drug-addicted prostitutes," Reimer draws attention to, while critically distancing herself from, the widespread tendency to blame the victims of this crime because of their alleged drug use, and underscores the fact that this stigma placed on sex workers is largely unspoken but manifested in the length of time it took police to begin treating seriously these cases of missing and murdered women. The reference to placing a "pussy" on the Canadian nickel not only brings the poem back to the reference to "beaver" in the first stanza (in addition to being another euphemism for female genitalia, the beaver is actually featured on the Canadian nickel), it also draws another correlation between female sexuality and the marketplace. Reimer seems to be suggesting, albeit sarcastically, that if we place a pussy on the nickel, children will learn that twenty "pussies" are worth one dollar. Here Reimer gestures to the ways in which women, and more specifically, those working in the sex trade on the Downtown Eastside, are seen by many as "cheap" and essentially disposable.

In developing poetic strategies that both expose and undermine the ways in which capitalism has appropriated female sexuality and female bodies for its own ends, Reimer engages one of the key poetic and theoretical vocabularies through which the female body has been explored in recent decades: the *écriture féminine* of Hélène Cixous. In fact, "Corporate Whores" can be read as an extended dialogue with and revisioning of Cixous's "Laugh of the Medusa" (1976). Reimer answers Cixous's call for women to "write the body," but does so in a way that heightens the negative affect of disgust. In a poem called "why is everybody such an asshole," Reimer writes:

i wanted to write a phenomenological poem but nothing
ever *happens* women are "always writing" about the body
bcz the body engineers subversive action ten-minute
intermission first gush of a two-day late menses oh, what a
shame
                                        write your name on your coffee cup
meet me at the intersection between Art and Commerce
(2010, 22)

Deploying abbreviations that are more commonly found in text mes-
sages than poetry, and writing in a deliberately unpoetic vernacular,
Reimer develops a mode of *écriture féminine* in which the body engi-
neers a subversive event (the arrival of a late period) that effectively
challenges the speaker's assumption that nothing "ever happens" in
a phenomenological poem and ascribes a kind of active agency to the
menstruating body. Instructing the reader to "write [her] name on
[her] coffee cup and meet [the speaker] at the intersection between Art
and Commerce," Reimer locates the menstruating body of the speaker
at the nexus of creative and economic forces. Rita Felski has argued
that "the celebration of feminine sexuality apparent in the writings of
Cixous and other French theorists tends to assume a separation of the
sexual from the social, embracing a metaphysics of desire which fails
to acknowledge the historical mediation of conceptions of the body and
of sexuality by culturally specific systems of signification" (2009, 37).
When Reimer writes the body, she writes a body that is materially
grounded and implicated in cultural, historical, economic, and corpo-
real processes.

"what makes you 'organized'?" a poem that rehearses a series of
common questions one might be asked in a job interview in a corpo-
rate setting, explores the limitations of the language of the corporate
office environment where neither the speaker's boss nor her comput-
er's spell-check recognize the word "conservatism," making it hard for
her to articulate a defense against the political forces to which she ob-
jects. The poem ends with four questions that foreground a connection
between writing and gendered bodies:

why are women always writing about the body why are men
always writing about the penis why are general managers always
writing policy why are housewives always writing grocery lists?
(Reimer 2010, 40)

Her questions invite the reader to consider the connections between
theoretical and literary considerations of gendered modes of expres-
sion and the kind of practical writing that people produce in the "real
world" of the office and the home, encouraging the reader to consider
how these more mundane forms of textual production are implicitly
and explicitly gendered.

The idealized, poetic, metaphorical body explored in texts like Cixous's
"Laugh of the Medusa," where white ink and menstrual blood become
the metaphorical tools through which a multivocal, nonlinear *écriture
féminine* is enacted, gives way in Reimer's text to a messy, unruly,
leaky, disgusting body caught in the quagmire of a capitalist culture.
This is not a rejection of *écriture feminine* so much as it is a rewrit-
ing that emphasizes the mundane over the metaphysical. While one
might be tempted to turn to Julia Kristeva's work on abjection in order
to understand the poetics of disgust in *[sic]*, as Ngai notes, even abjec-
tion "is eventually reconceptualized in the libidinal terms of 'want,'
'primal repression,' and self-shattering *jouissance*" (2005, 332), since
"*jouissance* alone causes the abject to exist as such" (Kristeva 1982,
9). Reimer's poetics of disgust is not rooted in abjection; it does not
lead to the dissolution of self, what Kristeva calls the "beseech[ing] and
pulveriz[ing] of the subject" (5) through a kind of unbearable *jouis-
sance* of the abject. Rather, the singularity of her poetics of disgust is
premised on a refusal that is very firmly rooted in the mundane and in
a kind of fixity that belies *jouissance*.

Polysemy, slippage, and multivocality are not absent from Reimer's
text, but the utopian vision that underscored Cixous's call for women to
write the body gives way in Reimer's text to a sober acknowledgment
of the ways in which female bodies and female desire have become ap-
propriated and commodified in the context of neoliberalism and late
capitalism. The body in these poems is framed and constrained by the

marketplace rather than liberated by *jouissance*. In spite of the near-constant references to sex and the body, Reimer's language is driven not by Eros but by something closer to disgust, which as Ngai argues, "does not so much solve the dilemma of social powerlessness as diagnose it powerfully" (2005, 353).

In her discussion of disgust in relation to capitalism, Sianne Ngai turns to language poetry. Drawing on Bruce Andrews's *I Don't Have Any Paper So Shut Up (or, Social Romanticism)* (1992), Ngai draws attention to Andrews's tendency to deploy proper nouns in his poetry as a way to "fix" language into place, since proper nouns are less prone to polysemy and slippage (2005, 350). Andrews's work is "insistently ugly" (348) and "crowded with the linguistic equivalents of . . . raw matter—expletives, onomatopoeia, and proper names," linguistic elements that are not particularly amenable to re-signification and polysemous slippage (348). According to Ngai, Andrews renders his poetry "intolerable to the extent that it can't be absorbed by the pluralist economy of an aesthetic eclecticism" with its "inclusive pull" (349). In occupying the position of the unconsumable (or what Charles Bernstein calls the "anti-absorptive" [1998]), his poetry is located outside the circle of neoliberal tolerance that dictates the market-driven consumption of art, offering instead an art that is radical in its unconsumability. Andrews's text is "crammed full with nothing less than the pluralist American public sphere itself and the culture industries in which . . . intensities . . . are so easily and eclectically mingled" to the extent that these elements become disgusting through overconsumption (Ngai 2005, 351–52).

Like Andrews, Reimer produces vaguely comical poems that display what Ngai identifies as a "complex relationship to a public sphere virtually coeval with the marketplace" (2005, 353). Reimer enacts a poetics in which sexuality and desire collapse into disgust; in doing so, she offers a feminist poetics of the body that both identifies and writes against the commodification of female sexuality in neoliberal, late capitalist cultures. As in Andrews's poems, meaning is fixed in Reimer's poems through the frequent use of proper nouns:

VEGAN CARNIVORE SQUATS AT SAFEWAY (20) . . .
prince charles never even asked to be my maxi-pad (20) . . .

they wanted to be the Tim Horton's© for the masses rather
than the Starbucks© for the masses (32) . . .
I'm going for the Gardisil© shot today!
(2005, 32)

It is no coincidence that many of these proper nouns refer to corporations or patented goods. The trademark symbol indicating that Gardisil is a registered trademark of Merck & Co. serves to further foreclose the possibility of polysemy not only by drawing attention to the proprietary interests of Big Pharma, but also by implying a connection between the pharmaceutical industry, women's bodies, and sexuality.[3] Reimer uses proper nouns to draw attention to the body, but rather than creating slippage, she develops a poetics in which words accrue a kind of stickiness akin to what Sara Ahmed describes as a contact zone where disgust creates a sticky residue that "becomes a quality of some surfaces, objects and signs" (Ahmed 2004, 89) and where disgust does not "move freely" but rather "sticks to that which it is near; it clings" (87).

However, Reimer's poems are not completely devoid of polysemy and slippage. Notably, Reimer deploys wordplay through punning. The most obvious pun occurs in the title of the collection. *[sic]* is the short form of "sic erat scriptum" or "thus it was written," an editorial comment inserted into a quotation to indicate that a quotation has been transcribed precisely from its source, errors and all. By inserting the editorial comment [sic], the author distances herself from the error, and in the process, seeks to establish her accuracy and authority. Similarly, Reimer titles her collection *[sic]* to distance herself both editorially and politically from the hyper-capitalist world represented in her poems; she presents this world to us "as is." "Sic" is also a homophone for "sick," suggesting a further link to a poetics of disgust. These poems are intended to make the reader feel somewhat queasy since they are not easily digestible at the levels of form or content, a point Reimer underscores when she proposes, in a poem called "a medical discourse," to "centre a poetics on irritable bowel syndrome" (2010, 28).

Reimer also uses puns to generate meaning within poems. "angry & militant" contains the line "maybe she's porn with it" (2010, 21), referencing the commercial jingle used to advertise Maybelline cosmetics:

"maybe she's born with it, maybe it's Maybelline." This pun both fixes the poem in relation to the capitalist-driven cosmetics industry and extends the meaning into new—but still related—terrain, exploring the connections among the female body, cosmetics, and the objectifying gaze of pornography, a connection invoked and ultimately resisted in the opening lines of the poem, which read, "never wanted a body either fleshy & 'asking for it'" (21).

Polysemy and wordplay also occur through the reworking of canonical texts. In "on spec," Reimer rewrites William Carlos Williams's famous imagist poem about the red wheelbarrow, both invoking and displacing Williams's picturesque red wheelbarrow glistening with rainwater beside the white chickens and installing something rather more disgusting in its place:

> so much depends
> an orange wheelbarrow
> sidle up reeking of dried menstrual blood, lilac wine, feet
> and where the fuck have you been?
> i've been to pussy to visit the queen
> (Reimer 2010, 27)

Imagist poems such as Williams's strove for precision and clarity of expression through the careful selection of sparse imagery; Reimer is also precise in her selection of images, but her precision leads not to an exploration of the purity of language, but rather to an exploration of the singularity of disgust. The poem continues with the invocation of another famous verse, "Pussycat, pussycat / where have you been? / I've been to London to visit the queen." The invocation and alteration of this children's rhyme compounds the poem's aim of polluting source texts in order to deploy an embodied poetics of disgust.

In [sic], Nikki Reimer problematizes the commodification of women in the context of neoliberal post-feminism by putting into practice a poetics of subversive bodily disgust. Her fellow Canadian poet Rachel Zolf writes out of (and against) a similar cultural and economic context in her 2007 collection of poems *Human Resources*. Although the form and compositional strategies of Zolf's poems differ from those of Reimer's, Zolf also develops a subversive, embodied, feminist poetics of disgust that advances a critique of late capitalism and corporate culture. I turn now to an analysis of Zolf's *Human Resources*.

Poetic, Libidinal, and Gift Economies in Rachel Zolf's *Human Resources*

Central to Zolf's poetic, aesthetic, and political strategy in *Human Resources* (2007) is a question posed by the poet Anne Carson in the context of an essay on the work of Paul Celan: "What is lost when words are wasted? And where is the human store to which such words are gathered?" (Zolf 2007, 31). Zolf cites Carson's question and responds with one of her own: "*Which* words are gathered, the wasted or the lost? . . . / When you 'cleanse words and salvage what is cleansed,' / do you collect what's been scrubbed off or what remains" (31). In *Human Resources*, Zolf collects what has been "scrubbed off," gleaning the dirt, the discarded language—the banal, the obscene, and the ugly—as part of her poetic practice, disrupting the association of poetic language with beauty and developing a poetics out of language that has traditionally been seen as unpoetic and abject. In so doing, she composes poems out of signs that have become tainted with what Sara Ahmed calls "stickiness" (2004, 91). Like Reimer, Zolf explores the political and poetic implications of disgust and creates a poetics of disgust that is predicated more on blockage than slippage.

The book is prefaced with an epigraph from a *Harvard Business Review* editorial that instructs readers to avoid complicated literary texts:

> Because literature concerns itself with the ambiguities of the human condi-
> tion, it stands as a threat to the vitality of the business executive, who must
> at all times maintain a bias toward action. . . . It is far safer to stick with
> throwaway thrillers, which at least provide a distraction from the stresses
> of the day. Forget the deep stuff. Read anything by Tom Clancy, Robert Lud-
> lum or Jeffrey Archer. . . . And while you're at it, read the Harvard Business
> Review. (Zolf 2007)

The impetus behind the poems in *Human Resources* came in part from Zolf's own work writing corporate communications for banks and insurance companies and the requirement in these fields to write in "plain language." The first poem in the book begins with the statement: "The job is to write in 'plain language.' No adjectives, adornment or surfeit of meaning" (Zolf 2007, 4). Zolf redeploys the kind of language she was required to use while writing for corporations, combining it with text pilfered from a variety of other sources and contexts. Zolf composes virtually unreadable, or what Ngai would call intolerable, poems out of material gleaned from a range of sources, including PowerPoint presentations from a continuing education course she took at the University of Toronto, Zolf's own freelance corporate communications work, Internet searches, literary theory, and philosophy; the only thing that seems to unite these disparate strands is the fact that most of them, with the exception of some of the philosophical and literary texts, are strikingly *unpoetic*, utilitarian, and in some cases, downright ugly.

Zolf works almost exclusively with found text in *Human Resources*. This practice of redeploying found textual fragments extends to her entire oeuvre; her more recent projects recombine, transpose, and splice preexisting material to enact powerful critiques of Israeli imperialism (*Neighbour Procedure*, 2010) and Canadian settler-colonialism (*Janey's Arcadia*, 2014). In *Human Resources*, she recycles existing text to challenge the equation of poetry with creative expression and to call into question notions of poetic value. *Human Resources* answers the American poet Laura Elrick's call for a poetics that "bring[s] about new ways of engaging in the practice of poetry, a poetics, in short, that points less toward a fetishistic valorization of 'the text' as object (form & content) and more toward an investigation of mediated textualities that intervene in (and experiment through) the mode of production, circulation, and exchange" (2010, 190).

The poems in *Human Resources* investigate the excess of text available through platforms like the Internet, advertising, and corporate communications and further consider how words are both commodified and wasted in these contexts. Zolf sees herself as a gleaner, reclaiming words that have been devalued through excessive use and circulation. She does not evoke nostalgia for a mythical time when words were valued. Rather, she plunders waste for its poetic possibilities, positing the poet as a "writing machine" that can "spew about anything: private jets, exquisite gardens, offshore-banking havens, the Great Ephemeral

Skin" (2007, 6). Zolf deconstructs dominant subject positions and un-seats Romantic notions of poetic authorship by deploying the Deleuz-ean notion of "becoming-machine," which, as Rosi Braidotti argues, is an attempt to rethink corporeality and subjectivity by situating the hu-man within a "nature-culture continuum," and in the process, "setting the framework of recomposition of bodily materiality in directions dia-metrically opposed to the spurious efficiency and ruthless opportunism of advanced capitalism" (2013, 92). In so doing, Zolf's poetics intersects productively with theories of critical posthumanism.

In spite of the book's engagement with cyber discourses and vir-tual communication, the body is undeniably present in *Human Re-sources* even if the theoretical, conceptual, and poetic frameworks Zolf uses to "write the body" are markedly different from those articulated by French feminist theory. In one poem in *Human Resources*, Zolf makes direct reference to post-structuralist theoretical discussions of polysemy, multiplicity, and desire; the "*écriture* chicks" whose femi-nist writing was inspired by these theories; and her own inability to write in that mode, an inability that she frames as being at least in part generational:

> ...   on our 35th birthday, in fact, the *New
> York Times Magazine* declared theory was dead—
> just when you'd gotten around to reading it. Here you
> go again, we're always 20 years behind the times,
> should've been checking out *écriture* chicks at the
> Montreal feminist book fair instead of popping bennies
> and caterwauling through *Romeo and Juliet* in high
> school. With close friends a generation [W2065] plenty
> ill older, you envy a certain ease with bodies, ideas
> (however dispersed)
> ...   Maybe if you'd
> come to writing through sex (or the other way 'round),
> she wouldn't feel so blocked about libidinal faro
> dnj[W54051] urng sitcoms economies, tackling *Desire in
> Language* or *Dissemination* for that matter. Get a grip,

they know her way around *jouissance,* you're game to
discharge some of that pulsion trapped in linguistic
structures, we're not so unattractive
(Zolf 2007, 16)

With the wry humor that punctuates so many of the poems in *Human Resources*, Zolf addresses a sense of belatedness in having come to feminist poetics and theory after the 1980s (the Montreal feminist book fair was held in 1988), but also a recognition of the need to develop poetic and theoretical frameworks through which to address the increasingly complex relationships among subjectivity, technology, capitalism, the body, and desire. For Zolf, this involves a critical examination of the ways in which online environments and market logic dictate language, bodies, and desires. Zolf invokes the close alignment of writing with desire in much of the French feminist-inspired poetry of that time period, at least in Canada, but posits her own approach to writing as more cerebral than libidinal and more prone to the blockage and stickiness of disgust than the playful slippage of desire.

Human Resources is composed with the help of computerized search engines and poetry generators. Specifically, Zolf deploys WordCount (a searchable Internet database of the most frequently used words in the English language), QueryCount (a searchable list of the words most often queried in WordCount), and Gematria of Nothing (a search engine that applies Hebrew numerology to English words). She also uses "Lewis LaCook's Markov chain-based Flash poetry generators" to compose a handful of the poems in the collection (Zolf 2007, 93). The use of WordCount, QueryCount, and Gematria of Nothing are sometimes indicated in the poems by the inclusion of a "w," "q," or "g" and a number that corresponds to the word's rank or value in the given database at the time the poem was composed. Many of the poems in the collection are so fragmented and disrupted by the letters and numbers that indicate the database values that they are virtually unreadable. Unreadability is a key poetic strategy in this text, as Zolf resists creating poems that might function as commodities of value or easily consumable goods. In this respect, *Human Resources* shares much in common with Bruce Andrews's writing, which Ngai describes as "intolerable to the extent that it can't be absorbed by the pluralist economy of an aesthetic eclecticism" (2005, 353), occupying instead the position of the deliberately unconsumable or anti-absorptive.

Brian Reed calls the poems in *Human Resources* "indelibly contaminated" and argues that they "could be said to court and exaggerate this process of degradation. Even when treating such high-minded subjects as Shakespearean drama and Puritan spiritual autobiography, Zolf's sentences are invaded by noun pileups, sloppy grammar, inscrutable abbreviations, and other quirks that she associates with corporate chatter" (2013, 18). Zolf's poetics of disgust is achieved in large part through this contamination and degradation, and is enacted in the service of an anticapitalist critique and a persistent questioning of the value we attach to particular words and things. By including WordCount and QueryCount scores next to specific words, Zolf draws attention to the way these words function in linguistic economies of value. Perhaps not surprisingly, the highest-ranked words in WordCount are among the most banal (a, the, and), while the most queried words are generally those related to sex, religion, and war. Also high in the rankings are certain common men's names, reflecting, perhaps, on the fact that men occupy public spaces—including the space of the Internet—more than women do.

In using WordCount and QueryCount, Zolf draws attention not only to the hierarchies implicit in how we engage with language, but also to the way in which language functions as an economy in which words circulate with assigned yet ever-shifting values. As Brian Reed points out, Zolf precisely documents WordCount and QueryCount rankings, but because these rankings shift constantly, the poems are out of date as soon as they are written (2013, 22). One poem is mainly comprised of the 100 highest-ranked words in QueryCount:

> Mass affluent consumers' key satisfaction drivers aspi-
> rational by most common queries of most-common-
> English-words engine: fuck Q1 sex Q2 love the shit god i
> penis cunt a ass jesus dog Q13 pussy hate bush john me
> hello vagina america bitch cat dick you war yes she like
> and cock no damn david gay man computer money

word mother michael poop Q42 happy mom asshole
orgasm he mike apple peace help one hi car bob fart cool
it chris microsoft crap woman what good is death hell
conquistador iraq james house mark butt porn cum girl
paul home dad work but of beer nigger andrew tom tit
tits usa anal baby stupid boy joe father kill mary school
sarah smith Q100 re-scoped the guestimate—the
generic one month is longer than 30 days. You can
control the reader's reaction without changing the facts
(Zolf 2007, 36)

The poem reads like a list of obscenities juxtaposed with numbers, military and religious references, proper names, and other common words, reflecting the ugliness of a patriarchal linguistic economy in which women are objects rather than subjects and militaristic and pornographic discourses are prized above most others. Zolf is not attempting to hold up a moralistic mirror to provoke our horror or contempt over how our culture uses or values language; rather, she makes poetry out of conventionally unpoetic language, reclaiming and recontextualizing the obscene and the ugly. Zolf reframes sexually explicit language, racist and violent language, clichés, colloquialisms, and the language of corporate capital, building poems that become part of a critical commentary on language and culture. I read this as a politicized, feminist reclamation of language that is at once ironic and irreverent, and that pushes back against a cultural discourse rife with sexism and homophobia. Zolf is a queer-identified feminist; her engagement with sexist and homophobic language subverts this language at its very core.

Zolf's strategy here is akin to Luce Irigaray's notion of mimicry as a kind of imitation that provides a critical distance. Irigaray articulates her notion of mimicry in *This Sex Which Is Not One*:

> To play with mimesis is thus, for a woman, to try to recover the place of her exploitation by discourse, without allowing herself to be simply reduced to it. It means to resubmit herself—inasmuch as she is on the side of the "perceptible," of "matter"—to "ideas." In particular to ideas about herself, that are elaborated in/by masculine logic, but so as to make "visible," by

an effect of playful repetition, what was supposed to remain invisible: the cover-up of a possible operation of the feminine in language. It also means "to unveil" the fact that, if women are such good mimics, it is because they are not simply resorbed in this function. *They also remain elsewhere*: another case of the persistence of "matter," but also of "sexual pleasure." (Irigaray 1985, 76)

Human Resources constantly draws attention to the ways in which female bodies, especially queer female bodies, are valued and devalued according to heteropatriarchal capitalism; it is also a profoundly anti-capitalist project that seeks to interrogate notions of value, commodity, and exchange.

Much of the language Zolf uses in this book is gleaned directly from the world of finance, business, and marketing, and Zolf skillfully oversees the collision of monetary, libidinal, and poetic economies, as is evident in the following passage:

> You know the drill, there is no writing that is not in economic W383 love W384 with commodity form, and there's stuff coming at me in all directions. Not the downward spiral of deferred want, not tied to lack or cost but generative and regenerative with the lesbian body, compound interest and the juice the spittle the fluids the fluxes the excrements the flatulence, the nerves. I was pretty sure she and I were on sync [sic], but nothing is not painful. Let's just use the void to think the full. Key her life positions that discovery of subject can be identity plentiful only while one never never never never never need old look home
> (Zolf 2007, 70)

Part of this poem is lifted from Monique Wittig's *The Lesbian Body* (*Le Corps Lesbien*) (1973), an experimental French novel written in the 1970s. Wittig's novel develops a language through which to write about lesbian desire that subverts and exceeds the limitations imposed on women's bodies by heterosexist articulations of corporeality and desire. Wittig configures the lesbian body through and in relation to a proliferation of erotogenic zones. Mixing language from Wittig's novel with textual fragments culled from other sources, namely popular idiom and the language of monetary economies, Zolf demonstrates the close relationship between economies of desire, language, pornography, and finance in late capitalist culture, and more specifically, in online environments. By developing a poetics of disgust, she attempts to counter this commodification of bodies and desires in the context of capitalism. It is worth noting that "economic" ranks as the 383rd most frequently used word in English and "love" ranks one behind it at 384; Zolf invites the reader to reflect upon the implications of both their proximity in WordCount rankings and also the fact that "economic" beats out "love" by one point.

In developing a poetics of disgust that dwells in the domain of capital, Zolf makes extensive use of Freud's observation of the symbolic connection between money and feces, a connection that Freud claims can be traced to the anal stage of psychosexual development in which the infant allegedly conceptualizes his or her feces as a gift of great value: "by producing them he can express his active compliance with his environment and, by withholding them, his disobeyance" (1991b, 103–4). The connection between feces and money is manifested again in the life of the adult neurotic, whose chronic constipation is linked to his or her anxiety regarding money (1991a, 213). The link between money and feces is evident throughout the poems in *Human Resources*, but is most directly invoked in the following poem:

> Retention Investments needs to know the keen relations among capitalist spirit, Brand Bible and anal stage. How one of the child's first Fisher-Price playthings is its feces, transformed into property, gift or weapon, depending on a fluctuating will and viral marketing strategy. We lived in a big house riddled with challenge and steepening and my compulsion to succorance. Okay, so good for Freud. Blame the excesses on parsimony and homosexuality on an unregulated anal babyQ91 stupid boy joe father stage. Ferenczi and his dedicated relationship

manager, on the other hand, will eat their own dog food
and bubble up a future-proofed thoughtform. It is what
it is, they say, tracing the origins of art and the advice-
driven market to that same kid's manipulation of his shit
(Zolf 2007, 24)

Zolf draws on Freud to further her inquiry into the relationship be-
tween waste and value, financial and libidinal economies, and desire
and disgust.

One of Zolf's key theoretical influences in the composition of *Hu-
man Resources* is Steve McCaffery's (1998) essay "Writing as a Gen-
eral Economy," in which he draws upon Bataille's notions of the general
economy, the gift economy, and the restricted economy to theorize the
play between, on the one hand, the desire for interpretation, closure,
and a singular reading of a text and on the other hand, the produc-
tive potential of letting go of the desire for mastery of a text and an
embracing of semantic multiplicity. McCaffery envisions a poetic "gift
economy" in which the "intense exchange within the textual experi-
ence . . . would manifest as a loss exchange among the signs them-
selves" (1998, 215). In imagining such a text, McCaffery invokes the
post-structuralist language of decentrality and multiplicity: "To envis-
age such a text would be to envisage a linguistic space in which mean-
ings splinter into moving fields of plurality, establishing differentials
able to resist a totalization into recoverable integrations that would
lead to a summatable 'Meaning'" (216).

Zolf is drawn to McCaffery's essay not only because she shares his
interest in open-ended and non-totalizing writing, but also because of
the way he conceptualizes language as an economy, and she uses this
notion in her own work. Values shift as words circulate in the econo-
mies of value established by WordCount and QueryCount, but eco-
nomic "value" remains a persistent and inescapable preoccupation in
Human Resources, as demonstrated through the frequent citing of
WordCount and QueryCount values. *Human Resources* does not fully
realize or inhabit the gift economy because words retain a stubborn
fixity through their association with the economies of WordCount and
QueryCount and the "value" attributed to words in these economies.

If the "gift economy" is something that exists, as McCaffery suggests, outside of capitalist modes of exchange because it disassociates wealth from investment and accumulation (1998, 215), then the gift economy remains out of reach to both Zolf and Reimer, who write from within (even as they write against) a capitalist economy. Reimer writes: "I would get in line for the gift economy but I have to / check with head office first" (2010, 38), suggesting the impossibility of getting away from the reach of capitalist authority embodied by "head office." Similarly, Zolf invokes the gift economy only to foreground the difficulty of participating in it:

> You had trouble accepting gifts, even a token from your
> lover at the bus stop. Haunted by the potlatch image
> of "swallowing" the visiting tribe by giving them blan-
> kets, or inducing shameful vomiting through excess
> feasting. Heads or tails, the more you copper allocated
> struggling shit the more face you save
> (Zolf 2007, 82)[4]

Reimer and Zolf each develop a radically anticapitalist poetics by creating texts that are not easily aestheticized as commodities or consumed by the reader. However, in their development of an embodied poetics of disgust, their poetry is grounded in an acknowledgment of the fact that there is no outside to capitalism, and that perhaps one of the most effective strategies of critique comes from appropriating the language of commerce, advertising, and corporations, and using it to construct a subversive, bodily poetics of disgust that sticks and clings more than it seamlessly circulates.

As this first part of *Poetry Matters* has shown, strategic embodiment is a crucial aspect of contemporary feminist poetics. This writing is indebted to a feminist intellectual, poetic, and theoretical tradition of writing the body, but extends articulations of corporeality into new realms by developing poetic strategies and vocabularies for addressing the complexities of embodiment in the context of neoliberalism, biogenetic capitalism, globalization, and networked environments. This occurs through a reclamation of matter and the feminine that disrupts philosophical and literary traditions that equate the female body with matter and passivity in *From Dame Quickly*; through an exploration of the maternal body as a metaphor for attachment and alienation in the context of communicative capitalism in *What Stirs*; through a hybrid, embodied posthuman poetics of dispersal, multiplicity and deferral in *sybil unrest*; and through the development of an anticapitalist poetics of bodily disgust in *[sic]* and *Human Resources*. These five books were all published in the first decade of the twenty-first century; they draw extensively on found material from popular culture and the capitalist marketplace, including websites, popular songs, advertising, news media, corporate communications, and pornography in order to critically examine the ways in which the female body is engaged in, and defined through, the structures, norms, and discourses of late capitalism.

In drawing on the raw materials of late capitalism, reframing and recontextualizing these materials, and presenting the reader with disjunctive, libidinal, mundane, and in some cases, disgusting articulations of embodiment, the poets discussed here display a canny awareness of capitalism's long reach into the affective and political registers of human experience. Herein lies one of the conundrums of contemporary feminist poetics: constructing a liberatory discourse that is immune to commodification is next to impossible. Consequently, one of the characteristics of recent feminist poetries is a move away from discourses of liberation and utopia toward a meditation on the tendency of neoliberalism to appropriate and commodify forms of political activism and resistance. Vanessa Place and Robert Fitterman point out that conceptual writing has flourished in the context of a repressive market economy in spite of the fact that there seems to be no escaping this economy because discourses of resistance are quickly subsumed and commodified by the capitalist regime itself (2009, 30). Neither feminism nor experimental poetry is immune to becoming a commodity in this context. For Scappettone, Christakos, Lai and Wong, Reimer, and Zolf the body and desire are implicated in and framed by a language of neoliberalism and market logic that seems impossible to escape. However, these poets each develop a corporeal poetics that strategically appropriates, agitates, distorts, and frustrates the language of the capitalist marketplace. This writing is not utopian, but it is also not devoid of hope for a better and more livable lifeworld, one where, in the words of Lai and Wong, we might "tilt the glass so that / it's half full & / hail the composting hero" and where "edible weeds retake / the city in which i lull you / out of consumerism / into loving the alien labour" (2013, 99).

PART TWO

Poetic Matterings: New Materialist and Posthuman Feminist Ecopoetics

FRUSTRATED WITH WHAT THEY PERCEIVE as the limitations of postmodern and post-structuralist feminism for an effective political engagement with materiality, many feminist theorists have sought to develop more materially driven critical frameworks for understanding the network of relations among biopolitics, the environment, capitalism, and globalization. As Stacy Alaimo argues, "from an environmentalist-feminist standpoint, one of the most unfortunate legacies of poststructuralist and postmodern feminism has been the accelerated 'flight from nature' fueled by rigid commitments to social constructionism and the determination to rout out all vestiges of essentialism" (2009, 237). This return to a consideration of materiality and nature, collectively referred to as "new materialisms," marks a distinct departure from feminist theories that tend to regard nature and matter "as an obstacle against which we need to struggle," that remains "inert, given, unchanging, and resistant to historical, social, and cultural transformations" (Grosz 2005, 13). Instead, new materialist theory seeks to understand the subject as what Rosi Braidotti describes as an embodied and embedded (2013, 67) being who is connected to and implicated in her environment.[1]

In this part of *Poetry Matters*, I place ecopoetics and new materialist thinking in dialogue not only to show how new materialist theory might offer a conceptual framework for reading contemporary ecopoetics, but also to consider how contemporary ecopoetics might contribute to new materialist thinking. By developing poetic, theoretical, and conceptual frameworks for understanding the relationship between language, materiality, and contemporary politics, I build on the concept of strategic embodiment explored in the previous chapters but expand materiality beyond considerations of the individual, corporeal body, instead examining matter as trans-corporeal and as actively challenging assumptions of human exceptionalism that position the subject as somehow discrete and separate from her environment.

New materialisms offer a productive framework for thinking about the ways in which politics, economics, and industry affect lived bodily experiences and identities. New materialisms seek to understand the complex interconnections and interdependencies of humans and other organisms, dislodging the anthropocentric epistemologies that have governed both traditional humanist philosophies as well as strands of post-structuralist and postmodern thinking. As Serenella Iovino and Serpil Oppermann argue, the "emerging paradigm" of new materialisms "elicits not only new nonanthropocentric approaches, but also possible ways to analyze language and reality, human and nonhuman life, mind and matter, without falling into dichotomous patterns of thinking" (2014, 2). This reconsideration of matter is "crucial for a materialist theory of politics and agency" (Coole and Frost 2010, 2).

Theorists of new materialisms are diverse in their approaches, but they share a belief in the political necessity of exploring the complex interconnections among human animals, nonhuman animals, and the material world, especially at this historical juncture when biogenetic capitalism, climate change, and globalization necessitate a politicized, ethical, and critical rethinking of the relationship between humans and the material world. Many of these theorists understand materiality as closely connected to the posthuman; in fact, one of the key elements separating "new materialisms" from "materialism" is new materialisms' desire to challenge aspects of humanism and embrace a posthuman subjectivity. This posthumanism is also distinct from the "anti-humanism" of post-structuralist theory because it takes a more materialist approach in its critique of the humanist subject (Braidotti 2013, 30). Karen Barad proposes the concept of agential realism to describe what she calls a "posthumanist performative approach" that explicitly acknowledges matter as dynamic and active (Barad 2007, 135). Barad's theory of "agential realism" challenges what she sees as the anthropocentrism of both humanist and post-structuralist approaches, questions the division between nature and culture, and subverts assumptions of nature as passive and devoid of agency. Jane Bennett's theory of "vital materialism" considers "human-nonhuman assemblages" and offers a critical framework for engaging with the material world not as a passive site in need of the protection of human agents, but rather as a site of vitality and interaction, and one in which human agency is understood as not taking precedence over nonhuman forms of agency (2010, 111).[2] Stacy Alaimo's theory of trans-corporeality offers a similar exploration of the interconnectedness of humans and their surroundings. Alaimo understands trans-corporeality as aligned with the "posthumanist sense of the human as sustainably and perpetually interconnected with the flows of substances and the agencies of environments" (Alaimo 2012, 476). Trans-corporeality "traces the material interchanges across human bodies, animal bodies, and the wider material world" and explores the subject's entanglement in "networks that are simultaneously economic, political, cultural, scientific, and substantial; what was once the ostensibly bounded human subject finds herself in a swirling landscape of uncertainty where practices and actions that were once not even remotely ethical or political matters suddenly become so" (476). Alaimo's understanding of the trans-corporeal, posthumanist subject intersects productively with Rosi Braidotti's theory of the posthuman. Like Alaimo, Braidotti understands the subject not as a discrete entity but as a being multiply interconnected with her environment: "to be posthuman . . . implies a new way of combining ethical values with the well-being of an enlarged sense of community, which includes one's territorial or environmental inter-connections. This is an ethical bond of an altogether different sort from the self-interests of an individual subject" (2013, 190). Alaimo, Barad, Bennett, and Braidotti understand the posthuman not as anti-human, but rather as positioned in opposition to the anthropocentrism of humanism. For Barad, the posthuman "is not calibrated on the human; on the contrary, it is about taking issue with human exceptionalism while being accountable for the role we play in the differential constitution and differential positioning of the human among other creatures (both living and nonliving)" (2007, 136).

In *Material Ecocriticisms*, Serenella Iovino and Serpil Oppermann bring new materialist theories to bear on literary ecocriticism, arguing that the "world's material phenomena are knots in a vast network of agencies which can be 'read' and interpreted as forming narratives, stories" (2014, 1). Indeed, nonhuman stories are embedded in the environment all around us. Material ecocriticism can considerably enrich ecocritical analyses of literary texts by offering an important set of conceptual tools for reading literatures that address the complex interrelations among nature, matter, science, and economics. However, rather than limiting one's focus to the *narratives* embedded in the world around us, one might expand materialist ecocriticism to include *non-narrative* forms like experimental poetry in which meaning is generated through process and interaction. In fact, contemporary innovative ecopoetics might constitute not just an object to which one can apply new materialist theory, but rather an additional dimension of new materialist thinking. To date, there has been very little dialogue between contemporary, experimental, process-oriented ecopoetics and new materialism. Iovino and Oppermann implicitly limit their consideration to narratively driven work; Rosi Braidotti turns to science fiction, which she sees as enacting a "displacement of our world-view away from the human epicenter" and "establish[ing] a continuum with the animal, mineral, vegetable, extra-terrestrial, and technological worlds" (2002, 183). Karen Barad is a notable exception, as she writes briefly about Alice Fulton's *Cascade Experiment* in *Meeting the Universe Halfway*.

Lynn Keller draws an important connection between global environmental crises and innovative poetry in the "Coda" to *Thinking Poetry*, where she sketches possible future political, critical, ethical, and aesthetic directions that poetry might take in the twenty-first century. Keller notes that Joan Retallack has responded to calls for a less anthropocentric nature poetry by advancing a "'poetics of reciprocal alterity'— that is, a poetics in which the imagination does not simply inhabit the supposedly empty spaces of otherness, but in which alterity has opportunities to 'speak back'" (2010, 183). Keller notes that for Retallack, proceduralism becomes an important tactic because it can mimic the processes and operations of the natural world (183). The poets I discuss in the following two chapters develop poetic processes, strategies, and aesthetics that resonate strongly with Retallack's notion of a poetics of reciprocal alterity.

It is my contention that innovative ecopoetics—a body of radically experimental writing that often utilizes procedural compositional techniques to mirror or amplify the agential processes of nonhuman actors—constitutes a vital but underexamined enactment of the posthuman. Contemporary ecopoetics establishes a continuum between and among humans, animals, and objects and considers the vitality and agency of nonhuman actants. Much of this poetry is unintelligible when read through traditional strategies of literary analysis, and the reader cannot always rely on established interpretive practices to make sense of the work. As Barad argues, traditional humanist accounts require "an intellective agent (that to which something is intelligible), and intellection is framed as a specifically human capacity" (2007, 149). In agential realist accounts, "intelligibility is an ontological performance of the world in its ongoing articulation. It is not a human-dependent characteristic but a feature of the world in its differential becoming" (149). I argue that innovative ecopoetics enacts new materialist and posthuman concepts not only at the level of content, but also at the levels of form and composition. In placing ecopoetics and new materialist theories in dialogue, I show not only how they illuminate one another, but also how they speak to and about issues of vital planetary and ecological interest. The utilization of poetic language and form to explore radical affinities and interconnectivities between humans and other organic and inorganic entities resonates with recent calls for a feminist mode of inquiry that takes matter into account. As Elizabeth Grosz argues,

> Feminist theory needs to turn, or perhaps return, to questions of the real—not empirical questions regarding states of affairs . . . but questions of the nature and forces of the real, the nature and forces of the world, cosmological forces as well as historical ones. In short, it needs to welcome again what epistemologies have left out: the relentless force of the real, a new metaphysics. (Grosz 2011, 85)

The poets discussed in this part take the material world as their object of inquiry, examining substances like water, oil, and Styrofoam, and attempt to think beyond and outside of epistemological frameworks that understand these things primarily in relation to their use value to humans and their role as commodities.

Specific features of innovative and experimental poetry, including procedural compositional methods and working with recycled text, are especially suited to a critical engagement with ecology and materiality. This poetry is devoid of the narrative continuity of most literary prose and the stable, coherent lyric voice of most poetry, but in the absence of formal cohesiveness, words attain a material quality, they develop systems, they inter- and intra-act, they become components in process-oriented transformations and manifestations. Timothy Morton, one of the few theorists affiliated with new materialism to write about poetry, suggests that there is something inherently ecological about poetry as a genre: "The shape of the stanzas and the length of the lines determine the way you appreciate the blank paper around them. Reading the poem aloud makes you think of the shape and size of the space around you. . . . The poem organizes space. Seen like this, all texts—all artworks indeed—have an irreducibly ecological form" (2010, 11). In his "Object-Oriented Defense of Poetry," he suggests that "to study a poem is not to study meaning alone, even if we expand 'meaning' beyond established parameters. To study a poem, rather, is to see how causality itself operates. A poem directly intervenes in reality in a causal way" (2012, 206); poetry has a kind of agency or ability to act in the world that sets it apart from other literary genres. He elaborates on the materiality of poetry in a more recent essay: "a poem has a physical architecture, a surface or volume on which or in which it is composed. . . . This medium could be electromagnetic waves (radio, television, light); it could be paper or metal or stone; it could be (human) breath. All kinds of nonhumans are already involved in the existence of the poems" (2014, 271). Morton emphasizes the materiality of poetry and the ways in which meaning in poetry is conveyed in large part through the location of words on the page and the conjunctions, disjunctions, and interactions between words. However, in his discussion of poetry in relation to new materialism, Morton turns to the work of Samuel Taylor Coleridge and William Carlos Williams rather than contemporary process-oriented or conceptual poetry.

Rather than focusing on wilderness and rural or pastoral settings, ecopoetics is intent on examining—and displacing—built human environments, urban spaces, and the language of science and technology. This writing often evacuates the role of human observer, thus challenging the humanist underpinnings of conventional nature poetry, where the natural setting typically becomes an occasion for the speaker to glean some kind of insight, or to experience a moment of self-exploration or reflection that serves to consolidate the speaking subject as a discrete entity marked off as separate from the environment. Lisa Robertson has identified poetry written in the pastoral and post-pastoral traditions, which have largely dominated nature poetry in Western literature, as particularly problematic in this regard:

> The evocation of feeling in poet or reader obeys a parallel planting of "nature" in the poem. . . . Appearing to serve a personally expressive function, the vocabulary of nature screens a symbolic appropriation of the Land. . . . A perversely topical utopia has always been the duped by-product of the ideology that blindly describes, thus possesses, a landscape in which people are imagined to be at peace with the economics of production and consumption. (Robertson 2002, 22–23)

While traditional nature poetry, specifically in its pastoral and post-pastoral forms, is imbricated in humanism and colonialism, the poetry discussed in this part directly problematizes humanism and colonialism and instead embraces a posthumanist politics and ethics.

This part of the book is divided into two chapters. The first chapter examines Yedda Morrison's *Darkness* (2012a) and Marcella Durand's "The Anatomy of Oil" (2008) through the lens of the posthuman. *Darkness* is a procedural rewriting of Joseph Conrad's *Heart of Darkness* (1902) that attempts to excise the human from Conrad's novel. In addition to using this text to launch a discussion of the displacement of the humanist subject and the decolonization of language—themes that are not only central to Morrison's text but also to the field of ecopoetics in general—I also use this text to draw attention to the importance of *process* and *interaction* in how ecopoetries generate meaning. I then examine Marcella Durand's "The Anatomy of Oil" to show how Durand deploys a kind of strategic anthropomorphism that points to the limitations of the epistemological, economic, and temporal frameworks through which we commonly understand oil. Durand deliberately anthropomorphizes the landscape in order to question the binary between "sentient and non-sentient" (Williams 2008) that allows us to exploit natural resources without feeling the need to be ethically accountable for our actions.

The second chapter in this section reads Rita Wong's *undercurrent* (2015) and Evelyn Reilly's *Styrofoam* (2009) through the lens of trans-corporeality. Rita Wong's *undercurrent* attempts to think "with" water rather than about water to advance a politicized poetics grounded in a commitment to environmental sustainability, decolonization, and anti-capitalist ideals. Evelyn Reilly's *Styrofoam* explores the molecular, ecological, and social dimensions of Styrofoam, a substance that is sublime in both its magnitude and its longevity.

I read all of these texts as enacting a new materialist, trans-corporeal, posthuman poetics which, while not always directly taking up issues of gender, is feminist in its posthumanism since, as Rosi Braidotti states, "the becoming-posthuman speaks to my feminist self, partly because my sex, historically speaking, never quite made it into full human-ity, so my allegiance with that category is negotiable and never to be taken for granted" (2013, 81). Stacy Alaimo calls trans-corporeality a form of "critical posthumanism" in its insistence "on the material inter- and intra-connections between living creatures and the sub-stances and forces of the world" and its refusal of human exception-alism through its consideration of "all species as intermeshed with particular places and larger, perhaps untraceable currents" (2016, 113). Alaimo understands trans-corporeality and new materialism as femi-nist in their emphases on the "material interchanges between bodies, consumer objects, and subtances" as "sites for ethical-political engage-ments and interventions" (2016, 9). The feminist politics that under-scores the work of all four poet discussed in these two chapters is first and foremost one of interconnectivity because it is crucial to see the interconnections "among the greenhouse effect, the status of women, racism and xenophobia and frantic consumerism. We must not stop at any fragmented portion of these realities, but rather trace transver-sal interconnections among them" (Braidotti 2013, 93). I turn now to a reading of Yedda Morrison's *Darkness* and Marcella Durand's "The Anatomy of Oil" as works of posthuman ecopoetics.

CHAPTER THREE

De/Anthropomorphizing Language:
Posthuman Poetics in Yedda Morrison's *Darkness* and Marcella Durand's "The Anatomy of Oil"

Rewriting the Default Grammar of Agency: Yedda Morrison's *Darkness*

"It seems necessary and impossible to rewrite the default grammar of agency, a grammar that assigns activity to people and passivity to things," writes Jane Bennett in *Vibrant Matter: A Political Ecology of Things* (2010, 119). Bennett draws attention in *Vibrant Matter* both to the importance of a radical rethinking of the attribution of agency solely to human subjects and the conceptual difficulty of such an endeavor. Yedda Morrison's *Darkness* (2012a) is a powerful example of a rewriting of the default grammar of agency that seeks to detach agency from the human, explore the possibility of nonhuman agency, and establish what Morrison calls a "bio-centric narrative" (Morrison 2012b, 177). *Darkness* is an "erasure poem," a poem composed by erasing select words in a preexisting text. The preexisting text with which Morrison works is Joseph Conrad's *Heart of Darkness*. Morrison erases or "whites out" (her tool of erasure is, literally, a bottle of Wite-Out) all words related to human agency in Conrad's novel, leaving behind words that are related to the natural world.[1] This process involves, at a very fundamental level, a careful consideration of the historical and ideological factors that connect agency to the human and that divide human from nature. More specifically, *Darkness* challenges and unwrites Conrad's conflation of humanity with white, European masculinity and his tendency to deploy landscape in his writing to "establish mood/perspective/bias, exploiting its ability to 'set the stage'" (Morrison 2012b, 177).[2]

The erasures in *Darkness* result in spare, pared-down poetry that eschews close reading but generates meaning through the use of blank space and through the meaning accrued in and through the deletion of certain words and the preservation of others. The opening passage of Conrad's novel, which reads: "The Nellie, a cruising yawl, swung to her anchor without a flutter of the sails, and was at rest. The flood had made, the wind was nearly calm, and being bound down the river, the only thing for it was to come and wait for the turn of the tide" (1987, 27), becomes in Morrison's text:

                            flood

           wind

     river.

                 tide,

(2012a, 3)

Visible also are faint traces of the Wite-Out that Morrison applied to the page (the Signet paperback edition of Conrad's novel, the pagination and layout of which carries over in Morrison's text); these brushstrokes visibly haunt the text, reminding the reader of just how many words have been erased and the extent to which human agency infuses every sentence of Conrad's novel. The sparseness of Morrison's *Darkness* is immediately apparent; some pages only contain four or five words, and the most text-heavy pages are still primarily comprised of blank spaces with small clusters of words grouped here and there. The white space of the page becomes a kind of blank screen upon which to meditate on both the words that are there and the act of erasure performed on the text. The end result of Morrison's erasures is visually and verbally striking.[3]

Water, trees, fire, ivory, and other dimensions of the natural world become agents in their own right in *Darkness*, untethered from human use value or concern. Morrison's political and aesthetic project in this regard aligns strikingly with Karen Barad's theory of agential realism and her attempt to understand the interplay of nature and culture, and the material and the discursive. Challenging post-structuralism's tendency to see matter as passive, inert, and immutable while granting agency to language, Barad proposes a "posthumanist performative" approach that acknowledges the dynamism of matter (2007, 135). She argues:

Meaning is not a property of individual words or groups of words but an ongoing performance of the world in its differential dance of intelligibility and unintelligibility. In its causal intra-activity, part of the world becomes determinately bounded and propertied in its emergent intelligibility to another part of the world, while lively matterings, possibilities, and impossibilities are reconfigured. Discursive practices are boundary-making practices that have no finality in the ongoing dynamics of agential intra-activity. (Barad 2007, 149)

The following passage from *Darkness* illustrates the exploration of nonhuman agency and the vibrancy of matter in Morrison's text:

```
ivory                        air
                             Trees, trees,
trees,               running up high;
          hugging the bank              stream,
crept                                   sluggish
beetle
small,    beetle crawl on—
     crawl
          leaking        crawl        slow.
forest  step        across the water
                       deeper and
deeper            darkness.     quiet
     night
          trees   run up the river
              hovering        air high
                              dawns
            chill stillness;
               low;          snap-
ping of a twig
```
(Morrison 2012a, 58)

Phrases like "trees hugging the bank," "run up the river," "hovering," and "stream crept" could be dismissed as anthropomorphizing nature and thus as a failed attempt to evacuate human agency and interest from the text. But as Jane Bennett argues, the relaxation "into resemblances discerned across the ontological divide" (2010, 119–20) that attends anthropomorphism can actually work to counter anthropocentric claims. Bennett writes:

> A chord is struck between person and thing, and I am no longer above or outside a nonhuman "environment." Too often the philosophical rejection of anthropomorphism is bound up with a hubristic demand that only humans and God can bear any traces of creative agency. To qualify and attenuate this desire is to make it possible to discern a kind of life irreducible to the activities of humans and gods. This material vitality is me, it predates me, it exceeds me, it postdates me. (Bennett 2010, 120)

Indeed, in *Darkness* the dimensions of the natural world—ivory, beetle, river, tree, twig, dawn—function as agents apart from human interest and activity; those anthropomorphic elements are "agentic" and describe actions that are irreducible to human activities and interests.[4]

Since there is no escaping the fact that the words that comprise *Darkness* were written down by Conrad and then selected by Morrison, and thus have undergone the filter of not one but two agential human minds (and undergo the filter of a third human mind when encountered by the reader), anthropomorphism functions in this context not only as an occasion to explore the creative agency of matter and the natural world, but also as a signal of the conceptual limits of our own thinking. Although written language is fundamentally anthropocentric, Morrison's procedurally based project removes words from their context within Conrad's sentences and brings them outside conventional measures of readability. Words attain a materiality separate from the logic of sentences and even of the poetic line; as a form of verbal, vibrant matter, these words generate new and unpredictable meanings. Divorced from authorial intention, lyric voice, and the formal concerns that dictate most poetry, the words on the page develop new meanings through intra-action. While Morrison may not completely succeed in eradicating human agency from the text since such an act is conceptually impossible, she does prompt the reader to reflect on the politics of human agency in relation to language and narrative, and in so doing, her work enacts, both formally and conceptually, a posthuman and anticolonial poetics.

Recent critiques of theories of the posthuman have drawn attention to the tendency of some posthuman thinkers to elide questions of race. Julie Livingston and Jasbir Puar argue that "much of posthuman thought . . . suffers from an often unmarked Euro-American focus and through that, ironically, a philosophical resuscitation of the status of the human as a transparent category" (2011, 5). However, because posthumanism is a critical response to humanism and humanism is inextricably linked to the European Enlightenment, it is necessarily tethered, albeit oppositionally, to humanism. Morrison's posthuman poetics is attentive to race, as is evident in the processes that inform her strategic unwriting of a novel that is structured in large part through the problematic contrasts it draws between the "whiteness" of Europe and the "blackness" of the Congo. In "whiting out" the human, Morrison ghosts whiteness *and* blackness from the page. As Morrison explains in her process notes that accompany a segment of *Darkness* reprinted in *I'll Drown My Book: Conceptual Writing by Women*, she wrestled with the racial politics of erasure as she composed *Darkness*: "erase whites only? Thereby erasing colonialism? So blacks are 'part of nature'? Erase blacks? As in erasing black history? . . . Worry about my ability to function ethically within the procedure" (2012b, 177). In the end, Morrison opted to strip all human action away in an attempt to attain a "nuts and bolts understanding of how colonialism and narratives of nature function at the level of syntax" (177) in Conrad's novel. The color line and the line between nature and culture that feature strongly in *Heart of Darkness* are excised in Morrison's unwriting; this excision allows the vibrancy of the nonhuman to come to the fore and detaches a vocabulary of the natural world from the ideological underpinnings of imperialism and colonialism.

Joseph Conrad's *Heart of Darkness* is a novel deeply engaged with colonialism; it represents Africa as a space to be explored, charted and mapped, its people colonized and resources extracted for economic benefit. Although it enacts a critique of the hypocrisy of European colonialism and imperialism and is specifically written as a critique of Belgian colonialism (Huggan and Tiffin 2010, 141), it is also a text that has come under criticism for its Eurocentric assumptions. The Nigerian writer Chinua Achebe argues that Conrad depicts Africa as a *terra nullius* or blank space and African people as being largely without language:

> Read as the animality lurking in the civilized European heart, Africa's darkness is made symbolic of Europe's fears of evolutionary reversion; tethered to this symbolism, Africans cease to exist as independent entities, becoming—as many animals do in fiction—representative of some earlier moment in evolutionary history or some primordial human trait. (Huggan and Tiffin 2010, 143)

Achebe further suggests that Conrad generally renders African people absent from the novel because "their role can only be as surrogates for a European malaise" (Huggan and Tiffin 2010, 143). In erasing words that contain traces of human agency, Morrison undoes what A. James M. Johnson calls "an ethnocentric narrative, based on the concept of time . . . that correlates the physical journey away from the European centre with a temporal journey away from the European present" (1997, 112). Gone from *Darkness* is the trajectory of the journey from the mouth of the Thames to the depths of the Congo that structures Conrad's novel.

As many critics have noted, Conrad tends to excessively anthropomorphize nature in *Heart of Darkness*; he denies the "faculties of mind" to Africans as individuals but transfers these faculties to the "imposing totality (the 'pensive forest') of which they are an unconscious part" (Johnson 1997, 122). Conrad's transferring of mental faculties to the natural world is *not* an anticipation of new materialist attempts to understand the natural world as agential. On the contrary, it is a manifestation of imperialist thinking steeped in humanist understandings of the white European male as the embodiment of reason pitted against a menacing terra incognita of which African subjects are understood as a part. European subjects, on the contrary, are understood as outside and separate from this "natural" world even as the very concept of wilderness is a construct of the European colonizer's mind. Yedda Morrison seeks to undo this dynamic in *Darkness*. This critical unwriting or erasure of a canonical text that is closely aligned with colonialism and imperialism challenges the legacy of the exploitation and commodification of "natural" resources such as ivory, and the violent acts committed against the inhabitants of regions like the Congo that occurred in the context of colonialism and continue, albeit in slightly different guises, in the context of globalization.

Morrison's *Darkness* can be read as a direct engagement with both Conrad's novel and the place it has come to occupy in relation to discussions of language and colonization. In erasing the words related to human agency in the novel, Morrison does not cast African subjects as part of the natural world; she does not reenact Conrad's tacit refusal to see Africans as fully human, thinking subjects. Rather, she removes Conrad's Eurocentric depiction of the colonial relation altogether by excising both colonizer and colonized from the text. In removing the colonial and imperial framing of Conrad's novel, a framing that sees resources as there for human exploitation, land as there to be charted and explored, and African subjects as primitive beings who exist outside of time and culture, what is left behind—things like ivory and wood—simply exist and are not framed as objects to extract or trade for human gain. The Congo River becomes important not as a means for the transportation of goods, but rather as an entity that exists for itself and for the plants and animals that depend upon it:

shore,

glittering river.

"The brown current ran swiftly out
darkness,   towards the sea

running swiftly, too, ebbing, ebbing
sea
(Morrison 2012a, 115)

Morrison creates a sparse, meditative reflection on nature as something with its own agency, its own "vibrant matter."

Some critics read *Heart of Darkness* as a commentary on the fragility of the boundary between human and animal, a fragility embodied in Kurtz's decline from esteemed ivory collector to "the condition of animality, characterized in the text by unbridled savagery and the temptations of the flesh" (Huggan and Tiffin 2010, 142). Jeffrey Mathes McCarthy reads Kurtz as embodying an "ontological intimacy with nature" that allows him to "step across the narrow social line dividing person from place and establish a kinship with nature that both distinguishes and destroys him" (2009, 634). In this regard, *Heart of Darkness* has been widely read as a novel about the "primitive instincts always lurking in the human heart, and the danger of atavistic reversion" (Huggan and Tiffin 2010, 142) and as "full of anxiety about allegiance to 'wild' forces that undermine the construction of a confident, imperial, and civilized subject" (McCarthy 2009, 635). *Heart of Darkness* "dramatizes modernity's destructive alienation from the natural world against the backdrop of the Congo's ecological collapse. More intimately, *Heart of Darkness* uses the competing constructions of nature in turn-of-the century Britain to haunt readers with a new version of themselves" (McCarthy 2009, 620).

Conrad's exploration of the fragility of the human subject is not an embracing of the subject's fragile state or an affirmation of his ontological intimacy with the natural world. The subject under threat of atavistic reversion in Conrad's novel is premised on frameworks derived from humanism. Rosi Braidotti defines the humanist subject as characterized by the "unique, self-regulating and intrinsically moral powers of human reason" and notes that this subject is predicated on eighteenth- and nineteenth-century renditions of classical antiquity and the Italian Renaissance embodied in Leonardo da Vinci's famous drawings of the Vitruvian man (2013, 13). European imperialism was largely justified through an adherence to specific humanist beliefs: "Humanism historically developed into a civilizational model, which shaped a certain idea of Europe as coinciding with the universalizing powers of self-reflective reason" (13). Colonialism was justified in part through a belief in "Europe" not only as a geographic location but also as a "universal attribute of the human mind that can lend its quality to any suitable object" (14). This is the philosophical and cultural backdrop that informs Conrad's depiction of Kurtz's demise and that Morrison attempts to undermine through her subversive "unwriting" of Conrad's novella. *Heart of Darkness* is premised on an investment in the primacy of the human and the separation of the Enlightenment subject from nature. Morrison's *Darkness* attempts to undo these investments by unwriting Conrad's novel from a posthumanist standpoint and, in the process, attempts to unwrite the fear of reversion and degeneration.

Descriptions of Kurtz on his deathbed in Conrad's novel that are written to provoke a sense of dread in the reader become, in Morrison's rewriting:

shade

hollow

mould of   earth

multitude of   trees

wilderness,

island.

morning

afternoon

lying   closed

quietly,

impenetrable darkness.

lying at the bottom
precipice where the sun never shines.

(Morrison 2012a, 116–17)

The dread of atavistic reversion present in Conrad's text is supplanted by a peaceful and meditative yet sparse text as Morrison excises the trappings of humanism and colonialism from the text and attempts to decolonize language.

In grappling with a poetics that attempts to erase human agency, one must acknowledge the inescapable matter of Morrison's agency as the poet with the bottle of Wite-Out making decisions about which words contain traces of human agency. Morrison's compositional strategy in *Darkness* can be said to place the agency of the human poet squarely at the heart of the project, thus problematically recentering the human.[5] Jane Bennett identifies the potential anthropocentric pitfalls inherent in using language to contest human agency or decenter human subjectivity, since the critique itself is being articulated by a language-wielding human agent: "It is not so easy to resist, deflect, or redirect this criticism. One can point out how dominant notions of human subjectivity and agency are belied by the tangles and aporias into which they enter when topics are explored in philosophical detail. One can invoke bacteria colonies in human elbows to show how human subjects are themselves nonhuman, alien, outside, vital materiality" (2010, 120). The contradiction Bennett identifies points to the limitations of our own epistemological frameworks, which, in spite of our best efforts, ultimately rely on language for their intelligibility. However, in their tendency to radically defamiliarize language, and to deploy fragmentation to undermine conventional understandings of clarity, readability, and signification, procedural ecopoetic texts like *Darkness* offer an exceptional opportunity to experience the disorientation and vastness of a perspective in which the drive toward readability, closure, and mastery is rejected in favor of the need to make language infinitely strange and to decenter the authority of the reading subject. When meaning resides less in the content of words and more in procedural and conceptual methods and systems, texts become understood less as narrative and more as an ecosystem or an environment where "the intellective human agent" (Barad 2007, 149) is limited in her ability to make sense of things; this limitation is both politically and poetically generative.

Of the four texts discussed in this part of the book, Morrison's *Darkness* is the only book not immediately concerned with late twentieth- and early twenty-first-century practices of resource extraction, manufacturing, and environmental devastation. However, Morrison's development of a posthuman ecopoetics that attempts to dislodge the primacy of the human subject and explore the possibility of nonhuman agency resonates deeply with the poetics of Marcella Durand, Rita Wong, and Evelyn Reilly. Morrison "unwrites" what is arguably one of the most widely read and widely discussed literary depictions of the convergence of colonialism and resource extraction, a convergence that she pries apart through her techniques of erasure. I turn now to Marcella Durand's "The Anatomy of Oil," another work of contemporary posthuman ecopoetics that seeks to critically examine the relationship between resource extraction and human agency.

Posthuman Anatomies: Marcella Durand's "The Anatomy of Oil"

"The Anatomy of Oil" is an eighteen-page poem that was originally published as a chapbook by Belladonna* in 2005 and subsequently published in Durand's book-length collection of poems, *Area*, by Belladonna* in 2008. Written in the early years of the twenty-first century, "The Anatomy of Oil" examines the geological processes that result in the formation of oil; the environmental impact of its extraction and transportation; and its role as a commodity, a source of fuel, and an ingredient in various petroleum-based consumer products. The poem also addresses the role of oil in geopolitics, touching on the U.S. invasion of Iraq and U.S. interests in Middle Eastern oil. While the setting is never directly named, references to Utes (Indigenous people living in what is now known as Colorado and Utah) and descriptions of Hoodoo rock formations suggest the poem is set in or near Colorado and Utah. The ecosystem in this region has come under threat in recent years due to the extraction of oil from tar sands.[6] Durand also makes reference to urban centers and to deserts in the Middle East in her attempt to offer a global "anatomy" of oil.

The word "anatomy" derives from the Latin *anatomia*, which means a cutting up or a dissection of something in order to understand its individual parts. Of the eleven sub-definitions of "anatomy" provided in the *Oxford English Dictionary*, the first nine refer specifically to the dissection of organisms, suggesting a close association between "anatomy" and the study of human and animal physiology as well as botany. The final two entries expand the definition beyond living organisms to include "the dissection or dividing of anything material or immaterial, for the purpose of examining its parts; detailed examination, analysis" and "chemical analysis." I begin my discussion of "The Anatomy of Oil" with a reflection on the term "anatomy" because I think it is important to foreground at the outset the extent to which the word "anatomy" carries a strong association with the dissection of living organisms to examine their component parts, but can also be expanded to consider the study of other kinds of complex systems. The ability to encompass both organic and inorganic systems that is reflected in the definition of "anatomy" is crucial to Durand's poetics and her attempt to develop an "anatomy" of oil whereby oil is understood not just as a source of fuel and a material used in the manufacture of plastics, but also as petrified shale deposits deep underground that predate and exceed anthropocentric understandings of oil as a commodity for human use.

Durand articulates a posthuman "anatomy of oil" in this poem. While the poem offers an extensive consideration of the harm humans continue to enact on the environment in the context of resource extraction in the anthropocene, it also displaces and decenters the human by offering an engagement with oil that is not solely predicated on its value to humans as a commodity and source of fuel. In so doing, Durand's poetry enacts what Rosi Braidotti describes as a "post-anthropocentric shift towards a planetary, geo-centered perspective" (2013, 81).

The poem opens with a reference to the effects of human activity on the landscape: "water cutting / out of reach, the deep rooms / upon rooms, in bands of red" (Durand 2008, 61). Durand seems to be describing the process of hydraulic fracturing or "fracking," whereby rocks are pulverized by high-pressure liquid (usually water, chemicals, and sand) in order to release and extract oil from the rock. Hydraulic fracturing has been associated with the pollution of air and groundwater, the release of methane, and the overconsumption of water in areas where water supplies are limited. References to drilling, mining, and other methods of resource extraction in which humans act upon and transform the natural world occur throughout the poem: "bobble-headed iron drills, thin threads poke into dry hearts—" (66) and further down on the same page:

> if gravel could be ground and rock extracted
> sand crushed and siphoned, flyaway soil captured
> snow and ice melted, rocky beaches compacted, and
> beneath the giant thumping machines small drops well
> and conglomerate into solid puddles, . . .
> (Durand 2008, 66)

The poem contains extensive descriptions of a landscape that is being irrevocably altered as it is mined and drilled for its natural resources. Yet Durand also seeks to expand understandings of oil beyond those limited to human use value; a key component of her "anatomy" of oil is its emphasis on the limitations of human frames of reference and measures of use value. In this regard, her project shares with Morrison's an interest in extracting the human from the nature poem in order to foster new epistemological and ontological relations to the natural world that do not revolve around the human as either a consumer of resources or as an environmental steward. Durand expands her consideration of oil beyond its immediate value as fuel and as a commodity that drives global economies. While oil "lights our lanterns / and forms our oars" (2008, 62), Durand offers a different perspective when she asks "but then what / is oil? but millions / of creatures crushed / into one another / shoulder / to shoulder" (72), defamiliarizing oil for the reader by invoking its geological origins and introducing frames of reference for understanding oil that exceed those structured around energy and the economy. Instead, Durand invokes connections and dependencies that cut across geological eras. Like the creatures crushed "shoulder to shoulder," the speaker describes herself and her human companion(s): "shoulder to shoulder we stand in our way / united and hungry our stomachs are full / we want something and take it from our neighbor" (73). In invoking a continuity between the fossilized remains of extinct creatures and the humans extracting oil through the shared descriptor "shoulder to shoulder," Durand invites the reader to make an implicit link between these groups, to ponder the possibility of our own extinction, and to realize the relative insignificance of humans in the face of the vastness of geological time and the fossil record. Through repetition, human subjects are aligned with the "giant sea-worms, tubes, mouth- / less and eyeless, under storm / of falling life" (62) whose petrified remains have become "fossil fuel" sandwiched between layers of rock.

The paradoxical claim to be hungry with a full stomach ("united and hungry our stomachs are full") reflects an unrelenting appetite for fuel that persists regardless of need. Toward the end of her description of hydraulic fracturing, she refers to the "depths of hunger / for which there is no resolve" (Durand 2008, 61). On the following page she describes the poem's "we" as "hungry   as we always are / as we   burn   *it*" (62). Frequent references in the poem to hunger and thirst suggest a perpetually unsatisfied appetite that persists even after nourishment has been provided and that will continue to persist even after all measures have been taken to extract every available ounce of oil from the ground. Toward the end of the poem she asks "Is our hunger / justified?" (78). While the answer to this question may be no, Durand notes her own complicity through the collective pronoun "our" and through repeated references to her own reliance on oil.

She writes extensively about geological history and formations, explaining the creation of oil as a geological process that predates humans by millennia:

> One layer over the next and another laid
> down over the first and others until all
> is lifted up—and as such climbs higher
> and creates within itself *voids*
>
> > and within these vast spaces
> > skeletons liquid and trapped
> > between water and air, mountain
> > and valley, held by such light
>
> (Durand 2008, 64)

Durand repeats the word "voids" on the next page to describe the pockets within the rock where oil is found: "one layer over the next and another / *creates within itself* voids like those / inside, those petrified objects, / heart, stomach, liver, brain" (Durand 2008, 65). In referring to oil deposits as voids, she creates a kind of inversion of value—in contrast to oil deposits as a product or commodity sought after by prospectors, they become a void in a geological formation, a "soft spot" between layers of hard rock. Also important to Durand's anatomy of oil is the reminder that oil deposits are formed from "heart, stomach, liver, brain" and thus from once-living creatures, creatures in possession of organs similar to our own. By establishing a link between human bodies and the bodies of prehistoric creatures based on comparable anatomies, Durand destabilizes attempts to separate human from animal and simultaneously explores affinities between humans and oil that are not based on the extraction and consumption of fuel. Durand also implies that our own remains might well become oil deposits in the post-anthropocene.

Tyrone Williams identifies Durand's deployment of anthropomorphism in her choice of phrases like "shoulder to shoulder" to describe the fossils of invertebrate sea creatures, and argues that it "puts into abeyance the sentient/non-sentient divide that 'allows' us to objectify, and thus exploit, 'our' natural resources" (2008). As Jane Bennett argues, anthropomorphism, though often dismissed as anthropocentric, can in fact forge alliances across species:

> A touch of anthropomorphism, then, can catalyze a sensibility that finds a world filled not with ontologically distinct categories of beings (subjects and objects) but with variously composed materialities that form confederations. In revealing similarities across categorical divides and lighting up structural parallels between material forms in "nature" and those in "culture," anthropomorphism can reveal isomorphisms. (Bennett 2010, 99)

Durand's deployment of anthropomorphism in her descriptions of the landscape and the resources extracted from that landscape is a central strategy in her attempt not only to delink oil from human use value and to place oil within a temporal framework that recognizes the environmental significance of oil drilling in the anthropocene, but also to draw attention to a geological history that opens up possibilities for engaging with oil in the context of a posthuman framework that exceeds anthropocentric epistemologies and temporalities.

The limitations of a human-centric approach to oil constrain the speaker as she repeatedly foregrounds her partial perspective. She invokes the "floating plates *under / us (but not written to us)*" and describes how "lines extend from continents / to seas unseen in this chasm" (Durand 2008, 61) in order to underscore the limited perspective of the human observer/speaker who is not an omniscient observer of a knowable landscape, but rather a tentative and speculative observer driving past "crushed abyss of *uncertain* / epoch" (66, emphasis mine) and encountering "what we *think* is oxidation" (69, emphasis mine), a "current / almost *indecipherable*, the / surface *unintelligible*" and a "substance . . . not secretive, but *untraceable*" (70, emphasis mine). Durand moves strategically between descriptions of resource extraction and descriptions of landscape and geology that eclipse or elude human influence, control, and interpretation.

In calling into question the binaries of human and nonhuman, and self and nature, and writing against an approach to the natural world that values the land as a source of revenue through resource extraction, "The Anatomy of Oil" problematizes ideological assumptions underpinning conventional nature poetry, which tends to deploy nature as a trope of self-exploration. Durand has written elsewhere about the limitations of conventional nature poetry and the need to rethink the relationship between the poet-speaker and her environment. In an essay called "The Ecology of Poetry," she argues:

> Traditional nature poetry, à la the human-subject meditating upon a natural object-landscape-animal that is supposed to function as a kind of doorway into meaning of the human subject's life is simply no longer possible. . . . Nature has changed from a perceptually exploitable Other—most easily compared to a book to be decoded by the (human) reader—to something intrinsically affected by humans. We ourselves are the wilderness destroying the very systems of which we are a part, in a role we utterly do not understand. (Durand 2010, 116–17)

Durand's claim that the human observer is in fact part of the ecosystems that he or she destroys is key to her framing of the speaker in "The Anatomy of Oil." Durand develops these ideas further in her essay by drawing on Lisa Robertson's observation in "How Pastoral: A Manifesto" that poetry that features a reflective self located in nature often functions to conceal a "symbolic appropriation of the land" (Durand 2010, 117). Durand works against these currents of conventional nature poetry and the pastoral, exploring both her own *complicity* and her own *limitations* as a human observer. The landscape does not function as a window onto the self or a springboard for self-reflection. Instead, both landscape and speaker remain opaque. Said another way, "The Anatomy of Oil" is not an attempt to understand the inner workings of the self, but rather an attempt to realize the self's complicity in environmental devastation. The speaker describes her own dependence on oil and thus acknowledges her complicity in an industry wreaking environmental havoc:

> the red rock comes straight
> down to the bank and is dry, as we speed by
> in our 4WD wide wheelbased SUV tinted windows
> following the RV with self-enclosed toilet, shower
> and small venting ribbons, a TV on dashboard camera—
> (63)

and

> we pass through, we are speeding
> through, we are in the middle of 120
> miles *without services* if we run
> out of gas we are in super-deep shit.
> (Durand 2008, 68)

Durand draws the reader back to the familiar terrain upon which we understand our dependence on oil. The speaker and her companion(s) travel through the desert by SUV, RV, boat, and foot, observing the landscape. However, in spite of her journey through it, the landscape remains fundamentally unknowable to the observer, whose perspective is bound by both human time and conceptual frameworks that understand nature in human terms. She writes:

> I love that rock and am amazed at how so large an uplift
> can look like a ship, it is the only thing I can think of

> to compare to this massive rock *thing* if only I could get
> out of the car to take a closer look if only he would
> stop and we could climb out of the car and take a closer
> look if only the highway would stop and we could climb
> out of the car and take a closer look if only the roads
> would stop and if only we could look closer at the rock
> if only we could stop the car if only we could look
> (Durand 2008, 74)

The speaker is stuck within an anthropocentric frame of reference in which rocks must be compared to ships (human creations) and where her access to the rock is framed and constrained by her dependence on a car, and by extension, the fuel that allows the car to travel close (but not close enough) to the rock formation.

In spite of the fact that the speaker's human perspective limits her access and understanding, she can also be read as a posthuman subject whose existence calls into question the distinction between human subject, environment, and machine, enacting what Rosi Braidotti calls a "new way of combining ethical values with the well-being of an enlarged sense of community which includes one's territorial or environmental inter-connections. This is an ethical bond of an altogether different sort from the self-interests of an individual subject, as defined along the canonical lines of classical humanism" (2013, 190). Durand's poetics enact what Braidotti, drawing on Deleuze, calls becoming-earth, becoming-animal, and becoming-machine. These three "becomings" are central to Braidotti's understanding of posthumanism and together entail the "recognition of trans species solidarity on the basis of our being environmentally based, that is to say embodied, embedded, and in symbiosis with other species" (2013, 67).

Being connected to the environment in a posthuman sense is not the same as being at one with nature; rather, it entails understanding subjectivity as an "assemblage that includes non-human agents" (Braidotti 2013, 82). This posthuman subjectivity is articulated in Durand's poem through an acknowledgment of the interconnectedness of humans and oil, and humans and machines, an interconnectedness manifested in the fact that the human body is understood through oil-laden images and metaphors: "My hand is the size of a tractor-trailer. / Between my thumb and forefinger, / a truck goes" (Durand 2008, 75–76) and "If I press here, my headache / goes away and fossil fuel comes out. / I buy vegetables at corner markets / and support the food wax industry" (76). Just as the speaker is described in machinic terms, machines are strategically anthropomorphized. Trucks carrying oil "sleep while underground / fuel tanks regenerate themselves" (76).

"The Anatomy of Oil" was first published in 2005, and was written during the U.S. military invasion of Iraq. Many have argued that the invasion of Iraq, justified by the Bush administration as an attempt to eradicate terrorism in the wake of 9/11, was in fact a war fought to protect U.S. economic interests in the Middle East.[7] No "anatomy" of oil written in the first decade of the twenty-first century would be complete without some reference to the ways in which oil, war, and geopolitics were mutually implicated at the time. She writes of "The ships in the thousands in the sea" (Durand 2008, 70), presumably in reference to American warships headed to the Middle East. Durand works to collapse the distinction between the Iraqi landscape and the American one: "he says each day he gets / information about chemicals / hidden in caves here or / there" (71), which could be a reference to the Bush administration's false claims that Saddam Hussein had in his possession weapons of mass destruction, or it could be in reference to activities Durand observes while traveling through the American desert. Durand draws connections between the deserts of the Middle East and the deserts of America: "Our desert calls to your desert. / Across the earth, one desert speaks / to another, just as water wicks away / into sky" (75) to further foreground their ecological and geographic similarities rather than dwelling on the geopolitical and cultural differences of their governing bodies.

Durand's anatomy of oil expands the definition of anatomy beyond its association with the body or organism as a closed system comprised of interconnected parts. Instead, Durand's "anatomy" presents oil as a multifaceted substance that is at once biological, geological, economic, social, and cultural. The poem's speaker is limited by her human perspective, but in foregrounding this limitation, Durand decenters the human, expands the reader's understanding of oil beyond its status as a commodity for human use, and advances a posthuman poetics that facilitates an exploration of oil that moves beyond the reference point of human use value.

Rosi Braidotti identifies a link between a critical posthumanism and a move beyond anthropocentrism (2013, 50). This involves a dismantling of species hierarchies that prioritize "man" as superior to other life forms. Yedda Morrison and Marcella Durand both enact a posthuman ecopoetics that strategically displaces the human and dismantles species hierarchies. Both poets embody what Braidotti would call a "post-anthropocentric" position, but curiously, both arrive at that point through a poetics that strategically anthropomorphizes nature in order to recognize forms of agency inherent in the environment and develop understandings of nature and natural resources that do not hinge on human perceptions or human use value. Morrison and Durand both use poetic form and process to foreground the importance of matter in ways that intersect productively with new materialist thinking. Because this poetry foregrounds process and materiality, it functions not just as a textual example to which new materialist theories might be applied, but also as an *active* site through which a return to matter is performatively conceptualized and enacted. I turn now to a discussion of two other recent books of poetry engaged with ecology and the posthuman. While Yedda Morrison and Marcella Durand enact a strategic de/anthropomorphism grounded in the posthuman, Rita Wong and Evelyn Reilly enact a posthuman ecopoetics rooted in understandings of trans-corporeality and interconnectivity.

CHAPTER FOUR

Water and Plastic: Trans-Corporeality in Rita Wong's *undercurrent* and Evelyn Reilly's *Styrofoam*

LIKE MARCELLA DURAND and Yedda Morrison, Rita Wong and Evelyn Reilly embrace an ecopoetics grounded in a posthuman political and ethical perspective that conceives of the human as coextensive with a vibrant, agential, material world. Whereas Durand offered an "anatomy" of oil in an effort to rethink, from a posthuman standpoint, the relationship between human and environment, Wong can be said to offer an anatomy of water and Reilly an anatomy of Styrofoam to address the relationship between humans and the environment. For Wong and Reilly, the objects that form the focus of their projects become metaphors through which to articulate a poetics of interconnectivity that I propose to read here in relation to Stacy Alaimo's theory of trans-corporeality. Trans-corporeality offers "a new materialist and post-humanist sense of the self as substantially and perpetually interconnected with the flows of substances and the agencies of environments" (Alaimo 2012, 476). Because "trans" indicates a movement across diverse sites, trans-corporeality "opens up a mobile space that acknowledges the often unpredictable and unwanted actions of human bodies, nonhuman creatures, ecological systems, chemical agents, and other actors" and "allows us to forge ethical and political positions that can contend with numerous late-twentieth and early twenty-first century realities in which 'human' and 'environment' can by no means be considered as separate" (Alaimo 2010, 3). Wong and Reilly's focus on the posthuman body could be read as an iteration of the kind of strategic embodiment that characterized the feminist poetics discussed in part 1 of this book, but one that specifically builds on and extends understandings of embodiment to foreground the body's interconnectedness with the world.

Fluid Interventions: Rita Wong's Poetics of Water

Vancouver-based poet Rita Wong enacts, through her entire poetic oeuvre, a sustained ethical and political critique of the toxic triad of colonialism, capitalism, and environmental devastation. Her collection of poems *forage* (2007) and her collaboratively authored poem (with Larissa Lai) *sybil unrest* (2013; discussed in an earlier chapter of this book) offer astute, linguistically innovative accounts of the devastation brought about by rampant and unchecked industrial development, genetic modification undertaken in the interests of profit without consideration of negative long-term environmental and heath effects, and systemic forms of inequality under global capitalism that disproportionally affect women, the colonized, and those living in countries like China and Bangladesh that have become sites of cheap manufacturing and exploitative labor. Her interest in the relationship between the racialized and gendered body, capitalism, and the environment is present in all of her writing. However, *undercurrent* (2015) arguably offers her most extensive reflection on the politics and poetics of transcorporeality.

undercurrent articulates its political critique through a sustained poetic engagement with water. Wong describes *undercurrent* as an attempt to write *with* and *for* rather than *about* water. Writing with water implies an ethic of coexistence and cooperation rather than a logic of domination or exploitation. Instead of treating water as a discrete object of analysis, she writes of water as a vital substance that connects all living things at a molecular level. Wong's endeavor to write "with" water is in many ways similar to Durand's "anatomy" of the various scientific and social dimensions of oil; both poets offer extensive examinations of natural resources and the environmental impact of their extraction and commodification. They also both consider the value and worth of these substances outside of anthropocentric frameworks.

Wong writes in *undercurrent* of local bodies of water close to her Vancouver home such as the Burrard Inlet and the Fraser River. She also writes about bodies of water further afield such as the Athabasca River and Gregoire Lake in northern Alberta; these two bodies of water have become severely polluted as a result of the extraction of oil from the Alberta tar sands. She writes of the displacement of communities and ecosystems along the Yangtze River in China where the Three Gorges Dam project artificially flooded parts of the river valley. In addition to writing of oceans, lakes, and rivers, she writes of rain, creeks lost to urban development in Vancouver, sewage treatment plants, and pipelines. Focusing on watersheds, oceans, and ecosystems as well as the role water plays in our bodies and in the bodies of all living things, Wong's understanding of water resonates with Mielle Chandler and Astrida Niemanis's approach to water as a substance that challenges Western notions of the human body as bounded, discrete, and separate from the world:

> The facilitative capacity of water—that is, water's facilitation of the inception, repetition, and proliferation of life in its potentially infinite plurality—throws into question Western thought's construction of "being." . . . Water both responds to a limited number of already-existent others and proliferates plurality in and beyond the human . . . water *models* a mode of sociality that we, as human sovereign subjects, repeat—dissolving the sovereign self in a becoming-responsive to others, both human and more-than-human. (Chandler and Neimanis 2013, 62)

Wong is especially interested in finding ways to counter understandings of the subject derived from a Western philosophical tradition that sees the self as a discrete, contained body that is separate from its surroundings because this has facilitated the treatment of the physical world as primarily existing for human use value and profit. She writes against the understanding of self in relation to environment that has legitimized activities such as damming and diverting water, strip mining, fracking, and logging in the interests of corporate profit. While humans have been altering the environment and extracting resources for as long as we have walked the earth, what Wong specifically objects to is the excessive plunder and extraction that has occurred in the interests of generating capital through oil and gas exploration and the bottled water industry. These practices, she notes, disproportionately affect Indigenous people, whose communities are flooded and polluted and whose traditional ways of life are disrupted by industrial development and resource extraction. In this regard, Wong's poetics is driven by a strong anticolonial ethos that is as prevalent as, but is also intimately connected to, an environmental and anticapitalist ethos. Her work is profoundly influenced by Indigenous ways of knowing and thinking about land, language, and subjectivity (Wong 2009, 347). The trans-corporeal body foregrounded in these poems is not the white, male body of Western humanism; Wong's trans-corporeal poetics is intersectional in the attention it pays to both race and gender.

Water functions as a rich and multivalent symbol in this book because of its centrality to all forms of biological life and also because, in the context of industrial capitalism, it becomes a conduit for toxins and pollutants. As Chandler and Neimanis explain,

> As it changes forms and cycles through various manifestations of bodies, societies, and politics, diffusing, spreading, and bringing back to us the very matter we cast away, water shows us that at every level we are of water. But to harm water is not simply to harm ourselves; it is, as so many ecologists have shown, to harm the conditions for the proliferation of life itself. If Western imperialism has muted the plurality of voices that would contest the worldview undergirding late capitalism's treatment of water, . . . water itself provides a starting point from which to rethink this worldview. (Chandler and Niemanis 2013, 62)

Writing with water implies, as Chandler and Neimanis suggest, "a particular kind of material sociality whereby we not only respond to others but also in turn comprise the fluid social gestational condition of possibilities beyond ourselves" (2013, 73). This is precisely what Wong achieves in *undercurrent*.

Thinking and writing with water manifests itself in *undercurrent* through the development of a fluid poetics as Wong's writing reflects qualities of water. As the opening lines of "pacific flow," the first poem in the collection, read: "water has a syntax   i am still learning" (Wong 2015, 9). *undercurrent* develops ways to use language creatively to explore the syntax of water. Concepts permeate each other, envelop objects, flow together, and collect in runnels just as water does; words dissolve into other words to form puns like "scar sands" and "bisphenol ache" that are rich in multiple meanings.

Although much of *undercurrent* is focused on the negative impact of human actions on water, Wong seeks to decenter the human by challenging assumptions of human exceptionalism and entitlement that facilitate the destruction of the environment. Mining, fracking, and other forms of resource extraction are framed in these poems as an ethical failure, a betrayal of what Wong understands as sacred bonds between humans and what Rosi Braidotti refers to as "earth others" (2002). Although the human is located at the center of this quagmire because humans are responsible for environmental devastation, the poems actively decenter the human and de-anthropomorphize nature by advancing a poetics of trans-corporeality and interconnectivity in which "the ostensible center is extended throughout multiple, often global networks" (Alaimo 2010, 16).

Wong's trans-corporeal approach to thinking with water is evident in "borrowed waters: the sea around us, the sea within us," the second poem in the collection. The piece begins with a description of the "great pacific garbage patch" which she refers to as a "dead albatross" that "mirrors us back to / ourselves" (Wong 2015, 10).[1] The "manmade" network of this patch of garbage "branch[es] into your bathroom" and into "plastic factories" and "fast food restaurants" (10), suggesting our shared complicity in the constant expansion of this island of garbage, and by extension, the consequences of our small, daily activities. Wong prompts her reader to think not just of the consequences for the ecosystem of seemingly innocuous activities like exfoliating our skin with microbeads or picking up lunch from a fast food restaurant; she also prompts us to reflect on and even embrace the fact that we share DNA with all living organisms and are thus connected at a cellular and genetic level to all living beings: "both the ferned & the furry, the herbaceous & / the human, can call the ocean our ancestor. our / blood plasma sings the composition of seawater" (11). In "declaration of intent" she refers to water as "a sacred bond, embedded in our plump, moist cells / in our breaths that transpire to return to the clouds that gave us / life through rain" (14). A "sacred bond" implies an ethical promise or imperative, a posthuman, trans-corporeal ontology premised on radical interconnectivity across life forms. The poem continues:

> a watershed teaches not only humbleness but climate fluency
> the languages we need to interpret the sea's rising voice
> water connects us to salmon & cedar, whales & workers
> its currents bearing the plastic from our fridges & closets
> (Wong 2015, 14)

To attain "climate fluency" entails learning the syntax of water, and by extension, "rewrit(ing) the default grammar of agency" (Bennett 2010, 119) that applies passivity to substances like water. Etymologically linked to the word "fluid," "fluency" comes from the Latin *fluentia* and *fluere*, which means "to flow," suggesting a link between "fluency" and the kind of intimate, embodied engagement with water that Wong advocates in these poems. The realization of the cellular connection to other life forms emphasizes the relative smallness of humans (it teaches humbleness) in this large network, but also the disproportionate role we play in terms of polluting and altering the delicate balance of ecosystems. In this regard, it also teaches remorse and hopefully instills a desire to stem the tide of environmental catastrophe.

The permeability of the bodies of humans and other living organisms is a persistent trope in this collection. Bodies are connected to their environment in part through the fact that they are largely comprised of water. Bodies are porous, absorbing environmental toxins and bacteria that fundamentally alter their composition. In "mongo mondo," Wong warns: "convenience not worth cancer's / long soft leak into lungs, brains, bellies" (2015, 12). Wong never loses sight of the bitter irony that humans are engineering their own environmental illnesses in the name of economic progress. The revenue generated by resource extraction and industry is eclipsed by the environmental and health-related costs—costs that cannot be factored in financial terms and whose burden will be carried disproportionately by future generations, the poor, and the colonized. Wong is attuned to the fact that the most marginalized people are often the ones most directly affected by pollution and climate change and that resource extraction is inextricably linked to colonial occupation. In this regard, trans-corporeality is not just a liberatory framework through which the poet or theorist learns to think about ontology differently; rather, trans-corporeality is also a conduit of colonial violence and capitalist exploitation.

The poem "body burden: a moving target" develops a trans-corporeal poetics in order to explore the multiple ways in which bodies are implicated in, by, and through the environment:

> eczema reminds
> fragile barrier, easily broken
> inner oozes out, itchy lymph
> fluids that came from
> swallowed water
> that came from
> a river that came from a lake
> that came from a glacier
> receding from industrial glare
> (Wong 2015, 40)

Again Wong underscores a trans-corporeal interconnectedness in which the embodied subject is coextensive with her environment. Eczema and other autoimmune illnesses can be exacerbated by exposure to environmental toxins and pollutants, since the body is a "fragile barrier" sustained by water, the source of which can be traced to watersheds that are threatened by pollution and climate change.

Central to Wong's fluid, trans-corporeal poetics is the use of puns. Puns create layers of meaning that signify in multiple directions; they crack words open. Wong's "bisphenol ache" is an obvious pun on "bisphenol a," a synthetic compound used widely in food packaging, water bottles, and other materials and that has been linked to a variety of health issues, including cancer, thyroid problems, asthma, and heart disease. Wong writes:

> bisphenol ache bursts a cell wall leaks plasma limpid, laden
> with toxic gifts courtesy of duped ontology   corporate cancer
> embedded in diets, morsel by muscle, blight by bite, gradually
> accumulated illnesses blossom in our bellies, breasts, bladders,
> intestines testify to trace amounts hoarded in blood & bitumen,
> brimming with slow malignant release, remind us that biology

is determined by chemistry cartels infiltrating our shampoos &
synthetic textiles, room deodorizers & tin can linings   receipt
paper coatings & hand sanitizers sing a slow song of poison by a
thousand exposures
(Wong 2015, 46)

Ontology, the philosophical study of the nature of being, is duped in
this context because toxins are altering our composition at a cellular
level to facilitate the growth of cancerous cells, or as Wong puts it,
"biology is determined by chemistry cartels." The internal rhyming
of "blight" and "bite" emphasizes the fact that these toxins enter our
bodies through pesticides and other chemicals in our food supply; that
which ostensibly nourishes us can also kill. Again she draws attention
to the gradual accumulation of toxins, the "chemical creep" that accrues
through daily activities like washing one's hair (with shampoo that
contains parabens) or collecting a receipt (which is coated in bisphenol
a) at the supermarket. Wong's poetics of strategic embodiment is at
once both profoundly materialist and anti-essentialist; she embraces
the body as biology, but is also attuned to the ways in which biology is
actively and negatively shaped by profit-driven corporations that are
indifferent to the consequences of their actions on living organisms.

In her effort to poetically conceptualize a posthuman, trans-corporeal
subjectivity, Wong presents the body, the physical self, as comprised, at
a very basic, fundamental, and cellular level, from the nonhuman. The
poem "the wonders of being several" is a "bivocal ditty to honour the
micro & the macro / as symbiotic bacteria outnumber our juicy cells ten
to one" (Wong 2015, 13). Wong acknowledges the role bacteria plays
in the facilitation of both health and sickness; these "bacteria buddies
swim throughout" our bodies but when "furbished with furans" or en-
vironmental toxins, they "revoke immunity" (13). The self is primar-
ily comprised of bacteria, becoming what Timothy Morton calls the
"strange stranger," or "the paradoxes and fissures of identity *within*
'human' and 'animal'" (2010, 41). Jane Bennett notes that acknowl-
edging the presence of "bacteria colonies" within our bodies helps to
"show how human subjects are themselves nonhuman, alien, outside"
(2010, 120). Following Morton and Bennett, Wong's celebration of the

bacteria within human bodies challenges Western philosophical per-
ceptions of the subject, underscores the permeability of bodies, and
draws attention to the vibrancy and agency of matter.

As Stacy Alaimo has argued, trans-corporeality marks a shift in un-
derstandings of human subjectivity: "As the material self cannot be
disentangled from networks that are simultaneously economic, po-
litical, cultural, scientific, and substantial, what was once the osten-
sibly bounded human subject finds herself in a swirling landscape of
uncertainty where practices and actions that were once not even re-
motely ethical or political matters suddenly become the very stuff of
the crisis at hand" (Alaimo 2010, 20). This dissolution of the subject is
profoundly different from the kinds of challenges to the subject posed
by post-structuralist theories because it is grounded not in semiot-
ics or discursive relations, but in a consideration of the raw stuff of
materiality.

Wong's poetics of connectivity and trans-corporeality involves a crit-
ical examination of the practices of resource extraction that lead to the
pollution of watersheds. Several of the poems in the collection address
the topic of the Alberta tar sands and their impact on Gregoire Lake,
the Athabasca River, and the Indigenous communities that rely on wa-
ters polluted by the extraction of bitumen from the tar sands. Many of
these poems were written during Healing Walks for the tar sands that
Wong participated in between 2010 and 2013. Wong describes one of
these walks in "fresh ancient ground":

> we walk for healing the scar sands, in a living pact with the
>   bears, the eagles,
> the muzzled scientists, the beavers who've built dams you can
>   see from outer space
> (Wong 2015, 18)

Her "living pact" is posthuman and trans-corporeal in its incorporation
of animals and "muzzled scientists." By strategically decentering the
human, Wong attempts to articulate an ethical relationship with land,
air, water, and animals that is premised not on assumptions of human
exceptionality or the primacy of profit, but rather on an understanding
of reciprocity and care. Scientists, whose role is commonly understood

as that of objective observers studying animals and the environment and thus as separate and even "above" their objects of study, here become part of a pact that emphasizes close connection. The "muzzling" of the scientists is a reference to attempts by the Canadian Conservative government (in office when Wong wrote this book) to tightly control information disseminated by scientists working on environmental and climate research (Chung 2013).

The poem "night gift" describes the sheer horror of observing the destruction of the tar sands and reflects on excessive oil consumption. Notably, Wong acknowledges her own complicity in this consumption when she notes that the very lenses she uses to observe the tar sands are made from plastic, a byproduct of petroleum.

> we burn ancient sunlight & petrified ancestors
> like there's no tomorrow
> dig & draw up dirt so relentlessly we tip toward stranglehold
> does capitalism's "progress" induce collapse?
> ed said, "everything's been touched by oil"
> i look through plastic glasses caught under
> petroleum by-product lenses
> (Wong 2015, 24)

Like Durand, Wong defamiliarizes oil by locating it in relation to its geological and biological origins. In referring to the fossils as "ancestors," she establishes a trans-corporeal continuity, a relationship to oil premised not on the consumption of fuel, but rather on a kinship with the fossilized remains of long-extinct organisms.[2] Wong goes on to diagnose our addiction to oil as a manifestation of "Stockholm syndrome." Stockholm syndrome, the psychological phenomenon of falling in love with one's captor, functions as a metaphor for a cultural dependence on consumption and consumerism that leads directly to widespread and long-term illness, disease, and environmental pollution.

Wong's anticolonial politics are intermeshed with her environmental politics; throughout *undercurrent*, she draws connections between the pollution of water and the violence of colonization. The poem "declaration of intent" begins with the lines "let the colonial borders be seen for the pretensions that they are / i hereby honour what the flow of water teaches us" (Wong 2015, 14). In its fluidity, water will not be contained by national borders, which are artificially imposed on the land and on Indigenous people whose ancestors lived on the land long before their movements were regulated by borders. While rivers, lakes, and other bodies of water sometimes become national borders, the meaning of these borders is imposed by a colonial regime intent on utilizing water and other natural resources for profit.

Closely related to Wong's fluid, trans-corporeal poetics is her use of language to enact a poetics of decolonization. "Q'élstexw" is a poem in which Indigenous words sprout up between English words in order to underscore the extent to which the land bears the traces of its original inhabitants: *"the city paved over with ~~cement~~ english cracks open, stubborn* Halq'eméylem / *springs up"* (Wong 2015, 59). The form of the poem enacts a reclamation of an Indigenous language that is local to the geographic space which is being described in the poem. The Indigenous words serve to remind readers of local linguistic histories, histories that have been lost due to colonization but that are here celebrated, recognized, and reestablished like plants pushing up through pavement. Languages that are Indigenous to a given location bear an intimate relationship to place, although that relationship is often suppressed through colonization.

In "dispatches from water's journey," Wong states that she lives "at the west entrance of a haunted house called canada" (2015, 64), further underscoring the ways in which the past ruptures the present. As Wong demonstrates repeatedly in this collection, resource extraction is a manifestation and extension of colonialism, and activities like mining, logging, and the transportation of oil through pipelines directly harm Indigenous communities and traditional ways of life.

Although the overarching tone of Wong's poetry is critical and cautionary, it is also characterized by an appreciation of the beauty of the world and an optimism for the future. She concludes *undercurrent* with reference to hope for the future in the poem "holders": "it is the children i will never see, but who i hope will live and / drink clean, wild water" (2015, 79). Wong's optimism is linked to her feminist politics; in "holders," the final poem in the collection, Wong imagines women joining in solidarity to resist the forces of environmental destruction.

These "women stand in / front of army trucks & policemen, uniforms & riot gear with / only their soft skin & clear eyes to protect their beating hearts. / the mothers, the sisters, the aunties, the grannies, the daughters / crack open the ugly pavement of unjust laws & find old rivers / underneath" (80). Wong positions these women as guardians of nature and protectors of the next generation. "holders" brings feminist activism and trans-corporeality to bear on one another in order to articulate hope and possibility. Wong writes, "the women lick their lips with gusto. they perch on the edge of / teetering cities. they jump into organic fields. the women build / homes with their beloveds. the women find ways to laugh even / when life isn't funny. the women remain" (2015, 80). Wong ends this final poem in the collection with these words, which suggest action and resiliency rather than paralysis in the face of what sometimes seems like an inevitable decline into environmental catastrophe.

This message of hope is continued in a short prose epilogue, a letter allegedly sent back in time from 100 years in the future. The letter indicates that in the year 2115, toilets compost rather than flush, and "we live in the world as if it were our only home . . . spontaneous compassion sprouts in / the cracks of collapsing systems" (2015, 87). Wong's imagining of 2115 is unapologetically utopian:

> three sisters sing louder in our guts & muscles. we learn the
> languages of roots & fungus medicines. dandelion, yarrow,
> burdock, lingzhi. everyone slows, attends to the waxing & waning
> moon each lunar cycle. balance quietly returns to the commons,
> . . . indigenous resurgence slows climate instability
> & deflates apocalyptic fervor. today people live & watch water's
> journey the way they used to watch the dow jones, as the flow of
> tao reaffirms ocean life. hych'ka.
> (Wong 2015, 87)

This critical optimism is necessary in order to galvanize change, and it resonates strongly with the hope and optimism underscoring new materialist and posthumanist approaches to politics and the environment. As Rosi Braidotti writes:

I live at the tail-end of bio-power, that is to say amidst the relentless necro-political consumption of all that lives. I am committed to starting from this, not from a nostalgic re-invention of an all-inclusive transcendental model, a romanticized margin or some holistic ideal. I want to think from here and now . . . from missing seeds and dying species. But also, simultaneously and without contradiction, from the staggering, unexpected, and relentlessly generative ways in which life, as *bios* and *zoe*, keeps on fighting back. This is the kind of materialism that makes me a posthuman thinker at heart and a joyful member of multiple companion species in practice. (2013, 194–95)

Optimism, joy, and celebration are key aspects of both posthumanism and materialist ecopoetics. Wong's poetics are characterized by love, wonder, and amazement as much as they are by a lament for extinct species and polluted lakes. Indeed, the book's activism is linked to a positive and hopeful investment in building a better future for the planet.

Evelyn Reilly's *Styrofoam* and the Poetics of Hyperobjects

If Wong's poetics of water is characterized not just by a critical engagement with the role of humans in the pollution of the watershed, but also by a utopian determination to imagine a better future, Evelyn Reilly's poetics of Styrofoam is eminently bleaker and more dystopian. Unlike water, which is connective, generative, and ultimately part of our bodies and the bodies of all living things even if it also carries toxins and pollutants, Styrofoam is inorganic and radically other even as it becomes part of ecosystems. Styrofoam is a synthetic aromatic polymer made from the monomer styrene, a liquid petrochemical. It is used in everything from home insulation to take-out food containers. It takes thousands of years to decompose and comprises an estimated 30 percent of the material in landfills (Little 2015). Evelyn Reilly's *Styrofoam* (2009) is a book of poems that reflects on Styrofoam's magnitude, its longevity, and its ability to permeate bodies and ecosystems. Styrofoam and other forms of plastic are large-scale nonhuman actants that take on a life of their own, surpassing and eclipsing the human. Like Wong, Reilly develops a posthuman, trans-corporeal poetics that is focused on a single substance in order to address, in nuanced ways, the complex relationship among biopolitics, industrial capitalism, and ecosystems, and to challenge understandings of humans as separate from their environment.

Reilly understands ecopoetics as a poetics of connection and interaction. In an essay called "Eco-Noise and the Flux of Lux," she defines ecopoetics as

> a relational poetics, one that reflects the shift from a classification biology obsessed with naming, to an ecological biology with its emphasis on processes of interaction and change, and, on the molecular scale, with randomness and contingency. Ecopoetics points to a poetry that attempts to trace the kinetics of whole systems, and to enact connections rather than to mark distinctions. (Reilly 2010, 258)

Through readings of several poems from *Styrofoam*, I aim to show how Reilly articulates a trans-corporeal poetics of relationality and connectivity that highlights the permeability of bodies, ecosystems, and chemical compounds and that attempts to come to terms with Styrofoam's magnitude, longevity, and "deathlessness" (2009, 9).

Reilly incorporates diverse found materials into her poems, some gleaned from literature and philosophy, some from the realm of popular culture, some retrieved from Google searches, and some from scientific articles. She also incorporates a range of photographs and illustrations, including a photo of birds scavenging at a garbage dump, close-up images of Styrofoam that look almost like a desert landscape, art made from Styrofoam, a picture of roadkill, canonical works of art, movie stills, and magnified cancer cells. Reading Reilly's poems requires tracing connections across this array of texts and images, although one need not be an expert in literature, philosophy, biology, art history, or chemistry in order to appreciate the scope and magnitude of her project.

The poems in *Styrofoam* are extremely fragmented and sparse. The speaker is fleeting and permeable and constituted in, through, and between diverse and fragmentary strands of text and image; she is "trans-corporeal," or "intermeshed with the more-than-human world" (Alaimo 2009, 238). Rather than using fragmentation to illustrate a lack of unity or wholeness, Reilly uses fragmentation in these poems to explore the interconnectedness of things. In other words, it is precisely *through* this radically fragmented form that Reilly is able to powerfully but somewhat paradoxically articulate a poetics of radical interconnectivity and trans-corporeality. Just as Wong's poetics formally mimic their subject matter as the poems flow, envelop, and carry like water, so too does Reilly's. Like plastics and thermoplastics, the jarring fragments of text in Reilly's poems permeate but retain a stubborn self-identity and a self-enclosed consistency even in their most minute manifestations.

Whereas Wong's poems took as their focus an element commonly associated with purity and life (even if most of the poems described water as carrying toxins and pollutants), Reilly's poems take as their focus a substance that is seen as antithetical to life and as always already associated with pollution. Unlike water, Styrofoam is *never* life-sustaining. It is *not* crucial to the functioning of biological organisms. However, as Reilly's poems make clear, Styrofoam and other plastics have become part of our ecosystems and have even entered our bodies and the bodies of other organisms by altering our endocrine systems and contributing to conditions like cancer and hormonal imbalances; they are here to stay, and we must learn to live with and alongside of them.

Reilly draws attention to the multidimensionality and ubiquity of Styrofoam and plastic. Styrofoam takes on different characteristics depending on the precise chemical compounds used to make it; it can be hard or soft, dense or light. As humans, we interact and intra-act with, depend on, and coexist with this synthetic material, which, despite the fact that it is our own creation, takes on a life of its own, acting *on* and *in* living organisms and promising to outlast humans by millennia. Underscoring *Styrofoam* is an ongoing reflection on the imperative to develop a kind of intimacy with this substance that has become part of our environment. Although Reilly acknowledges the responsibility of humans for manufacturing and using Styrofoam, she avoids ascribing a state of exceptionality to humans. On the contrary, the poems in *Styrofoam* emphasize the sublime magnitude and exceptionality of Styrofoam and the many lines of continuity between humans and other organisms affected by the presence of this substance in the earth's ecosystem.

Reilly's poems are animated by a series of implicit questions: What is Styrofoam? How does it interact with and affect its surroundings? How does it affect the health of living organisms? What can be done to manage the ever-increasing volume of Styrofoam on the planet? How long does it take to decompose? This last question is addressed in the opening lines of the first poem in the collection. "Hence Mystical Cosmetic Over Sunset Landfill" begins with an answer followed by the question: "Answer: Styrofoam deathlessness / Question: How long does it take?" (Reilly 2009, 9). The fact that the answer precedes the question could be read as an indication of the belatedness of the question; by the time one asks how long it takes to decompose, Styrofoam has already been piling up in landfills for years. These lines draw attention to Styrofoam's seeming immortality, its "deathlessness." The status of plastic as "undead" is a persistent thread in the book, linking plastic not only to "vibrant matter" but also to the horror genre, where the undead manifests in the form of zombies, ghosts, and other unkillable entities. I will return to Reilly's engagement with horror and the undead below, but first, I want to explore another implication of the deathlessness of Styrofoam: its status as a hyperobject.

"Hyperobject" is a term coined by Timothy Morton, who argues that in spite of the fact that capitalism is a "boiling whirlwind of impermanence," it

> creates things that are more solid than things ever were. Alongside global warming, "hyperobjects" will be our lasting legacy. Materials from humble Styrofoam to terrifying plutonium will far outlast current social and biological forms. We are talking about hundreds and thousands of years. Five hundred years from now, polystyrene objects such as cups and takeout boxes will still exist. Ten thousand years ago, Stonehenge didn't exist. Ten thousand years from now, plutonium will still exist." (Morton 2010, 130)

Morton argues that one of the pressing issues facing us today is figuring out how to care for and coexist with hyperobjects, and that in order to do so effectively, we must "imagine collectivity" (2010, 125) rather than thinking in individualistic terms. Hyperobjects "cause us to reflect on our very place on Earth and the cosmos. Perhaps this is the most fundamental issue—hyperobjects seem to force something on us, something that affects some core ideas of what it means to exist, what Earth is, what society is" (Morton 2013, 15). This act of imagining collectively necessitates thinking in terms of the trans-corporeal and bearing in mind the interconnectivity and permeability of ecosystems and bodies; Reilly's poetic project powerfully enacts a recognition of these factors.

"Hence Mystical Cosmetic Over Sunset Landfill" juxtaposes the chemical compounds used to make plastics with the effects of plastics on the environment and on living organisms:

[hat: 59% Acrylic 41% Modacrylic]
[ornamental trim: 24% Polyvinyl 76% Polyamide]

holding a vial
    enwrapped

Enter: 8,9,13,14,17-ethynyl-13-methyl-
7,8,9,11,12,14,15,16-octahydro-cyclopenta-diol
(aka environmental sources of hormonal activity

(side effects include tenderness, dizziness

       and aberrations of the vision
(Reilly 2009, 9)

Like Wong, Reilly develops a trans-corporeal poetics that traces the effects of chemicals on bodies. Reilly refers to landfills as "vast mummifiers / of waste / and waste's companions" (2009, 10), ascribing a kind of immortality to synthetically produced materials like Styrofoam and other thermoplastics which are preserved like mummies. "Waste's companions" here could refer to the birds, humans, insects, plants, and other ecological elements that interact and intra-act with the objects that end up in landfills. Reilly recycles into her poems textual fragments lifted from the Internet in which people discuss how to repurpose old Styrofoam:

Kristen J
A low oven and a watchful eye turns bits
of used plastic meat trays into keychain ornaments.
Monica T
Soft and satisfying for infant teething if you first freeze.
(Reilly 2009, 10–11)

Repurposing Styrofoam waste can be understood not just as a thrifty and environmentally conscious act of recycling that keeps Styrofoam, for the time being, out of the landfill, but also as an effort to mask the deathlessness of this substance; when Styrofoam is repurposed, it is given life as a new object, but its status as a hyperobject is temporarily deferred. However, given the carcinogenic properties of Styrofoam, this attempt to defer its deathlessness by transforming it into a teether for an infant must be read as morbidly ironic and unsettling.

The title "Hence Mystical Cosmetic Over Sunset Landfill" alludes to the speaker's observation that fine particulate matter in the air caused by pollution at a landfill actually enhances the beauty of the sunset, an observation that draws attention to the extent to which industrial pollutants have become incorporated into a dystopic aesthetic of the picturesque. Reilly rejects the binary structure of much traditional environmentalist thinking in which the natural world is positioned in opposition to culture and industry and is configured as a passive site in need of protection.

Reilly incorporates lines from Samuel Taylor Coleridge's "Rime of the Ancient Mariner," a text that she claims "haunts" this entire collection of poems (2009, 68), linking the killing of the albatross in Coleridge's poem to the extinction of plant and animal species as the result of pollution.[3] She includes Coleridge's line "(*for all averred, we had killed the bird*," and then adds her own words: "[enter albatross / stand-in of choice" (2009, 11) to suggest that the albatross functions as a kind of substitution for something else. Indeed, the word "albatross" has become a kind of idiom for an unshakeable psychological burden. Reilly's use of the albatross operates on at least two levels: the havoc wrought on ecosystems by thermoplastics is a metaphorical albatross that pursues the speaker and weighs on her conscience, but on a more basic level, thermoplastics literally kill birds.[4]

Timothy Morton considers "Rime of the Ancient Mariner" in his book *The Ecological Thought*, attributing the poem's "powerful ecological statement" to its uncanniness and its multifaceted exploration of the "strange stranger, who emerges from, and is, and constitutes the environment" (2010, 46). For Morton, Coleridge's poem is rife with unsettling, traumatic encounters with "strange strangers": the albatross, the Mariner, the Wedding Guest, the water snakes, and others. Morton argues that what the Mariner learns in this poem is essentially "how true sympathy comes from social feeling—the awareness of coexistence" and of the "entanglement of all strangers" (47) regardless of their status as humans, animals, or objects. The Mariner learns to love the inhuman, the "radically strange, dangerous, even 'evil'" (92), and this lesson is manifested in his blessing of the water snakes (92). Morton reads this as a manifestation of "ecological thought," or "intimacy with the strange stranger" (46). The ecological thought is a realization of the interconnectedness of all things, including living organisms, toxins, chemicals, and plastics that leach into ecosystems. Reilly's invocation of Coleridge's poem, and indeed her entire poetic project, resonates strongly with Morton's articulation of ecological thought as she seeks to probe the complex trans-corporeal relations between humans, other living organisms, and synthetic compounds like Styrofoam and plastic which can no longer be considered as separate from the environment or even separate from the self. *Styrofoam* can be read as a poetic reckoning with the ecological thought.

"Hence Mystical Cosmetic Over Sunset Landfill" includes a meditation on the word "foam," providing a definition that draws attention to its multiplicity. Foam is: "1 : a mass of fine bubbles on the surface of a liquid / 2 : a light cellular material resulting from the introduction / of gas during manufacture 3 : frothy saliva 4: the SEA" (Reilly 2009, 10). Foam is at once the property of a synthetic manufacturing process, a quality of the ocean, and a characteristic of a bodily fluid; as such, foam provides rich symbolism for mediation between the environment, human subjects, and synthetic materials like Styrofoam. The poem concludes with the lines:

What the sea brought: poly.flotsam.faux.foam

&Floam®

a kind of slime with polystyrene beads in it
that can be used to transform almost any object
into a unique work of art
(Reilly 2009, 12)

In the poem's concluding lines, "foam" morphs into Floam®, a substance made by Nickelodeon that contains polystyrene microbeads and is sold as a craft supply for children. By including the registered trademark symbol "®," Reilly emphasizes the fact that this product is owned by one of the largest cable television networks in the United States, and is marketed as a fun and creative product for children, but is ultimately created to generate profit without consideration of its negative impact on the environment. What seems like a harmless, creative toy becomes a pollutant, washed up with the tide. The microbeads found in Floam and other consumer products make their way through municipal water treatment facilities into lakes and oceans where they wash up on beaches and are ingested by fish and birds, disrupting ecosystems but becoming part of an environment that they irrevocably alter.

Styrofoam's vital materiality and status as a hyperobject is further articulated in the poem "Bear.Mea(e)t.Polystyrene," in which the longevity of thermoplastic is framed through discourses of religious ecstasy, female *jouissance,* and bodily pain that fragment and dissolve the subject. Through a complex constellation of references, the poem explores the disintegration of the subject who has been altered by the intrusion of thermoplastics into her psychic, social, and physical self.

The poem begins:

> Standing
>
> in the foreshortened
>
> space of
> impact on material
>
> amid immortality of plastic (the ex-
> of exhilaration (the ex-

of anonymity
ex(of nihil exhil
(Reilly 2009, 20)

Reilly plays across notions of nothingless (ex nihil) and exhiliration (exhil) and explores "the multiplicity of foam and foam's conditions" (2009, 20). The poem vacillates between reflections on the exhilarating magnitude of Styrofoam, the "pseudo-kindness" of polystyrene in its mundane, daily use (*"keeps food warm for the elderly"* [21]), and "a kind of narcissism / that reflects a white.cellular.polycarbonate.glow" (20–21) that references the individualistic thinking and self-absorption that impede an acknowledgment of trans-corporeality and the profound understanding and appreciation of the intricate connections between living organisms (including but not limited to humans) and the chemicals, toxins, and plastics that leach into bodies and ecosystems. Reilly explores these interconnections:

The smell of fumes

        & a yellow strip

of smoked.brilliance
orange pylons discarded
nickel cadmium batteries
and.sleet

like small rounded plastic
units that frost

the.terrain

of polished visitation.ecstasy   the interlaced
figures   abandonments and inter-
spersements.of

earth.clay.stone.foam.Floam®
(Reilly 2009, 22–23)

This is a landscape of "abandonments and interspersements" (23) where toxins leach from batteries into rainwater; plastic covers the ground like frost; and earth, clay, and stone encounter Floam®. But it is also a site of "ecstasy," a word used twice in the poem and linked to the notion of religious ecstasy through references to Saint Teresa, a sixteenth-century Spanish nun who experienced and wrote about religious ecstasy and whose presence is directly invoked in the lines:

> Teresa
>
> among altered alters
> at www.artnut.bernini/ecstasy.html
> (2009, 22)

The URL included in the poem, if typed into a web browser, takes the reader to a picture of Bernini's statue of Saint Teresa. An image of the statue also appears in the book immediately following this poem and preceding "Wing/Span/Screw/Cluster (Aves)," another poem in which Saint Teresa emerges as an important presence. "Wing/Span/Screw/Cluster (Aves)" includes several lines from Saint Teresa's *The Interior Castle* and lines from Gertrude Stein's *Four Saints in Three Acts*, a libretto Stein wrote for an opera by Virgil Thompson that features several saints, including Saint Teresa.

By invoking the figure of Saint Teresa in these two poems, Reilly explores the productive possibilities that lie at the intersection of a discourse on religious ecstasy and a reflection on industrial and consumer waste. If ecstatic religious experiences entail a kind of transcendence of the body and a sublime merging or union with a divine presence, then religious ecstasy is one model for thinking beyond the self and for understanding one's connection to something of great magnitude. Religious ecstasy differs from the kind of transcendence of self that is explored by Reilly, however, insofar as Reilly's attempt to go beyond the self remains firmly embedded in the material world and a poetics of trans-corporeal relationality, even if it requires the conceptual work of moving beyond and outside of human frames of temporal and spatial reference.

Through references to Bernini's famous statue depicting the ecstasy of Saint Teresa, Reilly also implicitly evokes Lacan's reference to this statue in Seminar XX, his attempt to explain female *jouissance* as something that is always in excess and outside of language (Lacan 1982, 142). Lacan describes Bernini's statue: "You only have to go and look at Bernini's statue in Rome to understand immediately that she's coming, there is no doubt about it. And what is her *jouissance* coming from? It is clear that the essential testimony of the mystics is that they are experiencing it but know nothing about it" (147). The experience is beyond, in excess, outside language; when Lacan says they "know nothing about it," he means it cannot be conceptualized through the symbolic order. *Jouissance* entails a kind of breaking down and disintegration of the discrete, bounded self and a breaking down of coherent meaning that can be seen reflected in Reilly's radically fragmented and non-referential poetics. Moreover, although theories of trans-corporeality and the hyperobject emerge from distinctly non-psychoanalytic intellectual lineages, in their articulation of theories of selfhood that exceed and challenge understandings of the self as stable, bounded, and finite, they intersect in productive ways with psychoanalytic articulations of subjectivity.

If the transcendence of the finite, discrete body is often understood through and in relation to discourses of religious ecstasy and *jouissance*, it is also frequently understood in relation to pain. Reilly's poem "Daffodil.Gondola.Polystyrene" borrows extensively from Elaine Scarry's *The Body in Pain* (1985) to further explore the dissolution of the boundaries between self and world as a kind of transcendent but unrepresentable phenomenon not unlike Lacan's articulation of female *jouissance*. Scarry argues that pain erodes the individual's stable sense of self, an observation Reilly incorporates into her exploration of the permeability and interconnectivity of living organisms through the incorporation of statements such as *"the self is experienced as participating across the bridge of the body"* (2009, 33), *"the body's attempt to secure / for the individual a stable internal space"* (33), and *"no important distinction between inside and outside"* (35). In framing the trans-corporeal subject's relationship to hyperobjects through recourse to discourses of bodily transcendence and dissolution that are linked to female pleasure, pain, and the divine, Reilly presents hyperobjects as a phenomenon that contributes to the dissolution of the subject, as well as a phenomenon whose magnitude and scope pushes language beyond the limits of semantic readability and into a realm where meaning breaks down and words become inadequate.

However, the magnitude of the divine is very different from the magnitude of hyperobjects like Styrofoam. Timothy Morton argues that religions like Christianity are ill-equipped to address the complexity and scale of hyperobjects: "With its apocalyptic visions and thousand-year itches, Christianity isn't ready for hyperobjects. Yet, thinking about these materials does involve something like religion, because they transcend our personal death. Living tissue is usually far more stable than chemical compounds. But hyperobjects outlast us all" (2010, 130). He goes on to argue that hyperobjects invoke a terror that cuts deeper than religious fear: "A massive cathedral dome, the mystery of a stone circle, have nothing on the sheer existence of hyperobjects" (131). While Morton may be right, the discourse of religious ecstasy and the dissolution of the self that it entails is perhaps the most accessible existing model of an articulation of the sheer magnitude evoked by the hyperobject and the demand that, in order to make sense of it, we must attempt to think beyond the discrete boundaries of the self as a stable entity.

The poem "A Key to the Families of Thermoplastics" begins with the language of religion before moving on to that of the horror film in its attempt to articulate the magnitude of the hyperobject and the human subject's relationship to it. The poem begins with a kind of mythic genealogy of plastics:

Polyethylene, Most Ancient of the Crystalline Polymers
gasoline tanks, water bottles, the plastic bag

Polypropylene, also called Mother of Abundance
carpet squares, garden furniture, automobile interiors

PVC, the Prince of Commodity Plastics
blister packaging, pipes and fittings, magnetic stripe cards

The Acrylics and their Most Adaptable Cousins
Ethyl, Methyl, Butyl, Stearyl and Laurel
(Reilly 2009, 48)

This passage seems to echo Morton's prediction that in the future humans will develop something like spirituality around the treatment of hyperobjects (Morton 2010, 132) and reads like an invocation of gods and goddesses from a classical epic. Plastics are categorized as a kind of family akin to the ancient gods from Greek mythology and are described in this poem as "families" grouped according to specific characteristics: "Family A: amorphous with random molecular orientation / in both molten and solid phase / Family B: semi-crystalline when molten and with dense crystallites / when solid" (Reilly 2009, 49). Reilly attributes a kind of agency or vitality to plastics, using adjectives like "adaptable" and "formative" (48) and describing them as "semi-rigid and very tough" (48), as possessing "exceptional clarity, but 'notch sensitive,'" and as "conform[ing] to the users grip" (51).

Plastic is ubiquitous and impossible to avoid; it enters our lives in the form of "shopping bag handles, cereal box liners, chemical drums / . . . carbonated drink bottles / . . . throw away condiment tubs / . . . yoyos, knobs, aerosol valves, paintball markers / . . . vacuum cleaner connectors, textile packaging / powder coating used in offshore drilling" (Reilly 2009, 51). The catalog of plastic items continues for three pages and includes items not readily associated with plastic: "superglue, encapsulation compounds, filament-wound / motor casings for aerospace applications" (52). In cataloging the multiplicity of plastics and their proliferation and use in everything from military operations to food containers to building materials, the poem illustrates an intimacy with plastic that verges on the erotic, but which also hints at a kind of destructive violence:

Look at the sample   *(touch the sample)*
Cut the sample   *(caress the sample)*
Burn the sample   *(stroke the sample)*

pass your hands feelingly
(Reilly 2009, 49)

The tone of the poem then shifts, as Reilly begins to link plastic, and specifically its "deathlessness" or longevity, to the undead from the horror film genre. Reilly incorporates quotations from Slavoj Žižek's essay "Troubles with the Real: Lacan as a Viewer of Alien" (2009) in which Žižek links the concept of the lamella to the "undead." Through her invocation of the lamella, Reilly builds on earlier Lacanian references in *Styrofoam* to further conceptualize plastic as a force that eludes or transcends human attempts at containment and mastery and that threatens the boundedness of the discrete subject. The lamella is libido or life instinct, something that is always already present and is essentially unkillable. Žižek describes the lamella as "an infinitely plastic object that can not only incessantly change its form, but can even transpose itself from one to another medium" and argues that the lamella anticipates Ridley Scott's film *Alien*: "the monster appears indestructible; if one cuts it into pieces, it merely multiplies . . . with infinite plasticity it can morph itself into a multitude of shapes." He further likens the lamella to the 1982 horror film *The Thing*. The lamella "stands in for the Real," it is the primordial abyss that consumes everything and dissolves identities (Žižek 2009).

Reilly links Žižek's discussion of the lamella to her own conceptualization of plastic as an ever-expanding substance that has the capacity to overtake the planet. Following Žižek, she invokes John Carpenter's *The Thing* (1982), "in which an abhorrent force of plasticity imitates / and destroys almost any form of life it encounters" (Reilly 2009, 57), as well as the 1958 film *The Blob* where "a young / Steve McQueen . . . confronts a translucent mass / of unquenchable desire and hunger" (2009, 58). She also invokes zombies and interjects lines from the "Purgatory" section of Dante's *Divine Comedy*, the section of the poem in which Dante and Virgil visit the island of Mount Purgatory and witness penitents being punished for each of the seven deadly sins. Like the penitents in *The Divine Comedy*, plastic occupies the space of the undead. It possesses the ability to transcend boundaries and change form; like the lamella and its filmic manifestations as amoeba-like blobs and zombie apocalypses, plastic is ever-present, its volume expanding continuously at it occupies more and more space on the planet. The poem concludes with the final lines from *The Blob*:

DAVE: I don't think it can be killed,
but at least we've got it stopped.

STEVE: Yeah, as long as the Antarctic stays cold.
(Reilly 2009, 58)

Although this film was made decades before climate change became a topic of discussion, the lines resonate with contemporary concerns about global warming; the twenty-first-century reader of Reilly's *Styrofoam* knows that the Antarctic is not necessarily going to stay cold.

Like Wong, Reilly foregrounds issues of gender and race in her trans-corporeal poetics. As I argued above, the feminine is invoked in *Styrofoam* through references to Saint Teresa and female *jouissance*; it is also foregrounded through references to the medical effects of thermoplastics on women's reproductive systems. "Plastic Plenitude Supernatant" is arguably the poem in which Reilly's interests in trans-corporeality, biopolitics, race, and female embodiment converge most powerfully. Reilly draws extensively in "Plastic Plenitude Supernatant" on a scientific publication titled "Evaluation of Styrene Oligomers Eluted from Polystyrene for Estrogenicity in Estrogen Receptor Building" (Reilly 2009, 68). In this poem she juxtaposes scientific research on the carcinogenic properties of Styrofoam and their effect on the female reproductive system with instances of everyday contact with polystyrene and references to Henrietta Lacks, an African American woman who had cervical cancer and whose cancerous cells, known in the scientific community as HeLa cells, were harvested without her consent and used widely in medical research. The notion of deathlessness in this poem is expanded to refer not only to Styrofoam but also to HeLa cells.

HeLa is what is known as an immortal cell line that was put into mass production in the 1950s and used around the world in multiple experiments. HeLa cells have been used in the development of the polio vaccine, advances in chemotherapy treatment, cloning, gene mapping, and in vitro fertilization, and they are still widely used in scientific research. There is no way of calculating the number of HeLa cells in existence today, but one scientist has estimated that if you laid all the HeLa cells ever created end to end, they would circle the earth three times

(Skloot 2010, 2). The Lacks case raises fascinating issues regarding bioethics, consent, race, and gender. Priscilla Wald has written extensively about the ways in which HeLa cells become anthropomorphized in scientific discussions of their deathlessness and aggressivity. She details how "these accounts register the confusion of Lacks with her cells, and the image that emerges from these quotations is of a bestialized, invasive, contaminating, sexually promiscuous woman" (2012, 251), thus showing how scientific discourse, though it claims objectivity, carries with it traces of racism and sexism that inform the research at multiple levels. Much of the discussion of HeLa cells and their ability to multiply endlessly treats them as if they are a substance akin to the Lacanian lamella.

The link between Styrofoam's "deathlessness" and HeLa cells is implied in the poem through Reilly's extensive use of a scientific article on the cancerous properties of Styrofoam that draws on data from experiments in which HeLa cells were used. Reilly's poem moves between the treatment of Lacks by the medical research community and the use of HeLa cells in research on carcinogens in Styrofoam, bringing these two strands together in order to probe the effects of chemical compounds on female bodies and to explore the ways in which the trans-corporeal body is inflected and informed by race, gender, class, and sexuality.

The poem begins with a reference to a carcinogenic compound in the Styrofoam packaging of instant noodles: "r e : *Identification of unknown ingredient in food contact polystyrene* / e g : noodle eating by pre, post, and presently pubescent / i e : sorry about that girls (er er, as per" (Reilly 2009, 42). The compound affects the bodies of women and girls, a fact underscored throughout the poem through references to xx (implying female chromosomes), and also the repetition of the word "period," which carries with it in the context of the poem a dual meaning as both a synonym for menstruation and a punctuation mark signifying the end of a sentence. Reilly works extensively with language gleaned from the scientific article, even including the "keywords" used by the scientific journal: "Polystyrene; Anti-estrogenic activity; / Endocrine disruptor; Uterotropic assay" (2009, 45). One of the lines lifted from the article and incorporated into the poem indicates that "*standard protocols using transfected HeLa cells*" were used in the research (42).

Lines like "the slightest Rub, Henrietta" and "one *fainted* in my palm, Henrietta" (2009, 43) imply that the speaker is directly addressing Henrietta Lacks. Reilly personifies HeLa cells, addressing "Henrietta" throughout the poem, calling her "mother of us all," "ethereal replicant" and "unearthly circuit," problematizing and complicating notions of lineage, kin, and the human ("replicants" are the biorobotic androids from the movie *Blade Runner*). Her name is invoked repeatedly: "(x-s to ex ex, Henrietta" and "(s-o-s, Henrietta" (43); both of these passages include open brackets as if to suggest HeLa cells' tendency to destabilize systems and divide endlessly. However, Reilly's personification of HeLa cells does not pathologize them for their ability to multiply endlessly; rather, it celebrates what Wald calls in her discussion of HeLa cells "the profound instability of the concept of 'being human'" (2012, 250), an instability that informs Reilly's poetic exploration of the trans-corporeal body throughout *Styrofoam*.

Evelyn Reilly's *Styrofoam* is a multifaceted examination of a substance that is manufactured by humans but that promises to outlast humans. Styrofoam and other plastic products are ubiquitous and have become indispensable, but at what cost to the planet and its ecosystems? Reilly's poetic project is driven by the question of how to live with the effects of these products, these hyperobjects, and how to grapple with the knowledge that this substance we have produced poses a threat not only to our own health, but also to that of the ecosystems with which we are so intimately connected. Like Wong, Reilly enacts a trans-corporeal poetics in which bodies are not discrete from their environments and in which ecosystems and endocrine systems are disrupted by human-made chemical compounds. Reilly's radically fragmented poems, which are composed using strands of texts gleaned from diverse academic, popular, philosophical, literary, and religious sources, paradoxically work to demonstrate an intricate and radical interconnectedness in which Styrofoam and thermoplastics are shown to play a fundamental role not only in relation to our daily lives, but also in relation to the lives of animals, the functioning of ecosystems, and the workings of cellular biology. Like the poetic fragments that comprise the poems in *Styrofoam*, the substance of Styrofoam maintains a stubborn consistency even as its chemical compounds enter and alter organisms at a molecular level.

For each of the four poets discussed in this section, developing an ecopoetics to address environmental crisis entails finding ways to challenge the humanist subject by underscoring that subject's posthuman and trans-corporeal identifications and connections with the world. Each writer utilizes poetic form and innovation to challenge assumptions of human exceptionality (and more specifically, the exceptionality of the consumer-citizen of the developed Western world), assumptions that are often deployed to tacitly justify environmental exploitation and pollution that occurs under the banner of consumer capitalism and economic growth. Each writer's work falls within Evelyn Reilly's definition of ecopoetics as

> a search for language that coheres with evolution, with our destiny as animals among other plants and animals. A search for a poetry that is firmly attached to earthly being and that is thus *dis-enchanted* in the sense of being free of the mesmerizing spell of the transcendent. For ecopoetics reflects yet another in a series of human decenterings, as from an ecological perspective, the self dissolves in a gene pool and the species into the ecosystem. (2010, 257)

Read together, these four texts illustrate how contemporary ecopoetics intervenes in and engages with new materialist and posthuman theories, and more specifically, they show how innovative poetics constitutes an important site from which to critique the universal, white male subject of humanism and to explore affinities and alliances that transcend species and displace the human.

While reading or writing poetry is not necessarily going to save the world from ecological disaster, poetry does hold the potential to powerfully alter our perspective, in this case by demonstrating ways of critically decentering the human by articulating a posthumanism and a trans-corporeal understanding of the relationship between self and world. Through redeploying and recycling text, parataxis, the use of procedural techniques, and other formally innovative approaches, these writers all use poetic form to advance a posthuman, trans-corporeal ecopoetics. In "An Object-Oriented Defense of Poetry" Morton explores poetry's unique position as a genre with the potential to embody a radical realization of transhuman interconnectivity:

> To write poetry is to perform a nonviolent political act, to coexist with other beings. This coexistence happens not in some eternal now, or in a now-point, however expansive or constrained. The "nowness" of a poem, its "spacious-ness," is the disquieting asymmetry between appearance and essence, past and future. With remorseless gentleness, a poem forces us to acknowledge that we coexist with uncanny beings in a groundless yet vivid reality with-out a beyond. This is what it means to compose an object-oriented defense of poetry. (Morton 2012, 222)

As Yedda Morrison, Marcella Durand, Rita Wong, and Evelyn Reilly each powerfully demonstrate through their ecopoetic practices, ac-knowledging and honouring trans-species and trans-corporeal alli-ances, thinking about our own selves in relation to the trans-corporeal and the posthuman, and understanding the world as a site of agential intra-action marks a crucial ontological shift away from the anthropo-centrism of postmodernism and toward a new materialist ecopoetics.

PART THREE

Geopolitics, Nationhood, Poetry

FEMINIST POETS IN THE EARLY YEARS of the twenty-first century have become increasingly interested in finding ways to use innovative and experimental language to engage critically with discourses on citizenship, nationhood, and democracy. Indeed, as Nicky Marsh has argued, "debates about citizenship and publicness" have largely "characterized feminism's third wave" (2007a 1). In the work of poets such as Dionne Brand, Claudia Rankine, Rachel Zolf, Juliana Spahr, Jen Benka, and Jena Osman, an antimilitaristic, anticolonial, and antiracist ethics and politics underscore a counter-public opposition to mainstream discourses of nationalism and patriotism. Each of these poets turns to strategies of documenting and witnessing; they engage with digital media, archival texts, and other materials in order to respond to the violence of the nation-state and to explore the disjunction between, on the one hand, the affective discourses of patriotism, nationalism, colonialism, and democracy that contribute to idealized popular discourses of national belonging, and on the other hand, the reality of the nation as an agent of militaristic violence founded on racism, genocide, and heteropatriarchal capitalism. Chapter 5 offers a reading of Juliana Spahr's *This Connection of Everyone with Lungs*, Claudia Rankine's *Don't Let Me Be Lonely*, and Dionne Brand's *Inventory*, three books written during the U.S.-led military invasion of Iraq. I read these books as affective engagements with intimacy and witnessing that chart an analysis of the critical importance of connection, affect, intimacy, and empathy as strategies to counter neoliberal individualism and military violence. Chapter 6 examines Rachel Zolf's *Janey's Arcadia*, Jena Osman's *Corporate Relations*, and Jen Benka's *A Box of Longing with Fifty Drawers* as texts that engage with foundational national documents to enact powerful critiques of nationalism and its attendant features of pride, nostalgia, and sentimentalism, and to explore the nation as founded not on principles of inclusion and equality, but rather on principles of exclusionary violence and discrimination. Together, these chapters chart a feminist poetics of global, national, and political engagement as it unfolds in the early twenty-first century.

CHAPTER FIVE

Not in Our Name: Intimacy, Affect, and Witnessing in Juliana Spahr's *This Connection of Everyone with Lungs*, Claudia Rankine's *Don't Let Me Be Lonely*, and Dionne Brand's *Inventory*

THE EVENTS OF SEPTEMBER 11, 2001 led to large-scale shifts in global politics and domestic security. Poetry, along with visual art and other forms of cultural production, functioned in the wake of 9/11 and in the context of these rapid geopolitical shifts as a space of dissent, a scene of witnessing, and a forum for processing trauma. As Ann Vickery notes in an issue of *How2* published shortly after 9/11, the terrorist attacks "left many wondering anew about the possibility of writing after trauma" (2002), but poetry was also positioned as more vital and more necessary than ever. As Elizabeth Frost writes in the same issue of *How2*, after 9/11, she "need[ed] desperately for language to be pushed outward or inward—to change and be changed, to be charged, remade. What might *that* new poetry look like?" (2002). This chapter examines three books of poetry written in response to 9/11 and the subsequent U.S.-led invasions and occupations of Afghanistan and Iraq. Each of these books creates an oppositional poetics that draws from media coverage of the Iraq War and that uses the media as raw, poetic material that is mobilized through de- and re-contextualization into a powerful critique of war. I frame this work as an affectively charged feminist poetics of witnessing that challenges conventional theories of poetic witness through its engagement with technology and the media. I draw extensively on affect theory in my discussion of a post-9/11 poetics of witnessing because affect theory offers a useful framework for drawing connections among intimacy, emotion, and large-scale geopolitical events.

As scholars, artists, and writers sought critical frameworks through which to make sense of both the trauma of 9/11 and the geopolitical changes that had occurred seemingly overnight, many turned to affect

theory as a productive site for theorizing these issues because it offered
a framework that could accommodate both a critical stance against war
and an acknowledgment of the deep personal grief that many felt not
just in relation to the events of 9/11, but also in relation to the actions
undertaken by Western governments in the name of national secu-
rity. Although the study of affect can be traced as far back as Baruch
Spinoza's *Ethics*, published in 1677, was further developed by Henri
Bergson and Gilles Deleuze in the twentieth century, and was an ongo-
ing area of study in psychology and cognitive neuroscience throughout
the latter half of the twentieth century, affect studies in the humanities
and social sciences emerged as a cohesive theoretical movement in the
early years of the twenty-first century in the context of a social and
political landscape shaped by the war on terror and the infiltration of
neoliberal modes of governance into the private lives of citizens. The
intersection between affect and geopolitics has been most clearly ar-
ticulated by scholars working in the areas of feminist and queer theory,
perhaps because "the personal voice has persisted as an important part
of feminist scholarship" (Cvetkovich 2012, 9). Sara Ahmed's *The Cul-
tural Politics of Emotion*, a book that takes as its focus the relationship
between emotions such as fear, disgust, shame, and anger and the poli-
tics of race, gender, and sexuality, examines how affect animated politi-
cal responses to 9/11 and the perceived threat of terrorism (2004, 75).
Ann Cvetkovich further explores the affective impact of geopolitics in
Depression: A Public Feeling, a book that directly links depression to
the forces of war, neoliberalism, homophobia, sexism, and colonialism.
Cvetkovich, along with Lauren Berlant, Neville Hoad, Kathleen Stew-
art, and other scholars and activists, collaborated through the "Public
Feelings Project" to draw attention to the affective impact of geopoli-
tics in the wake of 9/11. Cvetkovich explains:

> Begun in 2001 both nationally and at the University of Texas, our inves-
> tigation has coincided with and operated in the shadow of September 11
> and its ongoing consequences—a sentimental takeover of 9/11 to under-
> write militarism, war in Iraq and Afghanistan, Bush's reelection, and the
> list goes on. Rather than analyzing the geopolitical underpinnings of these
> developments, we've been more interested in their emotional dynamics.

What makes it possible for people to vote for Bush or assent to war, and how do these political decisions operate within the context of daily lives that are pervaded by a combination of anxiety and numbness? How can we, as intellectuals and activists, acknowledge our own political disappointments and failures in a way that can be enabling? Where might hope be possible? Those questions stem from the experience of what one of our cells, Feel Tank Chicago, has called "political depression," the sense that customary forms of political response, including direct action and critical analysis, are no longer working either to change the world or make us feel better. (Cvetkovich 2012, 1)

The Public Feelings group coheres around shared experiences of concern, fatigue, and "a seemingly low-grade or normalized version of the epistemic shock that is said to accompany trauma" (Cvetkovich 2012, 1). Building on an insistence on the value of bringing "emotional sensibilities to bear on intellectual projects" and a belief that sensibilities can inform and propel political projects, "affective investment" becomes a "starting point for theoretical insight" (10).

This chapter draws on scholarship associated with the affective turn to examine poetry written in the wake of 9/11; I aim to broaden Cvetkovich's claim to show how poetry can provide a productive space through which to explore the relationship between affective investment and political dissent. Through readings of Juliana Spahr's *This Connection of Everyone with Lungs* (2005), Claudia Rankine's *Don't Let Me Be Lonely* (2004), and Dionne Brand's *Inventory* (2006), I consider the poetic, affective, and political strategies these writers deploy as they interrogate and oppose military involvement in the Middle East. Each book foregrounds the poet as a witness located in the domestic setting, watching the news and reacting with helplessness, frustration, anger, and grief. This poetry challenges Carolyn Forché's claim that poetry of witness is defined by the direct experience of trauma (1993, 30); instead, it considers how, in the context of social media, the Internet, and the 24-hour news cycle, we all become traumatized witnesses of a sort, even if we have not experienced what Forché calls "extremity" in a personal, embodied sense (33). I read this body of poetry as foregrounding the domestic setting as the scene of witnessing. The domestic scene in which these three speakers bear witness to the atrocities of war can be seen as a traditionally female space; it is also the environment of the stereotypically depressed individual. The domestic is conventionally associated with privacy and intimacy, although in these poems the domestic is a fully networked space, rupturing the distinction between public and private, and global and intimate.

These three books are unified through a shared interest in exploring the affectively charged relationship between the private space of the home and the public space of the world event and are part of a much larger body of poetry that emerged as a crucial site of counterpublic opposition to military involvement in Afghanistan and Iraq.[1] This writing exhibits a self-reflexivity regarding the role of America on the world stage and a determination to interrogate the acts that the U.S. government has committed domestically and globally in the name of national security, specifically with regard to the suspension of civil liberties, the intolerance of political dissent, and the invasion and military occupation of Iraq and Afghanistan. The nation is invoked in the work of these poets in order to critically reflect upon American cultural hegemony and America's actions on the world stage, but also, for Spahr and Rankine, to grapple with the thorny question of the poet's own complicity as an American who benefits from her status as a citizen of the world's wealthiest and most powerful nation.[2]

Spahr, Rankine, and Brand each develop a powerful poetics of witnessing and dissent that responds to the calls for a politicized post-9/11 poetics as outlined by Elizabeth Frost, Linda Kinnahan, Kathleen Fraser, and others in the pages of *How2* in the wake of 9/11. This body of work can also be read in some respects as an offshoot of language poetry in its explicit critique of the nation-state. Language poetry cohered in opposition to the Vietnam War in the 1970s and remains a vital model of political protest poetry. Poetry written in opposition to the Iraq War builds on language poetry's tendency to incorporate textual fragments gleaned from popular culture, news media, and advertising as a means of social and cultural critique, although the sheer magnitude of news coverage stemming from multiple 24-hour news channels and the Internet in this post-9/11 context means that the contemporary poet-witness is shouldered with the task of wading through far greater amounts of information than her language poetry predecessors ever had to contend with. This glut of media soon became rich poetic fodder; Jeff Derksen notes that "as the strange militarized-religious language of the Bush Administration made its way into the media . . . a sickeningly rich semiotic cache was opened up. The engagement with the news (and not poetry as 'news') runs through many texts, drawing on the news as a primary text for semantic content, as well as refiguring the 'news' as subject matter" (2009, 76). The Bush administration was adept at manipulating language, creating such catch phrases as "shock and awe," "the war on terror," and "weapons of mass destruction." The mainstream media, which covered the war through the practice of embedding reporters inside the military, willingly and uncritically disseminated this language. Through acts of de- and recontextualization, antiwar poets "attempt to map out or imagine a counter-public that does not turn outside the existing public sphere . . . but points exactly to its distortion" (Derksen 2009, 75). This strategy is particularly evident in Brand's *Inventory* and Spahr's *This Connection of Everyone with Lungs*.

Because language writing eschewed an exploration of the interiority of the subject, it was oriented toward public culture and a critique of geopolitics and was in opposition to lyric poetry's consolidation of the self-reflective speaking subject. The post-9/11 antiwar poetry discussed in this chapter is distinct from language poetry in part because of its willingness to engage with the private and personal as well as the public and the political in order to show that the two realms cannot really be separated. In this regard, the writing draws from politicized feminist poetic traditions that eschew the schism between lyric and language; as Lynn Keller notes, "the mainstream/Language binary was from the outset being complicated or even collapsed from within, particularly by women writers" (2010, 7). While the counter-public imagined in this body of antiwar poetry is located within the public sphere, it is distinguished by a political and aesthetic determination to explore the connections between the public sphere of geopolitics and the interior affective landscape of the subject.

Spahr, Brand, and Rankine construct a poetics that draws from public culture and explores the affective dimensions of the private sphere.

They share an ability to move between and across the domains of the global and the intimate in their poetry. These poets draw on news media, but what sets their work apart, and what I am most interested in exploring here, is how they ground their poetic praxis and their critiques of war in an exploration of intimacy, emotion, and the domestic. In so doing, they offer a powerful, politicized, and affectively charged form of protest poetry. While embedded reporting was an attempt on the part of the Bush government to "regulate the visual field" (Butler 2009, 64) and mobilize affect in support of military action, the poets discussed in this chapter recontextualize those media reports in order to mobilize affect in opposition to military action.

Global Intimacy and Reluctant Complicity in
This Connection of Everyone with Lungs

> *I guess I am asking for a model that acknowledges poetry as intimate with crisis.*
>
> —JULIANA SPAHR, "Is Poetry Enough? Poetry in a Time of Crisis"

In an essay called "Poetry in a Time of Crisis," written shortly after 9/11, Juliana Spahr takes issue with the way in which poetry was being positioned in the months following the terrorist attacks of 9/11 as a site of solace and a form of writing that moves us inward rather than orienting us outward to the public and the collective (2004, 7). Instead, Spahr is interested in poetry's potential for facilitating connectivity and affective bonds on a global scale. She actualizes just such a poetics in *This Connection of Everyone with Lungs*, a book that reconfigures intimacy as a public and ultimately political relation rather than something private and divorced from the social, and addresses the affective and political complexities of accountability and connectivity in the context of rising global tensions in the early years of the twenty-first century. The book consists of two long poems simply titled "Poem Written after September 11, 2001" and "Poem Written from November 30, 2002, to March 27, 2003."

Spahr explains that she was drawn to what she calls the "political lyric" as she wrote these poems because of her conviction that "we must approach our politics with as much devotion as we approach our beloveds" (Bettridge 2005) and her desire to critically examine her "intimacy with things [she] would rather not be intimate with" (Spahr 2005, 13), including the U.S. military-industrial complex. In referring to *This Connection of Everyone with Lungs* as a "political lyric," she deliberately brings the lyric form to bear on a poetics engaged with public culture, media, and politics, disrupting the conventional schism between lyric and language poetry. If the lyric is a genre typically associated with love poetry, Spahr's "political lyric" is a kind of love poetry whose addressee oscillates between an expansive, political, world-making beloved and an intimate, albeit pluralized, domestic beloved. Through this continuous movement from the intimate to the global and back again, Spahr establishes an affective and politicized poetics of interconnectivity, complicity, and plurality.

The speaker in these poems is constructed through and in relation to a series of intimacies and an acknowledgment of uncomfortable complicities in order to advance a poetics of global intimacy.[3] The speaker is constituted as collective rather than singular, and as embedded, multiple, and dispersed through her devotion to both her politics and her "beloveds." Spahr addresses her "beloveds" repeatedly in the second of the two poems in this book, bringing global politics to bear directly on intimate spaces and developing the unconventional pronouns "yous" and "yours" to pluralize her addressee. The "disrupted center" or "dispersed lyric 'I'" (Mayer 2009a, 50–52) upon which Spahr builds the poems in *This Connection of Everyone with Lungs* rejects the singular voice in favor of a collective and hybrid "everyone with lungs" who together breathes the intimate "space between the hands / and the space around the hands and the space of the room" as well as the globalized "space of the troposphere and the space of the stratosphere / and the space of the mesosphere" (2005, 8).

The book's title comes from "Poem Written after September 11, 2001," a poem in which lungs function as a site of contact and interface with the world and thus as a powerful symbol of connection and community. Rather than beginning with a reference to hijacked airplanes, collapsing buildings, or mass casualties, "Poem Written after September 11, 2001" begins with the most basic elements of embodied subjectivity:

There are these things:

cells, the movement of cells and the division of cells

and then the general beating of circulation

and hands, and body, and feet

and skin that surrounds hands, body, feet.

This is a shape,

a shape of blood beating and cells dividing.

(Spahr 2005, 3)

As soon as Spahr orients the perspective of the poem through a meditative rootedness in the corporeal, she begins to develop a spatial poetics that connects body to world. Nicky Marsh has observed that Spahr uses air as a metaphor for local-global politics (2007b, 197). It is important to note, however, that Spahr uses the word "space," not "air," to explore the relationship between the local and the global. "Space" powerfully denotes physicality, orientation, and contact. Not only are subjects located in space in this poem, but space is also located within subjects. Space moves in, out, between, and among bodies, functioning as a dynamic metaphor for contact and affective bonds. Space becomes an entity that locates bodies in phenomenological and affective relation to one another; because it is shared and bodies exist together in it, space becomes a powerful symbol of connection. She describes the space outside the body as a "space in the room that surrounds the shapes of everyone's / hands and body and feet and cells and the beating contained / within" and one that surrounds and connects each body to all the others (2005, 4).

Jeff Derksen argues that poetry can function to "delineate and produce spaces that counter triumphal neoliberal narratives such as the purported demise of the nation-state and the attempted coronation of the individualized owner-citizen" (2009, 16); Spahr's poem actively engages with the "spaces and processes of globalization and neoliberalism" (2009, 17) to offer an alternative to the individualized neoliberal subject. Moreover, the political lyric subject is constituted through, and also works to establish, a collective rather than individuated sense of space, echoing Sara Ahmed's claim that "bodies do not dwell in spaces that are exterior but rather are shaped by their dwellings and take shape by dwelling" (2006, 9).

The discrete boundaries of the singular lyric subject are further challenged in this poem through the metaphor of shared breath. Human subjects are configured in relation to space that "goes in and out of everyone's bodies" (2005, 4) as

> Everyone with lungs breathes the space in and out as everyone
> with lungs breathes the space between the hands in and out
>
> as everyone with lungs breathes the space between the hands and
> the space around the hands in and out
> (Spahr 2005, 4–5)

Spahr develops a poetics of affective connection through repetition: "The relation of bodies and languages as systems of connection emerges in the use of the Steinian principle of repetition to provide a non- or anti-narrative thread or trace" (Mayer 2009a, 44). With chant-like, meditative repetition, she builds increasingly longer utterances that move from individual cell to body to community and eventually to world:

> as everyone with lungs breathes the space between the hands
> and the space around the hands and the space of the room and
> the space of the building that surrounds the room and the space
> of the neighborhoods nearby and the space of the cities and the
> space of the regions and the space of the nations and the space
> of the continents and islands and the space of the oceans and
> the space of the troposphere and the space of the stratosphere
> and the space of the mesosphere in and out.
> (Spahr 2005, 8)

The poem gains momentum as each iteration incorporates a new phrase and develops a new dimension of global interconnectedness and intimacy, illustrating the affective and "ethical bond" of a posthumanist subjectivity that rejects individualism in favor of a "non-unitary subject" that proposes an enlarged sense of interconnection between self and others (Braidotti 2006, 35). The lyric subject in "Poem Written after September 11, 2001" is a collectively constituted "everyone" engaged in what Braidotti, following Deleuze, might call a "flux of successive becomings" through its ability to incorporate an ever-broadening spectrum (Braidotti 2002, 70).

"Everyone with lungs" functions not only as a collective lyric "I" but also as the grammatical subject of the poem. However, toward the end of the poem, Spahr shifts the perspective, removing "everyone with lungs" from the subject position and installing in its place the world that passes through the lungs. This subtle but significant shift in perspective conceptualizes "everyone with lungs" as a porous space through which the world passes, and undermines the distinction between self and world. After expanding from the cellular to the global, the poem reverses course, contracting to the intimate space immediately surrounding the body:

> The entering in and out of the space of the mesosphere in the
> entering in and out of the space of the stratosphere in the entering
> in and out of the space of the troposphere in the entering in and
> out of the space of the oceans in the entering in and out of the
> space of the continents and islands in the entering in and out of
> the space of the nations in the entering in and out of the space of
> the regions in the entering in and out of the space of the cities in
> the entering in and out of the space of the neighborhoods nearby
> in the entering in and out of the space of the buildings in the
> entering in and out of the space of the room in the entering in
> and out of the space around the hands in the entering in and out
> of the space between the hands.
> (Spahr 2005, 9)

"Poem Written after September 11, 2001" moves from the particular to the universal and back again. Lungs function as a site of contact and interface with the world. Rather than reifying the body, and by extension, the lyric "I," as a closed, discrete entity, Spahr sees the world as constantly moving through the body while the body, in turn, moves through the world. "Everyone" is joined through this simple relationship between lungs and space. Spahr's anaphoric technique demonstrates the intricacies of global connectivity and the extent to which subjectivity is constituted in and through these connections. But lest we see this as a naive utopian vision of wholeness, Spahr is quick to remind her readers that the space that connects "everyone's lungs" is filled with harmful toxins. Spahr wrote this poem in New York in the days and weeks following 9/11 as she and her fellow New Yorkers inhaled the toxins released into the air when the World Trade Center collapsed:

> The space of everyone that has just been inside of everyone mixing
> inside of everyone with nitrogen and oxygen and water vapor and
> argon and carbon dioxide and suspended dust spores and bacteria
> mixing inside of everyone with sulfur and sulfuric acid and
> titanium and nickel and minute silicon particles from pulverized
> glass and concrete.
> (Spahr 2005, 9–10)

This description is followed by a blank space and then the poem's powerful concluding line: "How lovely and doomed this connection of everyone with / lungs" (2005, 10). As Nicky Marsh notes, the final lines of this poem are "devastating because of their destructive reversal of the universal possibilities suggested by the simple, shared, necessity of breath" (2007b, 198).

The second of the two poems that comprise *This Connection of Everyone with Lungs*, "Poem Written from November 30, 2002, to March 27, 2003," further probes the implications of global intimacies and affective bonds in the context of warfare and geopolitical relations in the early years of the twenty-first century. In her comments preceding the poem, Spahr states that in the months leading up to the U.S. invasion of Iraq, she turned to the news media in an attempt to make sense of world events, "I thought that by watching the news more seriously I could be a little less naive. But I gained no sophisticated understanding as I wrote these poems" (2005, 13). Spahr turns to the media not only for information but also for a sense of connection to the world. She seeks what Lauren Berlant calls an intimate public "constituted by strangers who share common texts and things" (2008, viii). Intimate publics provide a "porous, affective sense of identification among strangers that promises a certain experience of belonging and provides a complex of consolation, confirmation, discipline, and discussion" (viii). The mediatized intimacy Spahr seeks does little to clarify what is happening beyond the intimate space she shares with her beloveds. Instead, it confuses, distracts, and contributes to a sense of helplessness.

Spahr develops a poetics and politics of location that allows her to examine the relationship between the intimate and the worldly without resorting to a local/global binary, which, as Victoria Pratt and Gillian Rosner point out, has been criticized by many feminists for its tendency to "imaginatively construct the local as a defense against powerful global forces in a way that seems to confirm the force and inevitability of certain capitalist modes of expansion" (2012, 2). By developing a poetics of intimacy rather than a poetics of the strictly local, Spahr shows how the global and the intimate are "not defined against one another but rather draw meaning from more elliptically related domains" (Pratt and Rosner 2012, 2). Reading the poetics of intimacy established in this text in relation to the "affective turn" is fruitful because affect theory offers a critical and political context in which "intimacy and attachment are . . . being rethought in creative ways, and new globalized technologies are likely at the heart of some of this" (Pratt and Rosner 2012,15). "New globalized technologies" like the Internet and the 24-hour news channel are crucial components of Spahr's affective politics and poetics of intimacy in this book.

Spahr foregrounds her location on the island of Hawaii in her poetics of intimacy. As an island in the middle of the Pacific, Hawaii is isolated from the rest of the world and specifically from the continental United States. However, given its history of occupation by the United States, Hawaii is a site of colonial conquest; as a white person living on the island, Spahr must grapple with her own intimacy with this history: "How can we be true to one another with histories of place so deep, / so layered we can't begin to sort through it here in the middle of / the Pacific with its own deep unsortable history?" (2005, 50).[4]

Spahr's exploration of the politics of location, and specifically of her own location, is enacted through the juxtaposition of references to local flora and fauna with news stories that take place thousands of miles from her home.

Beloveds, the trees branch over our roof, over our bed, and so
realize that when I speak about the parrots I speak about love
and their green colors, love and their squawks, love and the
discord they bring to the calmness of the morning, which is the
discord of waking.

When I speak of the parrots I speak of all that we wake to this
morning, the Dow slipping yet still ending in a positive mood
yesterday, Mission Control, the stalled railcar in space, George
Harrison's extra-large will, Hare Krishnas, the city of Man, the
city of Danane and the Movement for Justice and Peace and the
Ivorian Popular Movement for the Great West, homelessness
and failed coups, few leads in the bombing in Kenya.
(Spahr 2005, 15)

Descriptions of plant and animal life situate the speaker of the poem
in Hawaii, while the constant stream of media reports connects this
remote island in the middle of the Pacific and the bed she shares with
her beloveds to the rest of the world. Spahr aligns the perspective of
the poem with the local and the intimate through her reference to
waking to the sound of the parrots, but then immediately broadens
that perspective: "when I speak of the parrots I speak of all we wake
to" (2005, 15), which includes economic and political news and celeb-
rity gossip.

"Poem Written from November 30, 2002, to March 27, 2003" reads
like a newsfeed or an aggregator (Mayer 2009a, 55). It presents the
reader with a paratactic and nonlinear litany of news headlines, rup-
tured by references to her beloveds, her bed, and her location on the
island of Hawaii. The constant stream of media images flattens the sig-
nificance of serious global events:

The Greenland glaciers and the Arctic Sea ice melt at unprecedented
levels and still a ship fuels up and slips out of port.

Winona Ryder has thirty prescriptions for downers from twenty
different doctors and still a ship fuels up and slips out of port.
(Spahr 2005, 40)

Spahr's documentary poetics provides a cogent commentary on both the ubiquity and limitations of contemporary mainstream media, as well as its tendency to distract us from events of real significance by offering a steady diet of celebrity gossip under the pretense of providing a constant stream of news stories. This mediatized environment manufactures a controlled intimacy, bringing disparate news stories into relation with one another—Winona Ryder and melting Arctic Seas—and into the intimate spaces of our homes. The media further functions as a key technology of connection, providing the link that Spahr seeks between her home on the relatively isolated island of Hawaii and the rest of the world. The comment about the ships fueling up and slipping out of port, surreptitiously tacked on to the end of each reference to a story reported in the news, indicates an event *not* revealed by the mainstream media but circulated via word of mouth: warships on their way to the Middle East to participate in the invasion of Iraq are refueling in Hawaii. The media's silence regarding this matter points to the significant gaps and oversights in the steady stream of media noise that distracts and renders complacent its audience.

Spahr explains in her prefatory note that she composed the poem during a time when

> The constant attention to difference that so defines the politics of Hawai'i, the disconnection that Hawai'i claims at moments with the continental United States, felt suddenly unhelpful. I felt I had to think about what I was connected with, and what I was complicit with, as I lived off the fat of the military-industrial complex on a small island. I had to think about my intimacy with things I would rather not be intimate with . . . (2005, 13)

Intimacy is configured as a way of conceptualizing connectivity and as a means through which to establish accountability and reciprocity. Intimacy involves, as Lauren Berlant suggests, "an aspiration for a narrative about something shared, a story about both oneself and others" (1998, 281). Intimacy, then, is both private *and* public and is shared between two or more individuals. Intimacy is not immune to "relations of power, violence, and inequality and cannot stand as a fount of authenticity, caring, and egalitarianism" (Pratt and Rosner 2012, 2). However, by examining the ways in which her "intimacy with things

[she] would rather not be intimate with" renders her complicit in global power relations, Spahr begins to unpack the relationship between intimacy, affect, global inequality, and ethical accountability.

The references to warships fueling up and slipping out of port raises the specters of complicity and connectivity upon which Spahr comments in the poem. Ironically, the connection she seeks to the rest of the world is realized through a reference to the warships, illustrating that connection can be as disconcerting as it can be comforting. Hawaii, though geographically remote, is connected to and implicated in the U.S. invasion of Iraq. Spahr, as a citizen of Hawaii, is in turn complicit even though she vehemently opposes the military action: "We sleep with levels of complicity so intense and various that our / dreams are of smothering and drowning and of the military outside / our door and we find it hard to get up in the morning" (2005, 63). Given this unwilling complicity, one might wonder about the extent to which resistance is even possible. Spahr's poem seems to suggest that agency resides in part in acknowledging a connection between the global and the intimate and developing a nuanced, politically responsible, and ethically accountable politics and poetics of intimacy and location.

Plurality and connectivity are developed through Spahr's address to her "beloveds." Her critical, probing, and at times difficult examination of complicity, intimacy, and collectivity and her conviction that "we must approach our politics with as much devotion as we approach our beloveds" (Bettridge 2005) are actualized through this ongoing address. While the lyric "I" remains intact in this poem, Spahr challenges the conventional mode of address common to most lyric love poetry through her address to plural "beloveds." Spahr emphasizes the plurality of her "beloveds" by bending grammatical rules to construct the unconventional plural pronouns "yours" and "yous" which are utilized repeatedly throughout the poem. The "beloveds," whom Spahr addresses directly at least twenty-four times in this poem, could refer to lovers and/or cohabitants; "beloveds" can also be read as a loose and indeterminate term that draws into an affective bond the reader and the collective "everyone," who, according to the book's title, are connected via their lungs:

Beloveds, we wake up in the morning to darkness and watch it
turn into lightness with hope. (15)

. . .

Beloveds, yours skins is a boundary separating yous from the rest
of yous. (19)

. . .

Beloveds, yours skins are of all colors, are soft and wrinkled,
blotchy and reddish, full of blemish and smooth. (23)

. . .

Beloveds, what do we do but keep breathing as best we can in this
minute atmosphere? (26)

. . .

Beloveds, today the UN commission searched all the square feet of
Hussein's office in a show of power. (27)

. . .

Beloveds, I keep trying to speak of loving but all I speak about is
acts of war and acts of war and acts of war. (28)

. . .

Beloveds, my desire is to hunker down and lie low, lie with yous
in beds and bowers, lie with yous in resistance to the alone, lie
with yous night after night.

But the military-industrial complex enters our bed at night.
(Spahr 2005, 63)

In her address to her "beloveds," Spahr works within the parameters
of lyric love poetry. However, her address to pluralized, ungendered
beloveds challenges not only the conventional address of the lyric love
poem to a singular "beloved" but also accepted notions of domestic in-
timacy that are structured around the nuclear family and the hetero-
sexual conjugal couple. As Elizabeth Povinelli argues, plurality offers
an alternative to the intimate couple who functions as a "key transfer
point between, on the one hand, liberal imaginaries of contractual econ-
omies, politics, and sociality, and, on the other, liberal forms of power in
the contemporary world" (2006, 17). "Beloveds" becomes a shifting, in-
clusive, and politicized term that moves far beyond the limits of domes-
tic intimacy, redefining what counts as intimacy in a global context.

Through the multiple connotations of the address to her "beloveds," Spahr reconfigures notions of public and private, constructing powerful metaphors that bring global and sexual intimacies together: "We say our bed is part of everyone else's bed even as our bed is / denied to others by an elaborate system of fences and passport- / checking booths" (2005, 30). Spahr shows how even the most intimate spaces we share with our beloveds are inflected with global politics, and how, in turn, global politics can function as complicated sites of intimacy. The next verse reads: "We wake up in the night with just each others and admit that even / while we believe that we want to believe that we all live in one bed / of the earth's atmosphere, our bed is just our bed and no one else's / and we can't figure out how to stop it from being that way" (Spahr 2005, 30). Sophie Mayer reads this as a critical examination of the "(ir)responsibility of the lovers' connection in a time of crisis" (2009a, 57), an attempt to reconcile the conventional tropes of lyric poetry (love, the beauty of nature) with the mediatized world of twenty-first-century warfare: "Connection, at once the narrative strategy needed for the poem to cohere and the political strategy urgently needed to divert war and violence, is found in intimacy, whose enaction is also an inaction" (2009a, 58). As Mayer suggests, the political efficacy of the bed is limited. However, rather than functioning as a refuge or retreat from the global politics that punctuate the poem, the bed Spahr shares with her beloveds is implicated in and shaped by these politics. The efficacy of Spahr's metaphor of collective or global intimacy lies in her examination of the ways in which global politics delineates intimate spaces and affective relations, since, as Geraldine Pratt and Victoria Rosner have pointed out, "intimacy does not reside solely in the private sphere; it is infused with worldliness" (2012, 3). This connection is reinforced by the fact that many of the references to physical and sexual intimacy in the poem are configured through military metaphors:

When I reach for yours waists, I reach for bombers, cargo, helicopters, and special operations.

When I wrap around yours bodies, I wrap around the *USS Abraham Lincoln*, unmanned aerial vehicles, and surveillance.

When I rest my head upon yours breasts, I rest upon the *USS Kitty Hawk* and the *USS Harry S. Truman* and the *USS Theodore Roosevelt.*

Guided missile frigates, attack submarines, oilers, and amphibious transport/dock ships follow us into bed.

Fast combat support ships, landing crafts, air cushioned, all of us with all of that.

(Spahr 2005, 75)

These lines mark the end of the poem; Spahr leaves the reader to ponder the ways in which sexual intimacy and global politics implicate one another. Pairing the global and the intimate in this manner helps to "expose patterns that recur when gender, sex, and the global imaginary combine" (Pratt and Rosner 2012, 2). Even if the lovers are powerless to stop the military buildup to the invasion of Iraq, their awareness of military action not only affects their most intimate moments but also shapes these moments.

Spahr develops numerous metaphors through which to conceptualize her politics of location and global intimacy and to explore the dialectic of connection and separation. One of the most compelling of these is the metaphor of skin. Skin functions as a "fleshy interface between bodies and worlds" (Ahmed and Stacey 2001, 1); it both protects us from others and serves as an intimate site of contact, "open[ing] bodies to other bodies" (Ahmed and Stacey 2001, 11). Spahr builds on this notion of skin as both the site of intimate contact and the boundary between self and other:

Beloveds, yours skins is a boundary separating yous from the rest of yous.

When I speak of skin I speak of the largest organ.

I speak of the separations that define this world and the separations that define us, beloveds, even as we like to press our skins against one another in the night.

(2005, 19)

She explores skin as a contact zone and posits the subject as permeable and collective rather than singular and solitary:

> When I speak of skin I speak of the crowds that are gathering all together to meet each other with various intents.

> When I speak of skin I speak of all the movement in the world right now and all the new boundaries of the right now that are made by all the movement of the world right now and then broken by all the movement in the world right now.
> (Spahr 2005, 22)

Skin also bears the specificity of race, and as such, it arguably functions as the most powerful social and cultural marker of belonging and separation. Spahr seeks to challenge divisions based on racial and cultural demarcations: "But when I speak of skin I do not speak of the arbitrary connota- / tions of color that have made all this brushing up against one another / even harder for all of us" (2005, 23). Instead of focusing on division, she explores cellular and genetic connection and contact: "Embedded deep in our cells is ourselves and everyone else. / Going back ten generations we have nine thousand ancestors and / going back twenty-five we get thirty million" (31). Spahr does not downplay the lived effects of racial oppression and discrimination. However, because *This Connection of Everyone with Lungs* seeks to establish a poetics of global connectivity and intimacy, Spahr is mainly interested in challenging the racial and cultural divisions that contribute to the global tensions and conflicts against which she writes.

Spahr's address to her beloveds and her exploration of lungs as a symbol of global connectivity are not attempts to establish a naive, utopian sense of unity and wholeness. Rather, *This Connection of Everyone with Lungs* is a critical examination of the "lovely" and "doomed" (2005, 10) affects and complicities of global intimacy in the context of war, mediatization, and advanced capitalism. *This Connection of Everyone with Lungs* establishes a collective lyric "everyone" connected through the fleshy interfaces of lungs and skin, the fiber optic cables that link our networked world, and the realm of global geopolitics.

Spahr casts out in search of connection, which can be read as a fundamentally optimistic and socially oriented act. Nevertheless, her "political depression" (Cvetkovich 2012, 80) is evident when she writes toward the end of the poem: "Beloveds, weeks ago the doubleness of the news broke me down / and I stopped writing and loving all humans, mainly / myself" (Spahr 2005, 57). On the next page she notes "Beloveds, before all my hope is burnt up, I should also remember / that eleven million people across the globe took to the streets one / recent weekend to protest the war and this gave us all a glimmer" (58). In spite of this glimmer, Spahr acknowledges that these protests are ultimately powerless to stop the invasion of Iraq: "a huge sadness overtakes us daily because of our inability to / control what goes on in the world in our name" (71). *This Connection of Everyone with Lungs* is both introspective and expansive in its poetic stocktaking of location, complicity, and accountability. It is also a melancholic text in its realization of the limitation of the poet's role. The poet can document and witness, she can develop a vocabulary of the affective complexities and difficult intimacies of global relations. While these acts are valuable and indeed vital, they cannot halt the invasion of Iraq. A similar sense of melancholia or political depression hangs over Claudia Rankine's *Don't Let Me Be Lonely*, the text to which I now turn.

"Thinking as if Trying to Weep": The Poetics and Politics of Affect in Claudia Rankine's *Don't Let Me Be Lonely*

Don't Let Me Be Lonely (2004) takes as its focus loneliness and depression as conditions of contemporary American life. It is a poetic articulation of what Kathleen Stewart calls "ordinary affects" or "public feelings that begin and end in broad circulation, but they're also the stuff that seemingly intimate lives are made of" (2007, 2). The book is subtitled "An American Lyric," situating it squarely in relation to nation and poetry. However, *Don't Let Me Be Lonely* is not strictly a work of poetry but rather a hybrid of poetry and essay that is comprised of short, often unconnected or loosely connected paragraphs. Rankine's argument advances through juxtaposition, collage, repetition, and the interplay of verbal and visual elements. Threads emerge, concepts are introduced and then revisited sometimes several pages later, and although the work offers little in the way of plot, Rankine's powerful and poetic articulations of what Sara Ahmed (2004) calls "the cultural politics of emotion" offer a compelling critique of contemporary American culture. The unusual form of this text allows for rich layerings and surprising and often unexpected connections, and it facilitates an exploration of post-9/11 American culture that is both expansive and focused.

Rankine's writing has a documentary quality; it incorporates labels from prescription medications, a pamphlet from the U.S. Postal Service about handling suspicious mail, photos, movie stills, and other fragments of American culture. The poem concludes with several pages of endnotes that provide fascinating supplementary information to the poem. Rather than setting up an opposition between the documentary fragments of American public culture and the private life of the speaker, the documentary and personal elements of the poem implicate and inform one another even though these connections are often inferred rather that directly stated. The fluid, rhizomatic structure of the text is poetic, but these qualities directly facilitate its sharp analytical focus and allow Rankine to trace surprising and powerful connections among geopolitics and the affective dimensions of private life. Indeed, affect and politics seem to become fused in *Don't Let Me Be Lonely*, a book that both politicizes affect and explores how affect becomes mobilized in support of politics.[5]

Implicit in the book's subtitle is a critical reflection on how "American" becomes deployed as an adjective to mobilize and regulate national affect. In the aftermath of 9/11, George W. Bush defined "the American way of life" as a "love of freedom." Donald Rumsfeld claimed that the goal of the so-called "war on terror" was to protect the "American way of life" (Grewal 2005, 204). As Inderpal Grewal notes, the U.S. government and discourses of American nationalism have "produced the term 'American' as a discursive regime in which oppositions like 'terrorism vs. security,' 'good vs. evil,' and 'civilized vs. barbaric' have captured popular and state discourse" (2005, 204).[6] The power of this discourse lies not just in its connection to military strength, but also

through cultural formations within which the close relation between con-
sumer culture and citizenship has allowed all kinds of identifications with
America. . . . If the phrase "American way of life" became one of the main
discourses used by politicians to justify a wide range of actions, from threats
of bombing to reductions of civil liberties . . . it is because this discursive
regime has circulated within a transnational network of consumption linked
to democratic citizenship. (Grewal 2005, 204–5)

Rankine's "American Lyric" is written against the backdrop of this
deployment of "American" as an adjective to mobilize national affect
in support of the so-called "war on terror." Although Rankine seeks
critical distance from this deployment of "American," through her
documentary exploration of American culture, she also explores other
possibilities for engagement with the nation, engagements that are
critical but also *invested* in America and "American" as sites of affec-
tive, albeit ambivalent identification.

Like Spahr, Rankine weaves together the intimate and the global,
although Rankine's exploration of intimacy is focused less on the inti-
macy of sexual or domestic relations between "beloveds" and more on
the intimacy of depression and grief. The speaker of the poem, a speaker
who is not reducible to the author but is rather a kind of persona or
assemblage, suffers from insomnia and depression and her television
remains on late into the night. She watches movies, news, and com-
mercials. She sees ads for antidepressants on late night television and
has filled a prescription for antidepressants that sits in her medicine
cabinet. She ventures into the world to see friends, including a woman
dying of cancer, a man in a nursing home who has Alzheimer's disease,
and another man on leave from work due to depression. Her sister has
recently lost her husband and children in a car accident. Personal crisis,
illness, and death permeate the book, and the loneliness of these condi-
tions is exacerbated by a national public culture of consumerism and
uncritical patriotism.

Like *This Connection of Everyone with Lungs, Don't Let Me Be
Lonely* addresses the ways in which the public realms of geopolitics,
capitalism, war, and neoliberalism alter the intimate landscape of the
subject. This is not merely another way of saying the personal is politi-

cal. Rather, it is an exploration of the ways in which politics infiltrates the affective sphere. In the context of a neoliberal culture in which the individual is made "fully responsible for her- or himself" (Brown 2005, 42), depression, anxiety, and loneliness are written off as personal failures rather than logical and understandable human responses to social inequality, precarity, and the erosion of democracy. By politicizing depression, Rankine refuses the neoliberal framing of depression as a private failure or weakness.

Rankine's engagement with depression resonates with Ann Cvetkovich's claim in *Depression: A Public Feeling* that depression, long understood as a private, individual condition, might instead be understood as inextricably linked to social and political factors. Cvetkovich offers a useful model for thinking about psychic and social, public and private, and the global and the intimate in and through one another. Depression, she argues,

> might not immediately reveal its connections to capitalism and colonialism, even if it's a structure of feeling for how they are experienced. It's a sensational story of a different kind, literally sensational because it's about the impact of the world around us on our senses—which include our bodies, our feelings, and our minds. It can be hard to tell the difference between inside and outside—between what's inside your body and what's out there, between what's inside in the house or outside in the neighborhood or on the other side of town, between your heartbreak and the misery in the world beyond. (Cvetkovich 2012, 158)

The speaker's "political depression" sets her apart as what Sara Ahmed calls an "affect alien" (2010) who is at odds with the discourses of American patriotism, American exceptionalism, and the American dream. She calls a suicide hotline she sees advertised on late night television; when the paramedics arrive, she tells them she had a "momentary lapse of happily" and reflects that "the noun, happiness, is a static state of some Platonic ideal you know better than to pursue" (Rankine 2004, 7). Rankine's speaker dwells in unhappiness as a space of political and personal dissent.

Rankine's speaker shares much in common with Sara Ahmed's trio of unhappy figures, the feminist killjoy, the melancholic migrant, and the unhappy queer. Through these figures, Ahmed offers a crucial framework for understanding unhappiness as a vital and productive site of political critique. For Ahmed, happiness "involves a way of being aligned with others, of facing the right way" (2010, 45). She who refuses this alignment resists the normative "happiness scripts" offered by a mainstream culture inflected by normative values (2010, 59) and becomes an affect alien and a potential revolutionary. The revolutionary refuses both happiness and the desire to be happy (2010, 192). As Ahmed explains, "The revolutionary is an affect alien in this specific sense. You do not flow; you are stressed; you experience the world as a form of resistance in coming to resist a world" (169).

In her poetic meditation on loneliness, unhappiness, and tension, Rankine explores how affects become unconsciously stuck or lodged in the body. The speaker recounts reading in the newspaper of the president of South Africa's decision to make anti-retrovirals available to HIV-positive South Africans: "My body relaxes. My shoulders fall back. I had not known that my distress at Mbeki's previous position against distribution of the drugs had physically lodged itself like a virus within me. . . . Such distress moved in with muscle and bone. Its entrance by necessity slowly translated my already grief into a tremendously exhausted hope" (Rankine 2004, 117–18). The distress that had lodged itself in the speaker is akin to what Ahmed calls a "sticky feeling." For Ahmed, emotions are located neither in the individual nor in the social, but "produce the very surfaces and boundaries that allow the individual and the social to be delineated as if they are objects" (2004, 10). The "I" and the "we" take shape through contact with others, and emotions circulate between bodies and allow "the individual and the social to be delineated as objects" (10), but when these objects become saturated with affect, they become sticky and get lodged within subjects as "sites of personal and social tension" (11). Rankine's speaker only realizes that this negative affect has become lodged or stuck inside her at the moment of its release; the passage about anti-retrovirals is powerful not only in its articulation of the ways in which negative affects or "sticky feelings" lodge inside the subject, but also in its identification of the hope that can accompany their dislodging, even if that hope is a "tremendously exhausted" one.

Other negative affects are borne on a more conscious level in the text. The speaker's depression is framed through world events like 9/11, the reelection of George Bush in 2004, and the systemic and ubiquitous racism that informs the criminal justice system and American public culture; she also observes these things through a kind of veil of loneliness and melancholy. Here is Rankine on the reelection of George Bush and systemic racism:

> Cornel West makes the point that hope is different from American optimism. After the initial presidential election results come in, I stop watching the news. I want to continue watching, charting, and discussing the counts, the recounts, the hand counts, but I cannot. I lose hope. However Bush came to have won, he would still be winning ten days later and we would still be in the throes of our American optimism. All the non-reporting is a distraction from Bush himself, the same Bush who can't remember if two or three people were convicted for dragging a black man to his death in his home state of Texas.
>
> *You don't remember because you don't care.* Sometimes my mother's voice swells and fills my forehead. Mostly I resist the flooding, but in Bush's case I find myself talking to the television screen: *You don't know because you don't care.*
>
> . . .
>
> I forget things too. It makes me sad. Or it makes me the saddest. The sadness is not really about George W. or our American optimism; the sadness lives in the recognition that a life can not matter. Or, as there are billions of lives, my sadness is alive alongside the recognition that billions of lives never mattered. I write this without breaking my heart, without bursting into anything. Perhaps this is the real source of my sadness. . . . I don't know, I just find when the news comes on I switch the channel. This new tendency might be indicative of a deepening personality flaw: IMH, The Inability to Maintain Hope, which translates into no innate trust in the supreme laws that govern us. (Rankine 2004, 21–23)

Rankine draws on Cornel West's distinction between hope and optimism and states that she is suffering from an inability to maintain hope (in the passage on the president of South Africa making anti-retrovirals widely available, she refers to her "tremendously exhausted hope," suggesting that her hope, though still present, has been under siege). However, although she cannot maintain *hope*, she does not claim to be devoid of *optimism*. Her optimism takes the form of what Lauren Berlant calls "cruel optimism," or the paradoxical position of desiring and maintaining an investment in the very object that prohibits one from flourishing (2011, 1). Rankine's speaker remains engaged in the social, political, and public landscape of America even as it contributes to her feelings of loneliness and her status as an outsider or affect alien. She remains invested in a wish for a less racist and more peaceful and equitable society, and the book is in part an attempt to witness and document the political and ethical shortcomings of early twenty-first-century American culture as the starting point in an effort to imagine other ways of being and other ways of relating under the sign of the nation.

The speaker claims at one point that she is writing a book about liver failure, a condition that, in spite of public perception, is more often induced by medications than by alcohol. Among the many images Rankine includes in the text is an image that looks like a drawing from an anatomy textbook of the abdominal organs. The drawing features the esophagus, stomach, liver, and, where one might expect to find the intestines, a map of the United States of America. The liver here might be seen as cleansing America of toxins, although the America depicted in Rankine's writing is not free from the toxicity of war, racism, and neoliberalism. She might be making a comment on the widespread use of prescription medications in America to treat conditions like depression, anxiety, and insomnia. The image could also be read as a reflection on how the speaker internalizes national politics to the point that they impact her affective landscape. She recounts the experience of telling a New York taxi driver that she is writing a book about the liver because she is "thinking as if trying to weep" (Rankine 2004, 89). Rankine's style of writing is a kind of "thinking as if trying to weep," a poetics that externalizes or articulates the connections between the affective interiority of the subject and the political dimensions of contemporary American life. We learn elsewhere in the book that "thinking as if trying to weep" is paraphrased from the poet César Vallejo; Rankine explains, "Vallejo comes closest to explaining that any kind of knowledge can be a prescription against despair" (2004, 55). For Rankine, knowledge does not exactly function as a "prescription against despair," since despair and loneliness intensify as fragments of knowledge accrue in the poem. However, these fragments do offer a critical conceptual framework for conceiving of negative affect as a productive and necessary site of social and political dissent.

Rankine's speaker demonstrates what it might mean to think as if trying to weep. The speaker bears witness to American racism as she watches her television. In addition to George W. Bush's apparent lack of interest in the dragging death of a black man in Texas, Rankine writes of the case of Abner Louima, who was sodomized with a broomstick while in police custody (Rankine 2004, 56), and Amadou Diallo, a Guinean man shot and killed by four police officers in New York (57). As Amadou Diallo's death is announced on television, she notes that "it felt wasteful to cry at the television set" (57). Instead of tears, she experiences a sharp pain in her gut: "Sometimes I think it is sentimental, or excessive, certainly not intellectual, or perhaps too naive, too self-wounded to value each life like that, to feel loss to the point of being bent over each time" (57). The speaker's visceral response is far from naive or anti-intellectual; it is a thinking as if trying to weep, an assertion of what Judith Butler would call the fundamental grievability of the precarious lives of these black men.

Rankine includes numerous television stills, some of which are taken from news channels and some from movies. These stills are literally framed by the image of a television screen, and together, they foreground the importance of television in the text and present the speaker as a kind of mediatized witness writing an "American lyric" in large part as a critical response to the images she sees on the screen. Every few pages we see the image of a TV screen clouded with static. Faintly visible is the outline of a face that looks to be, although one cannot be absolutely certain, that of George W. Bush. Images like this one function as visual symbols. The static could represent the speaker's state of mind. It could represent the way in which the mainstream media can

paradoxically obscure the events on which they report and, by exten-
sion, complicate the role of the witness who cannot be sure of what,
exactly, she beholds when she looks at the screen.

Like the speaker in *This Connection of Everyone with Lungs*, Ran-
kine's speaker is a mediatized witness observing world events on televi-
sion, but even the role of mediatized witness seems at times more than
she can bear. Although she does not withdraw from the world, she does
withdraw from watching the television news, programming her televi-
sion remote FAV button to select the Independent Film Channel and
HBO because neither channel carries news. She states, "This is what is
great about America—anyone can make these kinds of choices" (Ran-
kine 2004, 24). The choice to skip the news channel is primarily an act of
mental and emotional self-preservation rather than a protest or refusal
of the subjective and embedded reporting of the Iraq War. Her framing
of this act as a kind of freedom of choice that underscores American
national identity is clearly ironic; neoliberalism creates the illusion of
personal choice while eroding democratic freedom (Brown 2015, 108);
one can choose to skip the news, but one cannot change the way that
news is reported and delivered, nor can her refusal offer much in the
way of a counter-discourse. Rather than watching the news she watches
westerns, arguably the most stereotypically American film genre and
one steeped in colonialist and nationalist ideologies. However, she ob-
serves that the shoot-out at the end of *The Wild Bunch* that kills the
cowboys "releases all of us from the cinematic or, more accurately, the
American fantasy that we will survive no matter what. Though they
are handsome, white, leading men not dressed all in black, he liter-
ally shoots the life out of all anticipatory leanings" (Rankine 2004, 25).
After the "orgasmic rush" of the end of the film "we can just lie back,
close our eyes, and relax, though we are neither liberated nor fulfilled.
They are dead, finished, no American fantasy can help them now" (25).
The carnage at the end of the film provides the counter-narrative to the
fantasy of American victory, a counter-narrative largely absent from
the news channels she programs her television remote to skip over.

In writing of the events of 9/11, Rankine describes participating in
collective shock and mourning and going to the site of the World Trade
Center three days after the twin towers fell. Watching the rescue work-

ers she notes, "I see but do not hear them. The language of description competes with the dead in the air. My eyes burn and tear" (Rankine 2004, 82). Rankine articulates the complexity of experiencing grief, shock, and fear as a result of the events of 9/11 that make her part of a grieving populace, but she also describes being at odds, out of step with the discourses of nationalism and militarism circulating in the aftermath of the terrorist attacks, and she seems to watch as an outsider, observing. She reflects on the cultural shifts that have occurred since the 1990s and characterizes that decade as deeply inflected by consumer capitalism:

> To roll over or not to roll over that IRA? To have a new iMac or not to have it? To eTrade or not to eTrade? Again and again these were Kodak moments, full of individuation; we were all on our way to our personal best. America was seemingly a meritocracy. I, I, I am Tiger Woods. It was the nineties. Now it is the twenty-first century and either you are with us or you are against us. Where is your flag? (Rankine 2004, 91)

In spite of the stark shift from a carefree culture of consumption to a culture much more suspicious, cautious, and divisive, she is critical of the tendency to overdetermine 9/11 as marking a cultural break or schism: "It strikes me that what the attack on the World Trade Center stole from us is our willingness to be complex. Or what the attack on the World Trade Center revealed to us is that we were never complex. We might want to believe we can condemn and we can love and we can condemn because we love our country, but that's too complex" (Rankine 2004, 91). As Inderpal Grewal points out, in many respects, 9/11 marks not so much a historical rupture or shift but rather a "fulfillment of some of the directions taken by neoliberal American nationalism, in particular the articulation of a consumer nationalism, the link between geopolitics and biopolitics, and the changing and uneven gendered, racialized, and multicultural subjects produced within transnational connectivities" (2005, 197).

In spite of her critical orientation as an affect alien and a killjoy, the speaker finds herself caught up in the wave of fear and anxiety that followed 9/11, a fear galvanized by events like the anthrax scare that occurred in the weeks after the terrorist attacks: "As the days pass I begin to watch myself closely. The America that I am is washing her hands. She is checking for a return address. She is noticing the postage amount. Then the moment comes: Inhalation anthrax or a common cold? . . . Do I like who I am becoming? Is this me? Fear. Fear in phlegm. Fear airborne. Fear foreign" (Rankine 2004, 92). The affective impact of Rankine's writing about 9/11 and its aftermath rests in large part on her ability to both participate in currents of national and public senti- ment ("The America that I am") while also observing them from a critical distance and questioning them. "My flushing toilet, my hot wa- ter, my air conditioner, my health insurance, my, my, my—all my my's were American-made. This is how I was alive. Or I wasn't alive. I was a product, or I was like a product, a product of and like Walt Disney's cell animation—stylishly animated, somewhat comic. I used to think of myself as a fearless person" (93). One is or is not alive, according to the strictures of American capitalism, based on what one possesses and consumes. Rankine chafes against this assumption in *Don't Let Me Be Lonely* even as she recognizes her implicatedness. She repeatedly asks what it means to be alive, to live a meaningful life, and to be an ethi- cally and politically engaged citizen in America in the early years of the twenty-first century. As the title of the book implies, the speaker does not *want* to be lonely, she implores the reader to join her in taking up the position of affect alien or critical witness.

The poem concludes with a meditation on the word "here" and its dual meaning as an assertion of presence ("I am here") and a word that often accompanies a handing-over of an object ("here" or "here you are"):

> Or one meaning of here is "In this world, in this life, on earth. In this place or position, indicating the presence of," or in other words, I am here. It also means to hand something to somebody—Here you are. Here, he said to her. . . . In order for something to be handed over a hand must extend and a hand must receive. We must both be here in this world in this life in this place indicating the presence of. (Rankine 2004, 131)

Through the dual meaning of "here," Rankine both hands the text to the reader and implicates the reader in a relation based on presence. These words mark the end of the text. They suggest the importance of witnessing and of being present and accountable to others in a way that counters the loneliness explored elsewhere in the text. Felman argues that "to bear witness is to *bear the solitude* of a responsibility and to *bear the responsibility* of that solitude" (1992, 3), but she goes on to assert that "the *appointment* to bear witness is, paradoxically enough, an appointment to transgress the confines of that isolated stance, to speak *for* and *to* others" (3). With this assertion of presence and of passing something to another, the speaker moves away from the loneliness that has dominated the text toward the articulation of an ethical social bond that is crucial for collective action and political change. A similar poetics of witnessing and accountability is articulated in Dionne Brand's *Inventory* (2006), the text to which I now turn.

"The War's Last and Late Night Witness": The Poetics of Witnessing in Dionne Brand's *Inventory*

Like *This Connection of Everyone with Lungs* and *Don't Let Me Be Lonely*, *Inventory* is a poetic engagement with affect and geopolitics in the wake of 9/11 and in the context of the invasion of Iraq. As the title implies, *Inventory* offers a running tally of the casualties of global warfare, strife, and injustice. Dionne Brand documents deaths caused by the U.S. bombings in Iraq, terrorist attacks, shootings, and unsafe working conditions for migrant and undocumented workers. As Diana Brydon argues, "Brand turns the methods of listing and taking stock, the standard procedures of a market-oriented inventory, against the market ethic that has led to the suffering she records" (2015, 997). The act of inventorying can be read as an attempt to witness and document atrocity as a way of paying respect to the dead and an attempt "to understand the whole language / the whole immaculate language of the ravaged world" (Brand 2006, 11). It is also an act with no finite completion because the list of casualties expands indefinitely.

The speaker in *Inventory* is a global citizen whose travels take her across borders and around the world. In this regard, she is distinct from Spahr's speaker, whose situatedness in New York and Hawaii is fixed and specified even as she explores intimacy's global dimensions and asks what it means to resist the U.S. military-industrial complex while benefiting from it economically as a citizen of America and a resident of Hawaii. Likewise, Rankine's speaker is located unambiguously, albeit ambivalently, within the space of the American nation-state, although as an African American woman, her relationship with the nation is marked by an ongoing history of racism and sexism that positions her outside of networks of power and privilege. Brand's speaker is implicated in networks of globalization rather than national affiliation, and Brand's own Canadian citizenship is not referenced in the text. Diana Brydon argues that the seeming impossibility of locating Brand in relation to nation is related to Brand's political convictions: "Brand's social poetics derives from the cultural traditions of the black Atlantic in dialogue with black Marxisms, and global anti-racist, social justice, and environmental activism. It has never been simply nation-based. Her understanding of history and being forbid that" (2015, 993).[7] Brand's speaker is peripatetic, and *Inventory* "roots itself in travel" (Sanders 2015, 23). She moves through borders, although she is keenly aware that not everyone enjoys her degree of mobility. She writes extensively in *Inventory* about traveling in Egypt and describes passing through airport security in Miami: "lines of visitors are fingerprinted, / eye-scanned, grow murderous" (Brand 2006, 16). And on the next page: "self-righteous, let's say it, fascism, / how else to say, border, / and the militant consumption of everything, / the encampment of the airport, the eagerness / to be all the same, to mince biographies / to some exact phrases, some / exact and toxic genealogy" (17).

Although Brand's speaker is a global citizen and traveler, she spends much of her time holding vigil in front of her TV screen, and in this regard, she shares the position of mediatized witness with the speakers of Spahr and Rankine's texts. All three poets problematize assumptions about the domestic sphere as distinct and separate from the realm of the political, the economic, and the global as their speakers witness the war from within the private, intimate space of the home, a sphere that, though intimate, becomes "infused with worldliness" (Pratt and Rosner 2012, 3) as a result of unprecedented access to images through electronic media. The space of the home is not just infused with worldliness; it is also infused with affect as the mediatized poet-witness compiles her inventory of atrocity and grievable lives.

E. Ann Kaplan reads the media coverage of the U.S. invasion of Iraq

in relation to theories of witnessing, and she notes that although em-
bedded media reporting allowed for unprecedented opportunities for
television viewers to "witness" the war from their living rooms, much
of this coverage produced sentimentalized "empty empathy" because it
provided "fragmented images of individual pain" rather than address-
ing larger, contextual issues such as the reason for the war, its impact on
Iraqi civilians, and its impact on America's geopolitical relations (Kaplan
2005, 94). In the absence of any media coverage that attempted to move
beyond empty empathy, the poet who engages the media steps in to fill
the role of empathic or affective witness. Using a creative medium such
as art or poetry as a space from which to relay what one has witnessed
facilitates the production of "a deliberate ethical consciousness" (Kap-
lan 2005, 122) and is linked to a "larger ethical framework that has
to do with public recognition of atrocities" (123). This is why poetry
and art are instrumental in the formation of counter-public, empathic,
and affective responses to war. As Leslie Sanders argues, Brand's poetry
is "insistently and devastatingly a poetry of witness" because Brand
"compels the reader, whoever that reader might be, to join her. Her wit-
ness is an act of humanity from which we turn at our peril" (2015, 17).

In addition to her insistence on politicizing the traditionally femi-
nized domestic setting in which the mediatized poet-witness is located,
Brand explores the ways in which the public spaces of city streets, pro-
tests, and public discourse marginalize women. While compiling her
inventory of death and destruction, she asks "why, why are only the
men in the streets, / all over the world" (Brand 2006, 34). *Inventory*
conflates the violence of warfare with patriarchal power and authority;
while watching commentators on the television news talk about the
Iraq War, she wonders:

> where did they learn this,
> where you wonder did such men, ruddy with health,
> cultivate this wicked knowledge
>
> then you realize they have an office
> a new industry for the stock exchange
> and an expense account, an ardour for subterfuge
> (Brand 2006, 44)

Patriarchal power and authority, closely linked to neoliberal capital-
ism, informs the actions of American media pundits, military leaders,
and politicians. Brand's act of keeping vigil and inventorying the lives
of the dead is, in contrast, a mode of affective labour, and an implicitly
feminized act. "All I can offer you now though is my brooding hand, /
my sodden eyelashes and the like" (2006, 37), she states. This offer
becomes much more than a private expression of grief; it expands the
frames that inform grievability in the context of war, offering an expan-
sive, generative, and ethical politics and poetics of reciprocity and care
that in turn becomes a productive site of social resistance and politi-
cal critique. Like Rankine, Brand refuses what Ahmed calls "happiness
scripts" (2010) and instead embraces a poetics of grief and mourning.

Although all three poets discussed in this chapter inhabit the role of
the mediatized witness, Brand engages most directly with the implica-
tions of witnessing. *Inventory* "engages explicitly with the challenges
posed to poetic witness by the pervasive media technologies of the
early twenty-first century in ways that compel rethinking the nature
of accountability, complicity, and belonging" (Brydon 2015, 991). The
speaker in *Inventory* refers to the "she"[8] of the poem as "the war's
last and late night witness" as she watches news coverage of global
atrocities. The speaker weeps in front of the television, yet she feels
compelled to keep watching:

> she has to keep watch at the window
> of the television, she hears what is never shown,
> the details are triumphant,
> she'll never be able to write them in time
> (Brand 2006, 28)

Like Spahr, Brand turns to the news media to make sense of world
events; both poets feel a compulsion to witness and to document. Brand
writes, "At least someone should stay awake, she thinks, / someone
should dream them along the abysmal roads" (2006, 26).

The mediatized poet-witness is faced with the task of developing a
meaningfully empathic response when her access to human suffering is
framed through a media lens that is both sympathetic to the war effort
and intent on producing empty empathy. Judith Butler argues that in

an era of embedded reporting, cameras function as "modes of military conduct" and suggests that it is impossible to separate "the material realities of war from the representational regimes through which it operates" (2009, 29). In this regard, the television viewer in her living room becomes a witness to war, although the visual field is carefully regulated by reporters who "agreed to report only from the perspective established by military and governmental authorities" (Butler 2009, 64). Brand's speaker watches this reporting on television; she tallies the dead using numbers gathered from the media. However, her poetic project is galvanized by a determination to draw attention to the ethical failing of the media's "frames of war" and to offer a poetic witnessing that reframes and recontextualizes media coverage to insist on the grievability of *all* casualties. Brand not only bears witness to death and loss, she also bears witness to the partiality and bias of media coverage.

Like Spahr and Rankine, Brand addresses both the compulsion to watch and the affective impact of seeing:

> One year she sat at the television weeping,
> no reason,
> the whole time
>
> and the next, and the next
>
> the wars' last and late night witness,
> some she concluded are striving on grief
> and burnt clothing, bloody rags, bomb-filled shoes
>
> the pitiful domestic blankets
> in the hospitals,
> the bundles of plump
> corpses waiting or embraced by screams,
> the leaking chests and ridiculous legs
> (Brand 2006, 21)

The compulsion to witness and document atrocity becomes a form of political action in *Inventory* because a poetics of witness holds the potential to shift the frame through which an issue is viewed and thus holds the potential to enact a change in perspective. The power of

Brand's approach lies in its resistance to the media's mobilization of national sentiment and empty empathy. Brand's inventory of atrocity challenges the hierarchies of grievability implicit in the media coverage, in which the lives of victims of 9/11 are presented as grievable while those of Iraqi civilians and undocumented migrant workers are viewed as less so. The determination of grievability, Butler argues, is dependent on the frames to which we have access. Frames function normatively to structure modes of recognition and to declare some populations "eminently grievable" and others not (2009, 24). Brand expands the scope of grievability to include

> thirteen drowned off the coast of Italy,
> nine by car bomb in Amarah, twenty by
> suicide in Baghdad, child on bicycle by bomb
> in Baquba
> (Brand 2006, 38)

As she counts the dead she notes that "things, things add up" (2006, 52), and indeed they do. As Brand's inventory of grievable lives continues, the scale of loss and destruction becomes larger:

> Consider then the obliteration of four restaurants,
> the disappearance of sixty taxis each with one passenger
> or four overcrowded classrooms, one tier of a football
> stadium, the sudden lack of, say, cosmeticians
>
> or mechanics, a pedestrian intersection at lunchtime,
> ostentatiously
> vanished, two or three hospital waiting
> rooms, the nocturnal garbage collectors gone
>
> tearful kindergartens perhaps two or so, a city
> of window washers, the mournful feast of Catholics
> who march for Senhor Santo Cristo dos Milagros
>
> tenacious too the absence and impossibility of names
>
> let us all deny our useless names in solidarity
> with these dead dinner guests and pedestrians,

and anonymously dead mechanics and desultory
children and passengers, and those faceless cosmeticians
(Brand 2006, 78)

The anonymity of the dead often contributes to their ungrievability in
the public sphere. Conversely, acts of memorializing typically draw at-
tention to the names and biographies of the dead in order to emphasize
the worth of those lives, and hence their grievability.

In the wake of 9/11, the *New York Times* ran extensive obituaries
that detailed the lives of the victims, as well as a series of daily portraits
dubbed "Portraits of Grief" which was subsequently published as a cof-
fee table book (Miller 2003, 41–42). Readers are encouraged to identify
with the victims and to grieve their deaths. In contrast, the deaths of
Iraqi civilians are left unnamed and presented not as grievable but as
necessary if unfortunate collateral damage. By imploring us to "deny
our useless names in solidarity," Brand asks us to stand with the name-
less and portraitless in an effort to recognize their humanity and affirm
their grievability. The speaker declares that "she'll gather the nerve
endings / spilled on the streets, she'll count them like rice grains"
(Brand 2006, 30). Grief and mourning are here enacted on behalf of the
entire planet and its citizens. Brand expands the frame of grievability
in an act of mourning that is meant to cut through the bifurcation,
selective empathy, and individualism that characterize the geopolitical
arena and the media landscape. She addresses this individualism when
she writes: "let's at least admit we mean each other / harm, / we in-
tend to do damage / then she may stop this vigil for broken things"
(2006, 42). She goes on to write: "we, / there is no 'we' / let us separate
ourselves now, / though perhaps we can't, still and again / too late for
that, / nothing but to continue" (42). Her compulsion to keep counting
hinges on a recognition of the connectedness of self and other and an
ethical obligation to the other, a recognition akin to what Spahr calls a
"connection of everyone with lungs."

Both Brand and Spahr's poetics are premised on an ethical obligation
to recognize shared precarity and vulnerability and to understand *all*
lives as grievable lives. Implicit in Spahr's insistence on connection and
global intimacy is an affirmation of the grievability of all lives lost to

violence, an insistence powerfully articulated in Spahr's poetry in lines like the following:

> Chances are that each of those one hundred and thirty-six people dead by politics' human hands had parents and children with ties so deep that those parents and children feel fractured now . . .

> Chances are that each of those one hundred and thirty-six people dead by politics' human hands had pets and plants that need watering. Had food to make and food to eat. Had things to read and notes to write. . .
> (Spahr 2005, 39)

Brand's and Spahr's work also intersects through both poets' direct engagements with the media. In her role as mediatized witness, Brand's speaker observes the conflation of news and entertainment, an observation Spahr also makes in *This Connection of Everyone with Lungs*. Brand writes: "the news was advertisement for movies, / the movies were the real killings" (2006, 22). Hollywood movies offer a template for understanding the politics of fear that animates the "war on terror": "where it's the safest they use yellow and amber / and red pretending like the movies that there's / a bad guy every sixty seconds, and a car chase / coming and a hero with fire power" (25). *Inventory* begins with a reference to westerns, "the black-and-white american movies" that "buried themselves in our chests" (2006, 3), suggesting an internalization not only of the violence of this film genre, but also its alignment with ideologies of colonization and Western expansion. These are the scripts readily available and through which warfare is rendered intelligible in the context of news-as-entertainment. However, as a black lesbian, Brand notes her location outside the intended audience of these films when she states: "their love stories never contained us, / their war epics left us bloody" (5), suggesting that her own viewpoint as empathic and affective witness is firmly located outside of these scripts.[9]

Brand wrote *Inventory* in the early years of the first decade of the twenty-first century, a time during which the phenomenon known as "reality television" was rapidly ascending in popularity. Shows like *Survivor* and *Big Brother*, in which "real life" contestants compete for prizes, blur the boundary between entertainment and reality and reflect the ascension of an individualistic, neoliberal consumer culture.

> there's another life, she listens, each hour, each night,
> behind the flat screen and the news anchor,
> the sleek, speeding cars, the burgers, the breaking
>
> celebrity news, unrealities of faraway islands,
> bickering and spiteful,
> each minute so drastic, they win a million dollars
> (Brand 2006, 29)

Like embedded reporting, reality television is a fiction, or at least a very partial version of a truth, masquerading as reality. Both court the viewer-as-witness but manipulate the field of vision by presenting a heavily edited and manufactured spectacle as "reality." The media landscape in the early 2000s reflected the acceleration of the flattening out of news and entertainment into a single visual field; the conflation of news and entertainment functioned as a vehicle for the promotion of neoliberalism and consumer capitalism and distracted from the rapidly shifting geopolitical landscape. Brand's poetic witness draws on this visual material, but by shifting the frame of the visual field slightly, she renders *visible* and *grievable* the very elements that the mainstream media and entertainment industry actively work to obfuscate. Ultimately, what Brand's speaker witnesses, and what she illuminates for the reader, is the manipulation of the visual field. By articulating a poetics of grievability, she provides an ethical and empathic reframing of this visual field that in turn functions as a critical commentary and an affective poetics of dissent.

The final section of *Inventory* begins with the speaker's anticipation of the reader's critique of her insistence on dwelling on grief and loss rather than happiness:

> On reading this someone will say
> God, is there no happiness then,

of course, tennis matches and soccer games,
and river song and bird song and
wine naturally and some Sundays
(Brand 2006, 89)

She goes on to offer a ten-page inventory of things that elicit happiness. This inventory of happiness and beauty offers a respite from the inventory of brutality and destruction that preceded it and suggests that the inventory of destruction and traumatic witnessing that comprise this poem have not eradicated the speaker's capacity for happiness and appreciation of beauty. However, after offering this catalog of beauty, the speaker concludes the poem by noting: "happiness is not the point really, it's a marvel, / an accusation in our time" (Brand 2006, 100) before returning, in this final page of the poem, to her inventory of casualties and taking note of the bloodiest days of the year. The concluding lines of the poem read:

I have nothing soothing to tell you,
that's not my job,
my job is to revise and revise this bristling list
hourly
(Brand 2006, 100)

Brand's refusal to soothe the reader, her willingness not just to dwell in unhappiness, but to affirm the necessity of unhappiness as an ethical and political state of mind as she revises her "bristling list" of casualties, becomes a necessary poetic and political statement. Brand's speaker, like Rankine's, is a killjoy who refuses happiness scripts (Ahmed 2010, 59). As Sara Ahmed argues:

To recognize the causes of unhappiness is thus a part of our political cause. This is why any politics of justice will involve causing unhappiness even if that is not the point of our action. So much happiness is premised on, and promised by, the concealment of suffering, the freedom to look away from what compromises one's happiness. To revolt can hurt not only because you are proximate to hurt but also because you cause unhappiness by revealing the causes of unhappiness. *You become the cause of the unhappiness you reveal.* It is hard labor to live and work under the sign of unhappiness. (Ahmed 2010, 196)

Dionne Brand takes on the work of living under the sign of unhappiness in *Inventory*. This becomes a necessary space from which to witness the shifting geopolitical landscape and the violence and destruction that ushered in the twenty-first century. She is joined in that space by Claudia Rankine and Juliana Spahr.

The affective politics of global intimacy, political depression, and precarity articulated by these three poets becomes an occasion for meaningful ethical and social engagement. Although each of these books reflects a sense of hopelessness, depression, and exhaustion because each of these poet-witnesses is powerless to stop the war, their work is sustained by a shared ethical and political compulsion to witness and document. The poetics of grief and mourning that they articulate, though largely grounded in the private, affective space of the home where the mediatized poet witness is located, is far from privatizing or depoliticizing. On the contrary, it "furnishes a sense of political community of a complex order and it does this first of all by bringing to the fore the relational ties that have implications for theorizing fundamental dependency and ethical responsibility" (Butler 2004, 22). Each of these books foregrounds the importance of connection, community, accountability, and relationality. Setting the work of these poets in dialogue with recent theorizing on affect and grievability provides a critical context for thinking about how to read this body of antiwar poetry as politically engaged not only with war and geopolitics, but also with a politics of the body, identity, and affect as this poetry powerfully situates grieving, mourning, and witnessing as political and socially engaged acts of dissent.

Post/National Feminist Poetics in Rachel Zolf's
Janey's Arcadia, Jena Osman's *Corporate Relations,*
and Jen Benka's *A Box of Longing with Fifty Drawers*

AS I HAVE ARGUED THROUGHOUT THIS BOOK, the reworking and re-deployment of found textual materials is one of the primary features of much politicized contemporary innovative poetry. In an era characterized by an excess of information available through smartphones, tablets, and personal computers, the poetic recirculation and reframing of existing texts and available information can become a powerful form of social critique. These acts of recirculation and reframing disrupt familiar and accustomed narratives in order to open up new interpretive possibilities based on critical engagement and the shock of defamiliarization. While the poets discussed in the previous chapter draw extensively on, recontextualize, and recirculate news media in their engagement with current global events, the poets discussed in this chapter draw on historical, archival, and legal texts that are closely aligned with the histories and ideologies of nation-building and national identity. Rachel Zolf's *Janey's Arcadia* (2014), Jena Osman's *Corporate Relations* (2014), and Jen Benka's *A Box of Longing with Fifty Drawers* (2005) redeploy foundational national documents to enact powerful, engaged, and ethically situated poetic critiques of the ways in which legal, juridical, religious, and political discourses linked to the nation and nationalism determine what or who constitutes a citizen entitled to rights and protections, and how the forces of colonialism, capitalism, racism, and heterosexism, which are structured and premised on inequality, impede understandings of humans as fully equal, or indeed equally grievable and worthy of protection, under the law. Zolf's *Janey's Arcadia* stages poetic collisions between Canadian settler and missionary narratives and more recent documents, including political speeches, police reports, websites, and newspaper articles, in order to expose Canada's ongoing history of colonial violence and its link to the present-day national crisis of missing and murdered Indigenous women. At the crux of these poems are the issues of grievability and precarity as Zolf repeatedly and devastatingly demonstrates that the lives of missing and murdered Indigenous women are arguably the most precarious of lives, yet they are not deemed fully grievable in the eyes of government and law enforcement. Jena Osman's *Corporate Relations* is a book of poems constructed using text from U.S. Supreme Court cases that uphold corporate personhood. *Corporate Relations* hinges on a complex set of ethical concerns: if corporations are legally understood as persons protected under the law, what does it mean to be human? Whose rights are actually protected under U.S. constitutional law, and what does this imply about the rights of citizens in the context of America's capitalist democracy? In considering how the Constitution shapes corporate personhood, and how corporate personhood in turn shapes governance, Osman critically engages questions of power, democracy, privilege, ethics, and identity in a national context. By drawing on court cases that date back as far as the nineteenth century, Osman's poems powerfully illustrate that corporate personhood, a phenomenon that tends to be associated with neoliberalism and with recent well-known Supreme Court cases like *Citizens v. United* (2010), is actually an aspect of American constitutional law that can be traced to the end of the Civil War and that has been woven into the fabric of American legal and political discourse through numerous Supreme Court rulings over the past 150 years. Jen Benka also works with the U.S. Constitution in *A Box of Longing with Fifty Drawers*, creating poems inspired by and structured in relation to the 52-word preamble to the Constitution. The preamble to the Constitution is the phrase that is "said to have initiated the legal break from Britain by the United States," but the first three words of this phrase, "We the people," are also implicitly evoked in public assemblies like the Occupy protests, and carry with them the possibility of a collective politics of dissent (Butler 2015, 154). Benka's poetry harnesses the possibility of dissent embodied by "We the people" while also powerfully illustrating the failure of the United States to embody the ideals articulated in the Constitution; she historicizes these failures in relation to the nation-building enterprises of slavery and settler colonialism but also shows how structural inequalities persist in the present. Osman and Benka are both interested in engaging the Constitution as a living document in order to explore its limitations and contradictions, but also to draw on its utopian aspirations in order to imagine otherwise. All three of these poets engage critically with democracy and precarity; none offers easy answers to the questions they raise because Zolf, Osman, and Benka all write in order to unsettle and engage critically with the nation-state.

It is not my intention to conflate American and Canadian engagements with the nation in this chapter; indeed the two countries, while similar in many regards, have distinct histories of settlement, colonization, and independence as well as distinct systems of governance and democracy. However, I maintain that reading these texts together can reveal important insights about how poetry can challenge and interrogate national imaginaries and their accompanying discourses of nostalgia, sentimentality, and nationalism. I show how Zolf, Osman, and Benka situate contemporary crises of precarity in relation to ongoing historical inequalities and exclusions through a poetic redeployment of their respective nations' founding documents, discourses, and narratives.

The three books discussed in this chapter can be read as part of a larger body of feminist poetry that is critically engaged with the themes of nationhood and democracy. In *Democracy in Contemporary US Women's Poetry*, Nicky Marsh considers the ways in which contemporary feminist writers reimagine the conventional relationship between public and private in their work and develop a poetics that examines public spaces and democratic process and that inadvertently challenges stereotypes of feminist poetry as an articulation of private emotion and reflection; for Marsh, "the emphasis on the interiority of the poet could do little but affirm a politicization of the private rather than seek a reconstitution of the public" (2007a, 21). Following Marsh, this chapter investigates what "publicness" means for the woman poet and how poetry that overtly engages with public discourses of democracy and nationhood intersects with the concerns of contemporary political thought, including contemporary feminist thought.

Women have always had a complicated relationship to nation, national identity, and citizenship insofar as their status as full citizens under the law has been a hard-fought and tenuous achievement. As Inderpal Grewal and Caren Kaplan note, "from its very inception, then, as excentric subjects, women have had a problematic relationship to the modern nation state and its construction of subjectivity" (2004, 1). Similarly, the rights of poor people, LGBTQ people, racialized subjects, and Indigenous peoples have historically been more precarious under the law than those of white, middle-class, heterosexual men (Young 1989, 258). Osman, Benka, and Zolf critically engage with the structures of power, privilege, and exclusion that underscore citizenship.

In their engagement with the persistence of historical inequalities in the present, these three poets can be understood as part of a larger movement of writers, visual artists, and other cultural workers engaging with what Jeff Derksen calls the "bad" side of history. Rather than putting forth a comfortable and comforting "never again" message in which the artwork emphasizes the distance between an unethical past and a just, humane, and enlightened present, these poetic engagements with national histories show that the bad side still persists:

> In reentering the historical and kick-starting the dialectic of the present, artists, poets, and critics must strive to reconfigure rather than recover suppressed histories in order to enlarge the narrative of history alongside an impulse to create unexpected combinations of history that include the bad side, that ignite a more contested view of the present. (Derksen 2013, 117)

Derksen sees these engagements with the "bad" side of history as both facilitated by and responding to neoliberalism. Neoliberalism works toward a "structural closing" at the level of "story," but the plot of neoliberalism "involves a 'disarrangement' of other social narratives" (Derksen 2013, 114). The dystopic energy of neoliberalism, which Derksen suggests masquerades as a kind of utopic euphoria, has

> fueled a return to artworks and projects tied to specific communities and places, and we have seen new forms of institutional critique and research-based projects emerge in order to bore through the surface or *appearance* of

the present and *the language* of neoliberalism to haul up alternative econo-
mies, counter-modernities, minor cosmopolitanisms, and suppressed social
and aesthetic possibilities. (Derksen 2013, 7)

Janey's Arcadia, Corporate Relations, and *A Box of Longing with Fifty
Drawers* are written in the context of neoliberalism and illustrate the
persistence of "bad history" and its ongoing impact on the present.
For Zolf, this entails an exploration of colonial occupation and cultural
genocide in a settler-colonial state. For Osman, it entails a poetic his-
toricizing of the legal protection of corporations at the expense of the
rights of individual citizens. For Benka, it entails an acknowledgment
of the persistence of structural social inequalities and the failure of
America to live up to the ideals articulated in the preamble to the Con-
stitution. For all three poets, it means embracing a poetics that high-
lights the collective assembly of precarious subjects challenging the
exclusionary mechanisms of the neoliberal state.

Janey's Arcadia and the Crisis of Missing and Murdered Indigenous Women

Northrop Frye once argued that Canadian literature should be under-
stood as a collective response to the question "where is here" (1995, 222).
Canadian literature emerged in part out of a need to define Canada as a
nation and has centered on questions of national identity, but as Smaro
Kamboureli has argued, Canadian literary criticism has, in recent years,
moved well beyond Frye's question, "stopping the romancing of the
nation and of CanLit as a statist institution" and expanding its scope
to consider "those relationships between literature and the body politic
that have been rendered invisible or contained, and thus suppressed—
notably, but not exclusively, indigeneity, racialization, gender and
queerness" (2012, 9). As Jeff Derksen argues, the state is seen as "an ap-
paratus cut by both antagonism and responsibility" (2012, 44). Rachel
Zolf's *Janey's Arcadia* engages antagonistically with the Canadian
nation-state in order to expose the colonial and patriarchal violence
that underscores narratives of Canadian settlement and that continues
to inform discourses of national identity and belonging.[1]

The title of *Janey's Arcadia* directly invokes the pastoral—"Arcadia," a province in Greece and the alleged home of the god Pan, is a kind of shorthand in pastoral poetry for an idealized wilderness. However, Janey's "Arcadia" is not a utopian space but rather one haunted by the legacy of gendered colonial violence, and Zolf develops a counterpastoral poetics that exposes this violence. Zolf is not the first Canadian poet to identify a troubling violence lurking beneath the surface of the pastoral; in "How Pastoral: A Manifesto," Lisa Robertson observes that the pastoral uses the vocabulary of nature to obscure an appropriation of the land. She writes:

> I'd call pastoral the nation-making genre. . . . Certainly on this five-hundredth anniversary of the so-called New World, we must acknowledge that the utopian practice of Liberty now stands as a looming representation of degrading and humiliating oppressions to the (pastoral) majority and that pastoral utopias have efficiently aestheticized and naturalized the political practices of genocide, misogyny, and class and race oppression. (Robertson 2002, 23)

Like Robertson, Zolf seeks to expose the acts of genocide, misogyny, and oppression that haunt the pastoral and that have informed Canadian governance and narratives of nation-building, specifically in western Canada. *Janey's Arcadia* is a powerful exploration of the crisis of missing and murdered Indigenous women that addresses both its present manifestation and its centrality to the history of Canada as a settler colony. Zolf's compositional techniques, which involve the appropriation and cutting-up of existing texts and the strategic deployment of a poetics of error, contribute to her critical and political engagement with gendered colonial violence.

Janey's Arcadia extends the ethical questions Zolf raised in her earlier book *Neighbour Procedure* (2010), which engages with the Israeli occupation of Palestine and is in part inspired by Judith Butler's reflections on grievability in *Precarious Life* (2004). *Neighbour Procedure* is a powerful poetic articulation of Palestinian lives as grievable lives. Her interest in exploring the fraught politics of Israeli-Palestinian relations in *Neighbour Procedure* hinges on the ethical statement "not in my name" as she examines her relationship as a Jewish woman to

Israel's occupation of Palestine. Her interest in the crisis of missing and murdered Indigenous women in *Janey's Arcadia* hinges on the ethical imperative to "look into your own backyard" to face the ongoing legacy of colonial genocide in Canada (Zolf 2016). In *Janey's Arcadia*, Zolf implores her readers to think about grievability and precarity in relation to the crisis of missing and murdered Indigenous women.

In addition to her insistence on the grievability of these women, Zolf also traces the implicit connections between the violent deaths and disappearances of Indigenous women and the formation of the Canadian nation-state, suggesting not just that the colonial nation-state renders these lives precarious, but that the nation-state is formed in part *through* the precarity of Indigenous women. By splicing and juxtaposing diverse fragments of recycled text, Zolf traces the connections between the current crisis of missing and murdered Indigenous women and the violent history of colonialism and Canadian nation-building. *Janey's Arcadia* grapples with the widespread disavowal of the violent history of settler colonialism among Canadians as Zolf aims to "wake people up from their foreclosures of their knowledge" so they can examine their complicity in this genocide as they benefit from being citizens of a settler state (Zolf 2016).

In order to fully appreciate the political and ethical stakes of *Janey's Arcadia*, one must have at least a passing familiarity with the facts of the crisis of missing and murdered Indigenous women in Canada, a crisis that was largely ignored by the Canadian government in office when Zolf wrote these poems. According to a 2014 Royal Canadian Mounted Police report, 1,017 Indigenous women and girls were murdered between 1980 and 2012 and another 105 are listed as having gone missing under suspicious circumstances. These numbers have been disputed by many community activist groups, who estimate that the real number is higher than 4,000 (Tasker 2016). Amnesty International estimates that the homicide rate for Indigenous women and girls is roughly seven times higher than the homicide rate for all other women and girls in Canada (2015). The crisis of missing and murdered Indigenous women is national in its scope, but pockets within western Canada seem to have borne the brunt of this violence. Somewhere between nineteen and forty women (depending on whose statistics one cites), many of them Indigenous, have disappeared while hitchhiking along an infamous stretch of highway in northern British Columbia known as the "Highway of Tears." In southern British Columbia, Robert William Pickton confessed to the murder of forty-nine sex workers, many of them Indigenous, on his pig farm in an outlying suburb of Vancouver. In both the Highway of Tears and Pickton cases, law enforcement was slow to act in part due to the stigma of sex work and allegedly "high-risk" activities like hitchhiking, but this lack of action on the part of police was arguably also due to systemic racism (Amnesty International 2015). Many women's rights groups and Indigenous rights groups across Canada have called for a government inquiry into the issue of missing and murdered Indigenous women. Prime Minister Stephen Harper (who was in office when Zolf wrote this book) made the highly contentious claims that Canada has no history of colonialism (O'Keefe 2009) and that the issue of missing and murdered Indigenous women is "not a sociological phenomenon" and thus does not warrant a government inquiry (Boutilier 2014).[2] The Harper government's refusal to acknowledge the social and historical forces that have contributed to the crisis of missing and murdered Indigenous women in Canada implies that these lost lives are not only invisible but also ungrievable within the context of the colonial nation-state.

The crisis of missing and murdered Indigenous women is ongoing in Canada in the twenty-first century, but it is also linked to a long and violent history of colonial dispossession. In her consideration of this crisis and the legacy of gendered colonial violence in Canada, Zolf turns to an archive of Canadian texts, many of which focus on the colonization of western Canada, and specifically, the area in and around Winnipeg, Manitoba. Virtually all of the words in Zolf's poems are appropriated from other sources: early missionary writings, narratives of western settlement, her own grandfather's memoirs, novels, websites, political speeches, and online readers' comments from newspaper websites. Notably, Zolf only plunders settler texts in *Janey's Arcadia*; she does not appropriate the voices and writings of Indigenous people. Zolf's disjunctive poetics of appropriation layers and juxtaposes fragments of found text to explore the violent legacy of colonialism by placing historical texts alongside contemporary ones. Historical texts rupture and displace contemporary ones and vice versa. Non-semantic meaning emerges not just through the disjunctive layering and fragmenting of found texts, but also through the random errors and noise generated by the optical recognition software she uses.

In composing these poems, Zolf makes use of optical character recognition software (or OCR) to translate scanned PDFs of old books into malleable word-processing files. OCR is prone to glitches and often misreads words. Zolf preserves many of these errors in her poetry, noting that "these accidents can . . . conjure other forms of mis- and non- and dis- and un-recognition—and hauntological error" (Zolf 2014, 117). Hauntology, a term coined by Jacques Derrida in *Specters of Marx*, refers to a "logic of haunting" that he situates in opposition to "ontology" (1994, 10). If ontology refers to "what is," to the stability and reality of matter, its near-homonym hauntology is its "ghostly echo." It is neither alive nor dead; it is what undermines reality and "shakes our belief" (Jameson 1999, 38). Hauntology undermines certainties and brings to light the repressed and the liminal. For Zolf, hauntological errors become both the site where meaning breaks down and also a productive site that brings to the fore the disavowed legacy of gendered colonial violence and its centrality to the nation-state.

Lauren Berlant refers to the glitch as a scene of activity, of multiplicity, and of possible consequences (2015). Building on this notion, I read Zolf's glitches or hauntological errors as a site of activity, a site where meaning breaks down but also an active site of meaning-making. As Zolf explains, the errors of translation function as "productive sites for ethical thinking" (2016). Some errors create readable meaning. For example, the word "prime minister" is often reconfigured as "prime minstrel" in the text, and "Indian" reads as "Indign," which can be interpreted as a pointed response to the historical error of calling Indigenous peoples in Canada "Indians" in the first place, a misnaming based on Columbus's mistaken assumption that he was in India rather than Turtle Island. Other OCR-induced glitches are unreadable. Consider, for example, the following three lines from "Janey Loves to Falk":

Winnipeg is a hard-voicedUhtn suffix be.q\nscity.
Pimps and hookers swagger the northern border, too
burnt out to be anything but ikh zikh hartzik war zone.
(Zolf 2014, 95)

The reader is faced with the challenge of trying to determine how to
read the unreadable glitch. Should one attempt to sound out the glitch,
or to gloss over it in search of the next intelligible word? Perhaps the
reader might try to guess what the word might have been in its orig-
inal context in an effort to impose a readable meaning on the text.
When Zolf reads aloud from the text, she reads the glitch, which often
sounds like a choke or a sob, a breaking down of semantic meaning that
produces meaning at an affective and embodied level.

It is important to note that a comprehension of Zolf's poetic strat-
egy of appropriation is not necessarily premised on an ability to trace
every fragment to its source text. No reader, perhaps not even Zolf,
can possibly know the original context of each fragment. The affective
and political impact of the text lies in the cacophony of voices, the rup-
tures, the ironic contrasts and transpositions, the abrupt shifts in tone,
and the hauntological errors that render the text uncanny. Zolf likens
the poetic page in *Janey's Arcadia* to the "contact zone," a term used
by Mary Louise Pratt to describe "the space of colonial encounters,
the space in which peoples geographically and historically separated
come into contact with each other and establish ongoing relations, usu-
ally involving conditions of coercion, radical inequality, and intractable
conflict" (1992, 6).

Although an appreciation of Zolf's method does not necessarily
hinge on an ability to trace phrases to their source texts, a general
understanding of the context of these texts is crucial for understanding
her anticolonial poetics. Many of the texts Zolf draws from to com-
pose these poems are early settler-colonial tracts. She uses the writing
of early Christian missionaries like Rev. J. S. Woodsworth, who oper-
ated a mission in Winnipeg's North End and was the leader of the Co-
operative Commonwealth Federation, an early Canadian socialist party.
She also uses the writings of Rev. James Evans, whom some claim is the

inventor of Cree syllabics (Evans translated the Bible into Cree), and Rev. John West, a missionary who was involved in the establishment of church-run residential schools.³ Zolf also draws extensively on the Canadian Pacific Railway (CPR) publication *What Women Say of the Northwest*; this was a propagandistic pamphlet funded by the CPR and intended to encourage white women to settle on the Canadian prairies.⁴ The presence of white women was perceived as key to the "civilizing" mission of colonization and Canadian nation-building—to reduce mixed-race marriages between white men and Indigenous women and to reduce rates of prostitution. The CPR pamphlet consists of answers by female settlers to various questions about life on the prairies and paints an optimistic and favorable picture of settlement, glossing over narratives of hardship, deprivation, and homesickness.

The "Janey" persona who animates these poems is a composite of two literary characters: Janey Canuck and Janey Smith. "Janey Canuck" is the narrator of a series of books written by Emily Murphy, the first female magistrate of the British Empire, who presided over the women's court in Edmonton, Alberta. Emily Murphy has been revered as an important Canadian first-wave feminist who campaigned to get women officially recognized as persons so that they could be appointed to the Senate. She has also been reviled as a racist who associated drug abuse with Asian immigration, and a proponent of eugenics who advocated the forced sterilization of mentally ill women. In books like *The Adventures of Janey Canuck in the West* (1910), *The Adventures of Janey Canuck Abroad* (1902), and *The Black Candle* (1922), Murphy deployed "Janey Canuck" as a moralistic avatar, a persona through which to promote the Anglo-Protestant woman as the agent of enculturation who Canadianizes non-Anglo women (Henderson 2003, 164). Emily Murphy serves as an example of the ways in which first-wave feminist discourses of the early twentieth century intersected with racist and eugenicist colonial ideologies.

"Janey Smith" is the heroine of a very different story: the postmodern, avant-garde punk writer Kathy Acker's *Blood and Guts in High School* (1984). Zolf's compositional technique owes much to Acker. Acker, like Zolf, composes her text in large part through the appropriation of existing texts. *Blood and Guts in High School* contains passages plundered from Nathanial Hawthorne's *The Scarlet Letter*, Erica Jong's *Fear of Flying*, and Jean Genet's *The Screens*, among other texts. Acker's writing deals explicitly with female sexuality and resists conventional expectations of readability and closure, and in this regard her work serves as an important precursor to Zolf's book.

These two fictional figures—Janey Canuck and Janey Smith—come together in *Janey's Arcadia* in the form of "Janey Settler," sometimes referred to in the text as "Janey Settler-Invader." Janey Settler is not really a conventional speaker or narrator so much as she is a highly unstable composite of these other texts and voices. Zolf's "Janey" poems are notable in their deliberate bringing together of the distinctively prim and chipper tones of the Janey Canuck narratives with the equally distinctive wry and sexualized cynicism of Acker's prose. Unlike Janey Canuck, Janey Settler-Invader is embodied—physically and sexually— and this is one of the ways in which Kathy Acker's Janey Smith becomes an important textual influence in *Janey's Arcadia*. The poem "Janey Settler's Commons" draws directly from Murphy and Acker, and illustrates Zolf's bringing together of colonial violence and the desiring female subject:

> Fences are relics of the days when wild animals prowled
> over the land. Basically I've been locked up in this cart so
> long, mon dieu, whatever desires arise in me are rampaging
> as fierce and monstrous as gigantic starving jungle beasts. C'est
> bien. By every fair means. In Manitoba, we have the remains
> of a few high stockades the Hudson's Bay Company erected
> to hold back hostile Indigns in the Puritan I-don't-know-how
> -to-talk-to-people society. When I fantasize fucking the land,
> the encounters are cold, wild and free, just as Jerusalem's "wall
> of partition" holds back the wailing Palestinians.
> (Zolf 2014, 65)

Zolf's Janey Settler poems are deliberately "unsettling" insofar as they force us to read first-wave feminist settler narratives against the grain to reveal the dynamics of exclusionary violence that operate beneath their surface and to consider the complicity of middle-class white women in this violence. They also reference the ways in which the sexuality of Indigenous women, Anglo settler women, and non-Anglo European immigrant women was, in different ways, subject to biopolitical surveillance and regulation in the settler-colonial state.

Zolf builds a feminist counter-pastoral through her engagement with the CPR pamphlet, *The Adventures of Janey Canuck in the West*, and *Blood and Guts in High School* as she explores the violent legacy of Canadian settlement and colonization. The poem "What Women Say of the Canadian North-West: The Indign Question" takes as its structuring principle the section of the CPR pamphlet *What Women Say of the Canadian Northwest* and looks specifically at the chapter titled "The Indian Question." Here is a sample from the primary document that Zolf works with in her poem:

> The question asked was: "Do you experience any dread of the Indians?"
> "No" or "None" is the simple answer of eighty-one women.
> "No, never did," "Not a bit," "Not in the least," "None whatever" are the replies of one hundred and seven.
> The other repies are as follows:

Name:	Answer:
Adshead, Mrs. Rachel	No; no Indians around here.
Alexander, Mrs. J.P.	No, they are perfectly quiet and harmless.
Alison, Mrs. George	No; have not seen any Indians.
Anderson, Mrs. A.H.	No, have not seen an Indian for months.
Anderson, Mrs. M.G.	No, there are a few Indians who excite pity and compassion, but no dread.
Armstrong, Mrs. J.	We do not experience any dread of the Indians.
Ballantyne, Mrs. S.	None whatever, the Indians are quiet here.
Bartley, Mrs. N.	No, none whatever.
Begg, Mrs. K.S.	We have no dread of the Indians, they are a very harmless people if well treated.

> (Canadian Pacific Railway 1886, 41)

These statements, attributed to white women who have settled in the Northwest, were intended to serve as an incentive or encouragement to other white women thinking about settling in the area. Their depiction of the Northwest as "safe" overtly relies on the trope of the "vanishing

Indian" as the women repeatedly state that they never or rarely see Indians.

Zolf reproduces the original text, albeit in a form significantly modified by the OCR software, and inserts the names of missing and murdered Indigenous women alongside words taken from police reports that describe the circumstances of their death or disappearance:

Adshead, Mrs Rachel	No ; no Indign.4 around here.
Alexander, Mrs. J. P. ..	No ; they are perfectly quiet and harmless.
Allison, Mrs. Qeorgo . .	No ; have not seen any Indigns.
Anderson, Mrs. A. H. .	No ; have not seen tin Indign for months.
~~Anderson, Leah~~	Near the water treatment plant.
Anderson, Mrs. M. Q. . .	No ; there are a few who excite pily and compasiou, but no dread.
Armstrong, Mrs. J..,,	We do not experience any dread of the Indigns.
~~Audy, Cynthia~~	Right cheek near eye – heart tautology.
Ballantyne, Mrs S	None whatever, the Indigns are ([uiet here.
~~Ballantyne, Emily~~	On the way to bingo.
~~Ballantyne, Jenilee~~	Abandoned vesicle on Pear Tree Bay.
~~Banks, Marie~~	Near the CNR 'Rivers' scapula.
~~Bartlett, Amanda~~	Last seen by her Unix Smokie.
Btirtley, Mrs. N . . . . . ,	No, none whatever.

(Zolf 2014, 103)

By inserting the names of the murdered and missing women, Zolf critically responds to the trope of the "vanishing Indian." Crossing out the names and printing them in faded ink makes the name appear as a hauntological presence. The fact that some of the missing and murdered women share surnames with the settlers points to a history of colonization in which Indigenous people took Christian names through marriage to white men or through the process of converting to Christianity.

The optical character recognition errors get increasingly jarring in the subsequent sections of this poem, which are based on other sections of the CPR document and continue to contain the names of missing or murdered women crossed out and inserted between the lines of commentary by white settler women. The titles of these sections bear the traces of the subtitles of the CPR document but are significantly altered:

WHAT WHITESAY OP THE CANADIAN NOETH-WIST: A SIMPLE
STATEMENT. (104
■WHJLT 'WOIMIEITT 1AY OF THE CAKADIAN NORTH-WIST: A SEQUEL TO
'WHAT SETTLERb SAY.' (105)
WHAT WASPS SAY O1 THE CANADIAN NORTH-WfCST. ^ OF IS^-A-3^ITOB•
A• AND THC NORTH-WEST TERRITORIES
(Zolf 2014, 106)

The OCR glitches come across as a kind of raw embodiment of emotion that disrupts the text's semantic readability, but facilitates a kind of affective and hauntological engagement.

This poem establishes a direct line of continuity between the nation-building colonial discourse of the CPR pamphlet and the present-day crisis of missing and murdered Indigenous women. The Mohawk scholar Audra Simpson had argued that Canada "requires the death and so-called 'disappearance' of Indigenous women in order to secure its sovereignty," and that the emergence of Canada as a nation-state depends upon a heteropatriarchal violence embedded in the Indian Act and other forms of legislation designed to facilitate cultural genocide (2016).[5] Simpson sees violence against Indigenous women as an extension of the heteropatriarchal violence of the state and reads the relative indifference of government and law enforcement as a manifestation of state violence against Indigenous women. *Janey's Arcadia* makes a similar claim, advancing this argument through a poetic appropriation and redeployment of colonial texts.

Elsewhere in the book, Zolf provides handwritten lists of the names of murdered and missing women. She refers to these as "bodied inscriptions and grievable names" in the notes at the end of the book and indicates that they were inscribed by various women in Winnipeg, including the relatives of missing and murdered women from the area as well as local Indigenous writers and artists and white allies. Each page contains six names, each written in a different hand and with a different type of pen. The act of inscribing the names becomes one of community-building, collaboration, and memorializing; it reminds the reader that these lives mattered, that they are grievable, and it allows the names to be readable outside the context of the "What Women Say of the Northwest" poem where they are so violently erased.

Janey's Arcadia excavates the mechanisms of what Michel Foucault calls "biopower" and reveals its centrality to both to the history of settler colonialism and its ongoing manifestations in the present. As Janine Brodie notes, Foucault's lectures on biopower are useful for linking "state racism and the rationality of modern governance" (2012, 96). Even though Foucault did not write directly about settler states, his observation that "a biological and centralized racism" (quoted in Brodie 2012, 97) emerged in the nineteenth century around an expression of a new form of political power is useful for understanding the management of Indigenous peoples under colonial rule: "Biopower focuses on . . . the population or man-as-species. . . . The operation of power through the individual body and on the population is linked and rendered coherent by norms embedded in governmental rationalities and popular discourses" (97). The Department of Indian Affairs and its involvement in the creation of residential schools and the rules determining who was and was not a "Status Indian" are examples of how colonial government operated in a biopolitical register in its "management" of Indigenous populations in Canada.[6] Figures like Emily Murphy became agents of biopolitical governance through their advocacy of eugenics in the name of nation-building.

However, Zolf is not interested in developing a poetics that only historicizes biopower or links it exclusively to the management of Indigenous bodies by colonial governments in the nineteenth and early twentieth centuries. In addition to working with historical texts, Zolf mines present-day political speeches, online comments on newspaper websites, and other contemporary texts in order to demonstrate that colonial relations, colonial violence, and the operational strategies of biopower are an object of ongoing concern in Canada that cannot be contained within historical texts or relegated to the past. In "Concentration," Zolf transposes text from Stephen Harper's apology to residential school survivors in 2008 as well as his 2009 claim that "Canada has no history of colonialism" with commentary from the *Calgary Herald* website and lines from a letter published in the *Colonial Church Chronicle and Missionary Journal* in 1847:

> If little hope could be cherished of the adult Indign
> I stand before you today to offer an apology
> I'm pretty sure I saw her pounding down
> in his wandering and unsettled habits
> six Mama Burgers® at A&W® the other day
> of life, it appeared that a wide and most
> extensive Canada has no history of
> I wish the media would stop feeling
> field presented itself for colonization
> for this botched whale. The preservation
> in the instruction of n#tive children
> of your culture is your job.
>
> Therein ligaments the sediment Goy bless
> all of you of the great Rewrite and Gord bless
> our land sniffled the original the prime
> minstrel of the Mission Rivière Rouge
> (Zolf 2014, 20)

The political impact of Zolf's poetry is located in her arrangement of these fragments of text. The poem offers a kind of topography of the legacy of settler colonialism, and the general unwillingness of white Canadians to understand their complicity in this history. Zolf preserves the optical character recognition software's errors: God bless becomes "Goy Bless" and "Gord Bess," and the "a" in "native" is replaced by a pound sign. "Prime Minister" becomes "prime minstrel." Meaning emerges through the juxtaposition of fragments. Harper's statement about Canada having no history of colonialism renders his apology to the survivors of residential schools hollow and suggests that he lacks an understanding of just what he is apologizing for, or perhaps it suggests a kind of cruel indifference. Notable in the threads of racist online commentary that Zolf incorporates into the poem is an inability to understand the dynamics of colonialism; the reader can piece together the phrase "the preservation of your culture is your job" from among the fragments.

Some of the online comments Zolf appropriates in the composition of this poem were written in response to a *Calgary Herald* article about Chief Teresa Spence's hunger strike. In December 2012, Chief Spence went on a hunger strike to protest the deplorable living conditions in her community of Attawapiskat, and to demand a meeting with Prime Minster Harper and the governor general to discuss Canada's treaty relationship with First Nations.[7] In accordance with her own cultural tradition of fasting, she allowed herself a small amount of fish broth each day, a fact that led many skeptics to question the validity of her hunger strike. Audra Simpson has argued that Chief Spence's robust body, her fatness, her "failure" to starve to death as a result of her hunger strike was not read as a positive symbol of resiliency and strength but rather as an affront. Simpson explains:

> Teresa Spence's appearance, her fleshy appearance, was itself a site of ire by commentators on-line, in twitter flame wars, and in print journalism. . . . Why this link between fat, her fat in particular, and a resistance or refusal of domination? Because what she is required to do, with or without starvation, is to die. In fact, her very life, like the lives of all Indian women in Canada is an anomaly because since the 1870s they have been legally mandated to disappear. (Simpson 2016)

Several lines in Zolf's poem echo the general scorn heaped upon Chief Spence:

> I stand before you today to offer an apology
> I'm pretty sure I saw her pounding down
> in his wandering and unsettled habits
> six Mama Burgers® at A&W® the other day
> (Zolf 2014, 20)

Spence is also referred to in the poem as a "botched whale" (Zolf 2014, 20), which is likely an OCR translation of the phrase "beached whale." In placing these fragments together, the rage directed toward Chief Spence is layered over the prime minister's speech and a missionary journal in order to explore their connections and the ways in which they collectively illustrate the contemporary Canadian social landscape, where genocidal biopolitics continue to govern the bodies of Indigenous women. While Zolf does not explain the connections, she invites readers to *infer* the connections that emerge through the layering of these fragments and their proximity to one another.

Central to Zolf's poetics is an insistence that colonization is ongoing. Zolf draws lines of continuity between the writings and actions of nineteenth-century missionaries who established residential schools for Indigenous children and the present-day activities of Christian organizations in Winnipeg. The phrase "The / aboriginal / youth / community / is a / prime / area / for / development," a phrase Zolf lifted from the website of the organization Youth for Christ, is immediately followed by a quote from the Reverend J. S. Woodsworth describing plans for residential schools: "I drew / up a / plan for / collecting / a certain / number / of them / to be / maintained, / clothed / and / educated / upon a / regularly / organized / system" (Zolf 2014, 22), suggesting a line of historical and political continuity between the two source texts. The recently built Youth For Christ Centre, a lavish facility that boasts an indoor climbing wall and skate park, is located in Winnipeg's North End, an area of the city with a large Indigenous population. Youth For Christ has an evangelical Christian mandate; according to the organization's website, their mission is "to communicate the life-changing message of Jesus Christ to every young person in Winnipeg and the surrounding area" (Youth For Christ 2017). Built in part with public money, the Youth For Christ Centre has been a source of controversy since its inception. Zolf clearly understands the Youth For Christ Centre as an extension of the colonial mandate, since it provides outreach primarily to Indigenous youth. Zolf's OCR-imbued poetics of error morphs Youth For Christ promotional material into something only faintly recognizable:

> The Yuppie for Chrisp Centre For Youth Excellence is:
> - More than a drumstick in cervix
> - More than a wreath-class climbing waltz
> - More than an indoor skiff parody featuring Canada's only indoor Indign-conversion box

- Mordant a dandelion stump
- More than a fish-classic flagellating certainty

It's where we create hordes of placentas and encumbrant contagion!

(Zolf 2014, 40)

Although Zolf's poetics of error can be read as vaguely humorous in its absurdity as "Youth for Christ" morphs into "Yuppie for Chrisp" and "world-class climbing wall" becomes "wreath-class climbing waltz," it also hints at the violence that underscores the history of missionary work in the context of colonialism. "More than a drumstick in cervix" gestures to the sexual and physical abuse that was widespread in the context of residential schools, as well as the centrality of sexual violence to the crisis of murdered and missing Indigenous women. "Indign-conversion box" plainly states the underlying mission of Youth For Christ, a mission that is consistent with the goals and aims of colonization outlined by Christian missionaries in the eighteenth and nineteenth centuries.

In seeking to write about and understand the complexities of Winnipeg's North End as a kind of contact zone, Zolf also draws on her own grandfather's autobiographical narrative *On Foreign Soil: Tales of a Wandering Jew*—Zolf's grandfather, Falk Zolf, emigrated from Europe to Winnipeg in the early twentieth century as part of a wave of Jewish immigrants escaping persecution. Zolf's interest in writing about Winnipeg initially stemmed in part from her interest in documenting the transition of the city's North End from a predominantly Jewish neighborhood to a predominantly Indigenous one. The North End in the early twentieth century was a contact zone in which European immigrants and Indigenous people coexisted. Today, the North End is still a contact zone and is primarily home to Indigenous, Filipino, and African Canadian communities. Her engagement with the Jewish history of migration in poems like "Janey and Falk (and J.S. Woodsworth) Onboard," "Falk Stalks Janey," and "Janey Loves to Falk" complicates the colonial narrative. Jews and other European migrants occupied a contradictory position; they were complicit in the dynamic of colonial dispossession since they benefited from inclusion in the colonial nation-state, yet like Indigenous people, they were often subjected to biopolitical surveillance and management, and deemed morally and racially "inferior" to British immigrants according to the imperial and colonial discourses of scientific racism and eugenics that informed colonial forms of governmentality (Brodie 2012, 94; Henderson 2003, 176). Part of Zolf's effort to "look into her own backyard" in *Janey's Arcadia* involves an investigation into the complicated role of Jewish immigration in the context of Winnipeg's settler-colonial history.

The political impact of *Janey's Arcadia* lies not only in its engagement with history but also in its reflection on how that history lives on in the present. The text "brings to the surface disavowed colonial narratives about whiteness and indigeneity that continue to haunt the Canadian national mythos and identity" (Zolf 2016). In her effort to get readers to think about the ways in which the specter of colonialism haunts the national present, Zolf extends *Janey's Arcadia* beyond the page. She has made a short video translation of three poems from *Janey's Arcadia* using pilfered National Film Board of Canada (NFB) footage. The film "draw[s] viewers into a charged encounter with the images and ideologies that have formed them" (Zolf 2015) by underscoring the governmental role the NFB played in the colonization of Indigenous people and the cultural assimilation of non-Anglo settler immigrants. She has also orchestrated polyvocal performative actions in several cities in North America. These actions bring the poems from *Janey's Arcadia* into the fraught space of the contemporary settler city, where they become embodied, collaborative acts of assembly and resistance that confirm the political and ethical stakes of her approach to poetry and her ability to facilitate charged encounters that move her work powerfully from page to world.[8] Zolf forces her readers to confront settler colonialism not only as a historical event, but also as an ongoing national crisis that continues to unfold and in which all settlers are complicit.

Ontologies of Personhood: Corporations, Democracy and Constitutional Rights in Jena Osman's *Corporate Relations*

Like Rachel Zolf's *Janey's Arcadia*, Jena Osman's *Corporate Relations* (2014) draws on texts that are central to national identity and nation-building, this time in an American context, in order to raise ethical questions about rights, protections, precarity, and citizenship. While Zolf's poems address the question of what counts as a grievable life in the context of the nation, Osman's poems address the equally complex ethical question of who or what constitutes a legal person entitled to protection under United States law. Like her earlier collections *The Character* (1999), *The Network* (2010), and *Public Figures* (2012), *Corporate Relations* is part of Osman's ongoing interest in using poetic form to explore the intersections of nation, history, democracy, legal discourses, public space, and power relations. *Corporate Relations* engages the U.S. Constitution as a living document that shapes and limits personal and collective freedoms.[9] Specifically, the poems in this collection explore the ways in which legal interpretations of the Constitution expand rights for "juridical persons" (corporations) over and above the rights of humans. Each section of the book responds to a different constitutional amendment from the Bill of Rights and includes poems constructed from the language of Supreme Court cases that drew on those amendments to uphold corporate personhood and protect the rights of corporations, often at the expense of the rights of individuals.

Many of the legal cases from which these poems are comprised date back to the nineteenth and early twentieth centuries, emphasizing the fact that corporate personhood is not just a recent phenomenon linked to a neoliberal tendency to apply market logic to all dimensions of life, but in fact has roots in legal decisions from the 1880s and has become progressively embedded in U.S. law over the past 150 years.

Legal cases in which the Supreme Court has drawn on the concept of corporate personhood to uphold the rights of corporations at the expense of individuals raise ethical and philosophical questions not only about democracy, but also about what it means legally and ethically to *be* a person entitled to rights and protections under federal law. *Corporate Relations* goes beyond a mere critique of corporate personhood to ask questions about ontology and subjectivity. While Zolf uses the glitch to destabilize meaning and introduce a poetics of hauntological error that becomes the locus of political and social critique in her work, Osman uses the unsettling and uncanny figures of the automaton, the ventriloquist's dummy, the puppet, and the robot to destabilize subjectivity and to frame the "corporate person" as a profoundly uncanny entity whose powers exceed the reach of its creator. Osman mines popular culture, literature, and philosophy for examples of the blurring of human and nonhuman to explore the unsettling plurality and animatedness of the corporate "person," a legal entity that is comprised of groups of individuals registered as a corporation. In the notes at the end of the book, she observes that the "separation of the corporation from the individuals that make it up reanimates the age-old ideas of a mind-body split" and remarks that "we are simultaneously attracted and repelled by the cognitive autonomy of our own creations: their immortality, their limited accountability, the impossibility of their imprisonment, their tendency to change citizenship overnight" (Osman 2014, 73).

This instability and uncertainly regarding legal personhood is introduced in the opening poem, "The Beautiful Life of Persona Ficta." "Persona ficta" essentially means "legal personality" and is a term used to describe the prerequisite for having legal rights. One must be a "persona ficta" to enter a legal contract, which makes "persona ficta" the criterion for being recognized as human under American law. Legal persons are further subdivided into two categories: "natural persons," or biological persons who are recognized as legal persons by virtue of their having been born; and "juridical persons," which consist of groups of people that acquire the status of a legal person after they are incorporated. Each of the poem's verse paragraphs begins with an analogy that complicates the distinctions between corporations, humans, and machines. The poem opens with the analogy "a corporation is to a person as a person is to a machine" (Osman 2014, 11), but then goes on to complicate this formulation. The second verse paragraph reads:

> a corporation is to a body as a body is to a puppet
> > putting it in caricature, if there are natural persons then there are those who are not that, buying candidates. there are those who are strong on the ground and then weak in the air. weight shifts to the left leg while the propaganda arm extends.
>
> (Osman 2014, 11)

The poem enacts a slippage from person to machine and from body to puppet, and in the process, raises questions about the ontology of personhood: if corporations can be "persons" under the law, what does it mean to be human? If the corporation is a legal person, then what is its bodily form? Might it assume the form of a puppet, a robot, or some other vaguely unsettling entity that disrupts the boundary between animate and inanimate with its awkward, lurching stride and extended "propaganda arm"?

Osman builds on the legal definition of personhood and the distinction between natural and juridical persons. The poem goes on to present more complex analogies of personhood. The third analogy in the poem reads: "a corporation is to an individual as an individual is to an uncanny valley" (Osman 2014, 11). "Uncanny valley" is a concept developed by robotics engineers to describe the sense of unease that occurs when a robot seems *too* lifelike; the resemblance between robot and human that is too convincing prompts fear and disgust because it unsettles the boundaries of the human (Morton 2013, 130). In offering this analogy, Osman foregrounds the menacing aspects of corporate personhood; the corporation that comes to closely resemble the human becomes monstrous and threatening because it collapses the distinction between the human and the nonhuman, specifically in the arena of constitutional rights, where corporations are granted the same rights and protections as humans.

Many of the analogies in this poem ascribe affective and human qualities to corporations, and corporate and mechanical qualities to human subjects and human bodies, scrambling the distinctions between human and nonhuman and exacerbating the sense of uncanniness related to the blurring of human and machine and the humanizing of corporations. Here are the opening lines of five of the poem's remaining verse paragraphs:

> a corporation has convictions as a person has mechanical parts (11)
> a corporation has likes and dislikes as a body has shareholders (11)
> a corporation gives birth as a natural human births profit margins (11)
> a corporation has an enthusiasm for ethical behavior as a creature has economic interests only (12)
> a corporation is we the people as a person is a cog
> (Osman 2014, 12)

These statements are followed by descriptions of the mechanized monstrous body of the corporation: "they / create an eminent body that is different from their own selves" (Osman 2014, 11), suggesting that the corporate body functions as a kind of shell beneath which a group of people might assemble to seek protection, accumulate wealth, be exploited, or exploit others. Osman describes the lurching, mechanical movements of this body, "lead leg exaggerates the knee lift / of a normal stride. cordless microphones, remote control systems, hidden / tape recorders" (12). The distinctions between body and machine, human and corporation, collapse in the poem just as legal discourses of corporate personhood unsettle the distinction between human and corporation and ascribe to the corporation affects and emotions that are more commonly associated with the human, while ascribing to the human a kind of machinic and affectless quality: "a corporation warms the bed and wraps its arms around you and just wants / to spoon as a natural human wants to organize profits" (12). Osman's personification of the corporation is deliberately absurd in order to illustrate the ridiculousness of legal discourses of corporate personhood, yet it is also unsettling and uncanny as it plays on ontological fears about the fragility of human subjectivity and the ethics of creating artificial forms of personhood. Osman sees the juridical person as akin to an automaton breaking away from its master and wreaking havoc on its creator.

The remaining sections of *Corporate Relations* each take as their focus a constitutional amendment and the Supreme Court cases in which these amendments were invoked to uphold corporate personhood. Cumulatively, the poems in *Corporate Relations* powerfully demonstrate how corporate personhood, validated and enshrined through Supreme Court rulings and interpretations, has functioned to erode democracy and human rights in America and render precarious the lives of those who under the law are known as "natural persons." While this kind of critique could be achieved in the form of an expository essay, Osman's use of the poetic form is unique in its direct engagement (through procedural compositional strategies, poetic redistribution, and philosophical reflection) with the language of the court cases. In a review of *Corporate Relations*, Kent Shaw argues that the poetic form of this text is crucial to the ethical and political critique it advances. Shaw writes:

"How I feel this book needs to be poetry, and can succeed most fully in its lyric form, is to open the Bill of Rights as a human document intended to protect humans living in the United States from powerful humans or the organizations powerful humans are often employed by as they inevitably reach past common decency for their own selfish gains." With each amendment, Osman "makes clear the moral consequences of depersonalizing the constitution or personalizing the corporation" (Shaw 2014). In fragmenting, weaving together, and rearranging the speech of Supreme Court lawyers and judges, legal testimony, and legal rulings, Osman constructs poems that are grounded in the facts of the legal cases to which she refers (each section of *Corporate Relations* contains long explanatory paragraphs anchoring the reader's understanding in relation to the relevant legal cases, and the book includes an appendix that provides concrete explanations of all of the constitutional amendments invoked in the poems) but that also defamiliarize, recontextualize, and open up the language of these legal cases, transposing this language into poems that offer ethical and political insight and reflection.

"First Amendment Rights," the sequence of poems that address rulings in favor of corporate personhood based on the First Amendment rights of freedom of speech, freedom of assembly, freedom of religion, and freedom of the press, includes a poem based on the 1978 court case *First National Bank of Boston v. Bellotti* in which it was decided that corporations could make contributions to ballot initiative campaigns. As Osman explains, the lawyer representing the bank argued that because corporations do not have actual mouths, advertising was the only way they could disseminate their opinions. The Suprme Court ruled in favor of the bank, not because corporations have a right to free speech, but rather because humans have a right to *hear* speech. The poem begins:

the rights of the listener

limiting the stock of information

mental exploration

a megaphone

today, I will address the mootness question

what will happen in the future

I certainly hope so your honor, they owe me some money

the corporation can not have opinions   that is unanimous

money is speech and speech is protected

it cannot squelch

the right of the public to hear
(Osman 2014, 15)

The poem is constructed from various aspects of the court case and not just the majority ruling. Osman disarranges the logic of the legal ruling, opening its language to new interpretations by transposing and juxtaposing the voices of lawyers, witnesses, and Supreme Court justices. She concludes the poem with a quotation from the dissenting legal opinion from Justice Rehnquist in the *First National Bank* case, in which he quotes an 1819 legal ruling: "A corporation is an artificial being, invisible, intangible, and existing only in contemplation of law" (Osman 2014, 17). Many of the poems incorporate dissenting opinions, adding to the polyvocality of the text and underscoring the fact that these rulings were contentious. The inclusion of the dissenting opinions could be read as a testament to democracy, an assertion that dissenting opinions can be registered and acknowledged. However, because these are minority judicial opinions, they also serve to reinforce the fact that the majority ruled in favor of corporations.

Osman engages with the high-profile 2010 Supreme Court case *Citizens United v. Federal Election Commission* in which it was decided that limits on corporate and union expenditures during an election campaign are an impediment to free speech. Wendy Brown writes extensively about *Citizens United* in *Undoing the Demos: Neoliberalism's Stealth Revolution*, arguing that the court's ruling rested on an understanding of speech as capital. Brown argues that neoliberalism made this ruling possible because under neoliberalism, all dimensions of life are reduced to a framework governed by market rationality. Brown identifies a rhetorical slippage in Justice Kennedy's legal ruling in which speech is figured as analogous to capital in the political marketplace, and the accumulation and circulation of speech is understood as an unqualified good and an essential human right (2015, 173).[10] Osman's compositional strategy of recirculating speech can be read as an ironic enactment of speech-as-capital; her recombinatory poetic strategy recirculates legal speech in a poetic economy that mimics and subverts the political economy and market rationality that informed Justice Kennedy's ruling. However, *Corporate Relations*, with its focus on cases dating back to the nineteenth century, also suggests that the verdict in *Citizens United* was made possible not just by a neoliberal understanding of speech as capital, as Brown argues, but also by a long history of legal rulings in favor of corporate personhood in the United States. The conditions under which speech becomes thinkable as capital are not simply produced by neoliberal ideology; rather, rulings in favor of corporate personhood have created an environment in which a neoliberal market rationality can thrive and become understood as a component of democracy even as it actively works to undo democratic principles.[11]

The preoccupation with machines, robots, puppets, and other nonanimate entities that mimic living humans introduced in "Persona Ficta" continues in the section of poems on First Amendment rights. Through repeated references to automata and other nonhuman objects that assume human form and even mimic human speech, Osman explores the unsettling and uncanny dimensions of artificial life, especially when "juridical" persons are granted rights and protections denied to "natural" persons. Many of these poems address the First Amendment rights of freedom of speech and the right of the people to peaceably assemble (Osman 2014, 75). As the distinction between artificial and natural persons becomes blurred, corporate speech mimics, replaces, and overwrites the speech of actual individuals. "A Mouth" begins with the lines "no mouth / a human person torn down from the platform / permission to speak denied" (2014, 18), suggesting the suppression of public speech and the right to public assembly for "natural" persons and the simultaneous proliferation of corporate speech. Corporations, after all, are mouthless according to the courts, and are thus allowed to make their opinions known through other means. Those who are mouthless must attain a proxy mouth in order to put their words into the mouth of another; for Osman, the mouth of the ventriloquist's doll becomes a powerful extended metaphor for corporate speech. The poem continues with a detailed description of the physiology of ventriloquism and links ventriloquism to corporate speech:

> the voice appears to come from various points and not from the actual speaker
> teeth closed and lips only slightly parted
> placing a hand at the back of the political neck or within the hollow
> congressional body and moving a lever with the thumb
> voice thrown
>
> (Osman 2014, 18)

The ventriloquist functions here as a powerful symbol for the veiled voice of corporate America whose opinions are articulated by stealth and whose influence on Congress is concealed.

The collapse of the distinction between human and nonhuman also informs "Gag Order," a poem that begins with a reference to Descartes's unsettlingly lifelike automaton Francine (Osman 2014, 22). Descartes sought to establish a philosophical basis by which humans could be differentiated from other animals; he believed that automata could replicate "lower animals" but never the complexity of human speech (22). His famous observation—*cogito ergo sum*, "I think therefore I am"—a concept central to the formulation of Cartesian dualism or the mind/body split, was developed in part as a response to the "growing body of research that pointed to the overwhelming physical commonality between humans and animals" that made it "imperative to locate the immortality of the soul in the human mind" (Grenville 2002, 14).[12] As previously stated, Osman sees corporate personhood as a "reanimation" of Cartesian dualism (Osman 2014, 73). She offers a description of the laborious physical process of animating the jaw of a ventriloquist puppet in order to mimic the movement of authentic speech:

a downward movement pulls the mouth open
by means of a picture wire
or gut string,
a spring
causing the jaw to close
as the wire is relaxed
a slot in the back of the head
(Osman 2014, 22)

Speech is presented as far from natural, yet as the persistent references to ventriloquism throughout the text suggest, the "corporate person" or persona ficta is a kind of animated doll, a fake, proxy person voiced by the corporation hidden in the shadows that goes to great lengths to both animate the persona ficta's body and to conceal the source of its speech. Corporate speech is depicted as awkward, lurching, and mechanical but legally protected, often to a greater degree, than the speech of natural persons.

"Manchurian Candidate" again revisits the theme of ventriloquism; here Osman depicts the mechanics and structure of the ventriloquist's doll using somewhat violent language:

a straight piece of wire driven through the side of the face
from cheek to cheek
a spiral spring strong enough to pull the mouth shut smartly
after being opened by a tug on the picture wire below
a wire driven through the neck stick
the head readily removable for packing
(Osman 2014, 27)

The speaker cautions: "when you are ready to try this voice in public / take your position as far from the company as possible" (Osman 2014, 27) so as to lessen the appearance of corporate interference in the democratic process. Ventriloquism becomes a powerful metaphor for both the body of the "juridical person" and corporate influence in law and politics, where one never quite knows whose interests are being prioritized or whose unseen hands and voice are animating the uncanny figure at the podium.

Subsequent sections of the book include poems composed from Supreme Court cases that draw on Fourth, Fifth, Sixth, Seventh, and Fourteenth Amendment rights to uphold corporate personhood. In each case, Osman powerfully illustrates the ethical shortcomings of these legal rulings; amendment rights that were implemented with the intention of protecting all citizens are consistently used to deny rights to the most precarious while enshrining the rights of corporations. The poem "Santa Clara v. Southern Pacific Railroad" engages an 1886 Supreme Court case in which the railroad company's defense for not paying taxes invoked its Fourteenth Amendment rights, which guarantee freedoms of equal protections of all persons (Osman 2014, 65). The lawyers for the company argued that this law also applied to corporations and that under the Fourteenth Amendment, it was discriminatory to have different taxes and different laws in different states. As Osman explains, this amendment was originally intended to grant equal protection to former slaves, the most precarious of citizens, yet the ruling was used in practice to shore up the power of those who were already among the wealthiest and most secure. This poem is unusual in its form because it is primarily comprised of prose passages, including a lengthy explanation of the case, a note by Abraham Lincoln criticizing the way that "corporations have been enthroned" and warning that "an era of corruption in high places will follow" (2014, 66), as well as several quotations from lawyers and judges. The poem concludes with a quotation from Justice Hugo Black's dissenting opinion in a similar case in 1938 in which Black states: "of the cases in this Court in which the Fourteenth Amendment was applied during the first fifty years after its adoption, less than one-half of 1 per cent invoked it in the protection of the negro race, and more that 50 per cent asked that its benefits be extended to corporations" (67). The speaker warns that "citizens may become subject to the unrestrained power of those who possess / the machinery of government" (66). Those who possess the "machinery of government" are, of course, the corporations, which are themselves presented as machinic, uncanny, and unsettling in their attempt to mimic human form.

Corporate Relations draws attention to the persistent ethical failures of American democracy and the American justice system to protect the most precarious of citizens. Time and again, these poems suggest, the rights of the corporation trump the rights of the individual as constitutional amendments meant to protect citizens and ensure equality are perversely interpreted to ensure the opposite. But the text is not entirely devoid of optimism. In the notes at the end of the text, Osman remarks that while the American "plus one," the corporation as an entity with constitutional rights, seems threatening and monstrous, we might conceptualize other forms of the "plus one" that are more subversive and generative and that might counter a neoliberal individualism:

> I thought about tales of resistance, how people can band together to fight against the odds. How a group of people can form a crowd, a surge, a wave. How the crowd can seem to have a mind of its own.
>
> Must the plus one always be a monster? (Osman 2014, 73)

How, under other circumstances, might the coming together of people speaking as one function to disrupt hegemonic power? Large protests like Occupy, Tahrir Square, Gezi Park, the Water Protectors resisting the Dakota Access Pipeline, and the round dances that occurred in the context of Idle No More come to mind as examples. *Corporate Relations* was published in 2014 and written while the Occupy Movement was taking place. The human microphone deployed by those involved in Occupy and other protest movements also functions as a concrete example of people speaking as one.[13] Jodi Dean frames these protest movements as "crowds" that have "disrupted the settings given by capital and the state" (2016, 6) and as "fronts in global communicative capitalism's class war" (16).

Forms of public assembly involve, as Judith Butler argues, the "performative enactment of bodies" (2015, 177) and an insistence on a collective identity as "the people." When people take to the streets in protest, assembling under the assertion "we the people,"

> they are asserting that they, those who appear to speak there, are identified as "the people." They are working to ward off the prospect of oblivion. The phrase does not imply that those who profit are not "the people," and it does not necessarily imply a simple sense of inclusion: "we are the people, too." It can mean "we are *still* the people"—therefore, still persisting and not yet destroyed, or it can assert a form of equality in the face of increasing

inequality; participants do this not by simply uttering that phrase, but by embodying equality to whatever extent that proves possible, constituting an assembly of the people on the grounds of equality. (Butler 2015, 181)

Occupy, along with other recent anti-precarity demonstrations, are powerful, performative, embodied enactments that call for a new form of sociality (Butler 2015, 183). An assembly of persons as "we the people" in the context of political protest is radically different from the assembly of people under the mask or shell of the corporation, yet both are manifestations of the "plus one," the collective of bodies uniting under a single cause or entity.

Corporate Relations concludes with a poem called "Industrial Palace" which focuses on the relationship between the individual and the collective and the split between the mind and the body. On the one hand, this poem conceives of the human body as a kind of factory or machine in which "air is carried by pulley or wheel" and "the liver is a chemical plant" (Osman 2014, 72), echoing Descartes's understanding of the physical body as a kind of machine. On the other hand, it complicates this formulation by locating the "plus one," the assembly of "we the people," *within* the context of the body (the body here could be read as a metaphorical "body politic"). If the automaton or puppet is monstrous and nonhuman because at its core one finds only wires and string and its movements are controlled by an unseen force like a computer programmer, a ventriloquist, or a corporation, at the core of the body in "Industrial Palace" one finds, in contrast, a collection of homunculi working as a collective to facilitate the body's biological processes:

> six at the table of the teeth
> cutting, puncturing, sawing,
> grinding, rolling, grating
> further down the line
> four in black convert sugar to starch
> with the help of ladders they lift the blocks
> onto the conveyor belt
> (Osman 2014, 72)

The body-as-factory in "Industrial Palace" is populated with workers; each "person" in this factory has a job to do:

> the one at the ear has his ear to a wire
> connected to a large web of sound
> one stands behind the bellows camera of the eye
> ready to pull the shutter
> (Osman 2014, 71)

These workers could be read as exploited laborers at the mercy of the "suited one [who] reads alone in the office of sensation" (Osman 2014, 71); we learn that the "pistons, pipes, and turbines" that carry the body's oxygen are "property of the corporators" (72). However, the poem presents a rather more ambiguous reflection on the possibilities of collaboration and collective action. Osman reflects on different kinds of group formations and their potential to act in and on the world. A "group of persons are authorized to act as one / a group of persons combine in one body" (71) could describe a corporation, but it could also describe other forms of collective action like the Occupy protests or the round dances that occurred in the context of the Idle No More protests.

Osman refers in this poem to "a group of persons as a tamed institution" (2014, 71) but goes on in the next line to describe "a group of persons as secretly exerting power" (71), suggesting the possibility of agency and resistance within any form of assembly. She draws a distinction between a collection of *persons* (a corporate relation) and a collection of *individuals* working in harmony (a public assembly): "a collection of individuals serves the greater good / a collection of persons serves profit only" (72). *Corporate Relations* moves from an understanding of the "plus one" as the monstrous body of the juridical person to an exploration of the potential of the plus one as a form of peaceful assembly and collective action. "Industrial Palace" considers the actual human subjects behind the mask of corporate personhood, human beings who may uphold the ideas and values of the corporation, who may be oppressed by the corporation, but who might also hold the potential to rise up in protest; the "plus one" is not necessarily a monster, and perhaps it can form a "crowd, a surge, a wave" that "seem[s] to have a mind of its own" (73), a collective form of assembly like Idle No More, the Arab Spring, or the Occupy Movement.

Through her engagement with the U.S. Constitution, and specifically with constitutional amendments, Osman explores the irony of the fact that the Constitution, a document written with the intent to ensure the protection of citizens under the law, is often interpreted by the Supreme Court in ways that radically undermine the principles of democracy and the rights of citizens. "We the people," a phrase from the preamble to the Constitution, is implicitly invoked in *Corporate Relations* to assert not only the danger of including corporations under the banner of "the people," but also the potential for collective forms of assembly and dissent in which "the people" can push back against corporate influence.

A Box of Longing with Fifty Drawers: Jen Benka's Poetics of Dissent

If "we the people" is invoked implicitly by Jena Osman, it is invoked explicitly by Jen Benka in *A Box of Longing with Fifty Drawers* (2005), another book of poems that engages with the U.S. Constitution and American democracy in order to enact a poetics of dissent. *A Box of Longing with Fifty Drawers* consists of 52 poems, inspired by each of the 52 words in the preamble to the U.S. Constitution. The single-word title of each poem reflects, in sequence, the words of the preamble, which reads: "We the people of the United States, in order to form a more perfect union, establish justice, insure domestic tranquility, provide for the common defense, promote the general welfare, and secure the blessings of liberty to ourselves and our posterity, do ordain and establish this Constitution for the United States of America." At the time of its inception, the preamble to the Constitution functioned as a performative assertion of America's legal break from Britain (Butler 2015, 154). Within both legal and popular contexts, it further functions as an articulation of the general aspirations of the Constitution, and is consulted by lawmakers to determine the intent of the Constitution. It is a statement of great importance to American culture and identity, yet, as Benka's poems powerfully illustrate, in many regards, America fails to live up to the promises and intentions that are articulated there.

In *Notes Toward a Performative Theory of Assembly*, Judith Butler writes extensively about the first three words of the preamble to the Constitution, arguing that "We the people" has a performative force. "We the people" signifies a "people coming together, forming a way of speaking as a collective, and demanding a change in policy, exposing the absence of state legitimacy or the dissolution of a government" (Butler 2015, 155). "We the people" is invoked in public assemblies like Occupy, assemblies that come into being "precisely as public space is either sold off or subject to various kinds of securitarian control" (154). Published in 2005, Benka's book predates Occupy and most of the other widespread protest movements that have emerged in the early twenty-first century, but it is written in opposition to the same culture of precarity that galvanized the Occupy movement and, like Occupy, its assertion of "we the people" designates a plural subject, an assembly of precarious bodies "working to ward off the prospect of oblivion" (Butler 2015, 181).

As a set of rules, laws, and aspirations, the Constitution functions as a kind of organizing principle to consolidate the legal, ethical, and ultimately utopian vision of the new country and to performatively declare independence from England. The poem "Constitution" refers to the writing of "the first words / there in the blind dark of our history" as a kind of "order sprung from the center of chaos" (Benka 2005, 48). Throughout *A Box of Longing with Fifty Drawers*, Benka weighs the utopian promise of the Constitution against the lived historical and contemporary realities of American class structures, racial hierarchies, and heteropatriarchal structures of privilege. As she explains in the poem "Justice": "one theory suggests / that all theories / in their translation to practice / rely on innocent people / to pay the price for progress" (17).

The fifty-two poems that comprise this collection paint a picture of America as a nation in many ways unable to realize the utopian aspirations of the Constitution in spite of the Constitution's legal and symbolic importance as a living document. "We the people," as Butler notes, operates through terms of both inclusion and exclusion; Benka's poems address the inclusionary, exclusionary, and hierarchical structures of citizenship enacted within the context of the nation called into being as "We the people." Benka's poems move between past and present to show that the failure to live up to the ideals espoused in the Constitution is a historical constant even if the specific conditions of that failure change over time. This failure has been manifested in the context of settler colonialism, slavery, racial segregation, institutionalized homophobia and heterosexism, systematic discrimination against women, the failure of the welfare state, and in the maintenance of a capitalist system that facilitates the consolidation of wealth in the hands of the most privileged members of society. "We," the first poem in the collection, acknowledges a shared complicity in the kind of inequality that these poems seek to explore, repeatedly asking "where were we during the convening / two hundred years ago or yesterday," as if to suggest a long history of complacency among "we, not of planter class, but mud hands digging" (Benka 2005, 1). She cautions, "these words, are missing / the tired, the poor, the waylaid" (1), naming just some of those left out of the pledge of equality and justice issued in the preamble to the Constitution.[14] Other poems address the history of colonialism. "States" depicts the settlement of the area now known as the United States of America as an act of thievery; the poem reads in its entirety: "this land has no name / not taken, thieves / tracing rivers and t-squares / more borders" (7). Benka also focuses on more contemporary manifestations of inequality and oppression. "Welfare" explores the assumptions regularly made with regard to people who collect welfare: "says all winter long they have babies / so they don't have to work / says makes me sick" (30).

Most of the poems in this collection explore the public and the historical as the locus of inequality and exclusion, but some address the private and intimate. The poem "For" (Benka 2005, 22) describes a sexual encounter between two women. While this poem does not explore a scene of inequality so much as it explores an erotic encounter, it is an encounter between two women who are not entitled to the rights and benefits afforded to their heterosexual counterparts under federal law. The Defense of Marriage Act (DOMA)[15] is never directly invoked in *A Box of Longing with Fifty Drawers*, but much of Benka's poetic oeuvre is devoted to critiquing this piece of legislation. Her chapbook (coauthored with Carol Mirakove) titled *1,138* (2007) engages critically with

DOMA; the title of the chapbook refers to the 1,138 rights afforded to heterosexual citizens and denied to same-sex couples. In the context of this collection, "For" points to the ways in which structural social inequalities, written into federal legislation, can encroach on the most intimate of relations.

The title of the collection, *A Box of Longing with Fifty Drawers*, refers to the fifty states in the union as "drawers" and the nation as a "box of longing." As a "box of longing," the nation is an affectively charged space, a space of longing and desire, and a space with fifty points of entry, or, depending on one's understanding of the function of drawers, fifty enclosed spaces in which to conceal or obscure things. The title comes from the final lines of "America," the concluding poem in the collection. In this poem, citizens participate in the "delusion of discovery" of this "promised land lemonade stand":

> the dreams:
> of corn field wheat field tobacco field oil
> of iron cage slave trade cotton plantation
> of hog farm dairy farm cattle ranch range
> of mississippi mason-dixon mountains
> of territories salt lake lottery gold
> of saw mill steel mill coal mine diamond.
>
> topographic, economic
> industry and war.
>
> a box of longing
> with fifty drawers.
> (Benka 2005, 55)

But what is "longed for" in this formulation? Freedom? Wealth? Territory? Military might? Perhaps nationalism or patriotism can be configured as a kind of longing for one's country; the nation becomes a "box" that contains the collective longing of its citizens, longings that may be contradictory and incoherent. Perhaps the Constitution itself is a site of longing that is reflected in its idealistic articulation of a just society. Longing might also refer to the critical stance of the poet who longs for a more just society, one that lives up to the ideals embodied in the

Constitution. The poems in *A Box of Longing with Fifty Drawers* hold all of these meanings in tension as the nation emerges as a fraught site of struggle and inequality.

By working directly with and responding to elements of the U.S. Constitution, Jena Osman and Jen Benka both develop a poetics of dissent to illustrate the fact that the American ideals of democracy and equality espoused by the Constitution do not necessarily translate into actual equality and democratic freedom in the context of day-to-day living. Both engage the Constitution as a living document, and both write poems that critically reflect on *who* or *what* is granted protection under the law and has the right to public assembly, domestic tranquility, welfare, and security. Both investigate the processes by which these rights are withheld or deployed in ways that ensure the concentration of wealth, power, and freedom in the hands of select citizens.

Janey's Arcadia, Corporate Relations, and *A Box of Longing with Fifty Drawers* explore the disjunction between, on the one hand, juridical-political national discourses that emphasize civility and the rights of citizens and, on the other hand, a heteropatriarchal, exclusionary violence closely aligned with discourses of capitalism and nation-building. All three writers undermine nostalgic and sentimental attachments to the nation, and for each of these writers, articulating a poetics of dissent involves not just identifying this disjunction, but building poems that critically embody it through their direct engagement with primary texts that are closely aligned with national identity and history. All three of the writers discussed in this chapter participate in what Joan Retallack calls "a poetics of responsibility with the courage of the swerve. . . . Swerves (like antiromantic modernisms, the civil rights movement, feminism, postcolonialist critiques) are necessary to dislodge us from reactionary allegiances and nostalgias" (2003, 3). They defamiliarize texts that are deemed nationally significant in an effort to reflect critically on discourses central to national identity, ideology, and history, and through procedural methods, recontextualization, and redeployment, they detect possibilities and strategies for reading these historically and nationally significant texts differently. All three writers frame public assembly and protest as crucial for a poetics of dissent that insists upon the grievability of all citizens and pushes against the forms of precarity that are instituted by the capitalist, colonial state. For Zolf, this means advancing a politics and poetics of decolonization. For Osman, it means developing a politics and poetics that grapples with the strange, pluralized entity known as the corporation and asks fundamental questions about ontology, personhood, and the possibility of collective action. For Benka, it means thinking seriously about the tension between the ideals articulated in the Constitution and the historical and material inequalities that characterize American public life and culture. I am wary of collapsing these somewhat different projects together because, as Juliana Spahr warns, "looking at formal (or aesthetic) similarities can run the risk of depoliticizing, of totalizing, or of eliding asymmetries of power." However, while drawing analogies and connections can lead to oversimplified readings of formally and politically complex texts, they can also point to "the possibility of shared forms assembled, used, or reinterpreted among groups" (Spahr 2001a, 155). Perhaps Zolf, Osman, and Benka can be read, at least provisionally, as a poetic "plus one," an assembly of poets united in a politically driven documentary procedural poetics that critically engages with nationhood while also challenging the terms by which categories like "person" and "citizen" are established and maintained in the context of the colonialist and capitalist nation-state.

Coda

THE POETRY DISCUSSED in these pages maps a critical feminist space in opposition to the neoliberal, militaristic, and individualistic currents of the early twenty-first century. Much of this poetry is documentary. Much of it works with found text. It advocates embracing the materiality of language, bodies, and things. It is critical of hetropatriarchal capitalism, and of the ways in which nationalism is deployed in the interests of militarism and sometimes even genocide. It intersects politically and conceptually with recent theoretical work on affect, new materialisms, and the posthuman. All of the books discussed here were published in the fifteen years between 9/11 and the election of Donald Trump, a time that saw increasing political destabilization in the Middle East in large part due to Western military intervention and occupation; the intensification of news-as-entertainment and its circulation in digital environments, which eventually led to the rise of "fake news" and the refusal of mainstream media to engage with policy issues in any depth; the increased deregulation and privatization of public services; the rise of white nationalism and neofascism; renewed attempts to outlaw abortion and regulate women's bodies and sexuality; the intensification of destructive forms of resource extraction, often at the expense of the health and well-being of Indigenous communities; the expansion of the prison industrial complex; the growth of a culture of conspicuous consumption fueled by global capitalism; the hollowing out of the middle class in North America and Europe; and the intensification of a culture of precarity. The bulk of this project was completed prior to Trump's surprise victory in the 2016 American presidential election, but I finish my last revisions as Trump finishes his first year in office. Trump's presidency signals a shift in the American political landscape that I could not have anticipated while writing this book, but in retrospect, the poetry explored in this volume critically documents and opposes the cultural and social shifts that created the conditions for Trump's victory.

I write this from Canada, a country connected to the United States culturally, economically, and geographically yet also at a remove. Canada remains governed by a neoliberal political party that shares much in common with the Democratic Party in the United States. There is much to criticize about the Canadian government, from its arms deal with Saudi Arabia to its approval of the Kinder Morgan Pipeline expansion to its continued oppression of Indigenous peoples; the Trudeau government has not presented an alternative to the neoliberal status quo. Nevertheless, the political situation in Canada at present is not as volatile as that in the United States, nor are its citizens as polarized. Much of this book has argued for reading innovative American and Canadian feminist poetries together, yet given the events of the past year, once might wonder if the issues facing Canadians and Americans will diverge, and whether this will be reflected in our national protest poetries, since Canadian poetry might remain anchored in opposition to a neoliberal state founded on colonial genocide,[1] while American poetry might respond to the rise of a racist and heteropatriarchal kleptocracy that has no exact parallel north of the border (although right-wing populist and white supremacist movements are on the rise in Canada as well [Dangerfield 2017]).

The election of Donald Trump signals an alarming convergence of capitalism, xenophobia, and antidemocratic tendencies. In the words of Henry A. Giroux, America is "at war with itself":

> Democracy is under assault, and undisguised manifestations of violent proto-fascims are being propelled to the forefront of national political life. As this occurs, we bear witness to a media system that is enriched by a repugnant escalation of intolerance and violence. Today it's immigrants, communities of color, Latinos, Muslims, and protestors. But the list is constantly under review, and if you are progressive and you are not already on it, you may be tomorrow. Given those conditions, it becomes frightfully clear that the conditions for totalitarianism and state violence are still with us, attack-

ing multiculturalism, criminalizing protest, smothering critical thought, ridiculing social responsibility, foreclosing the ethical imagination, and dismissing democracy itself. (Giroux 2017, 227)

One could declare that poetry did nothing to stop the rise of Donald Trump and right-wing populist movements around the world; perhaps energy would be better spent marching in the streets, occupying public spaces in protest, and calling and writing to elected officials rather than writing or reading poetry. However, poetry and art have always accompanied protest and are crucial dimensions of political dissent. Poetry may not enact direct political change or facilitate revolution; however, poetry *can* provide a space of documentation, reflection, witness, and resistance. Poetry holds the potential to help us develop new forms of agency for engaging contemporary politics, and new literacies for reading our world.

A creative praxis of dissent, one that involves poetry as well as other art forms, is increasingly urgent, and must occur in tandem with grassroots activism and protest. In a recent article called "Poetry and Agency under Trump," David Micah Greenburg argues that although it is too early to determine how writers and artists will respond to a Trump presidency, poetry is a crucial form to watch because

> poetry explores the nature of agency itself—what it means to summon the presence to act effectively and in relationship to others. Poems are intense, memorable, and require interpretation, in the same way that agency requires will, direction, and judgment. Poetry's concern with voice draws attention to issues of speaker and audience, in the way that action, by definition, must occur alongside and along with others. And just as agency brings together intention and experience, poetry elevates language to draw attention to the experience of text, even as the reader simultaneously interprets ways that formal and linguistic choices demonstrate some intention. (Greenburg 2017)

Greenburg argues that now is the time to pay particular attention to poets who devote much of their time to activism because they in particular will find ways to "bring a sense of agency to poetry."

A poetics that explores the political dimensions of affect; demonstrates an understanding of subjectivity as posthuman and transcorporeal; critically reflects on the impact of capitalism on queer, racialized, female, disabled, and non-normative bodies; and develops an ethical vocabulary for reimagining the nation-state and critically engaging with issues of democracy and citizenship is now more urgent than ever. The poems discussed in this book bring a sense of agency to poetry; they seek new vocabularies and dissenting critical and aesthetic frameworks for thinking across issues of gender, materiality, capitalism, the toxic convergences of nationalism and racism, and the decline of democracy. This is poetry that *matters* both in its political urgency and in its attentiveness to the world as "matter," as a material entity under siege; it could not be more urgent or more relevant.

PERMISSIONS

The section on Juliana Spahr's *This Connection of Everyone with Lungs* originally appeared in 2014 in *Mosaic, An Interdisciplinary Critical Journal* 47, no. 2: 203–18.

The section on Rachel Zolf's *Human Resources* developed from a chapter that initially appeared in 2015 in *Public Poetics: Critical Issues in Canadian Poetry and Poetics*, 65–86 (Waterloo, ON: Wilfrid Laurier University Press).

The section on Margaret Christakos's *What Stirs* developed from an article that originally appeared in 2011 in *Contemporary Women's Writing* 5, no. 2: 89–106.

Coach House Books and Rachel Zolf have kindly granted permission to reproduce three poems from *Human Resources* in this volume.

NOTES

INTRODUCTION

1. Lending libraries have since become an important element of protest sites, cropping up in park occupations, including the occupation of Gezi Park in Turkey in 2013 (Oneofthelibrarians 2013).

2. In spite of the fact that *Zong!* is composed using constraint-based methods, M. NourbeSe Philip resists a reading of her text as conceptual poetry because such an alignment elides the important influence of Caribbean postcolonial traditions on her work. See Evie Shockley's "Is 'Zong!' Conceptual Poetry? Yes It Isn't" (2013).

3. Kate Siklosi refers to political poetry that deploys conceptual techniques to advance an antiracist and decolonizing praxis as "Poetic Terrorism," a term she borrows from Hakim Bey. She defines poetic terrorism as "the use of 'found' poetic material to combat dominant scripts of his-tory and enact sociopolitical change on the ground of our contemporary reality" (2017). Siklosi names Jordan Abel, Bhanu Kapil, Harryette Mullen, Mark Nowak, NourbeSe Philip, Shane Rhodes, and Rachel Zolf as practitioners of poetic terrorism. As Siklosi explains, "Acts of Poetic Terrorism are meant to 'shock' people out of their day-to-day lives by extracting different possibilities from aesthetic experiences outside the sanctions of law and state." Poetic terrorism is political precisely through its fusing of "social activism and aesthetic praxis." Siklosi's deployment of this term offers a useful distinction for thinking about the poethical potential of constraint-based and procedural poetry outside of the depoliticized realm of conceptual poetry.

4. Although my study includes a number of queer writers, none of these writers identifies as trans, although I would like to make clear that my definition of feminist poetics includes the work of trans-identified writers like Trish Salah and kari edwards.

5. Some women engaged productively with elements of language writing, recognizing that their active participation in the language movement was key to opening it up to more participation from women. As Ann Vickery argues: "Even though Hejinian and Howe may have seen L=A=N=G=U=A=G=E as limited in addressing feminist concerns, they saw their own involvement as necessary to changing its approach" (2000, 31).

6. See http://www.vidaweb.org/category/the-count/ for more information on the activities of this group.

7. See www.cwila.com for background information on CWILA's "count" and the other initiatives with which this group is involved.

8. Carmine Starnino dismissed CWILA's annual count as a "panicky response" in an interview published in the literary magazine *CV 2* (Bowling 2013). Thoughtful critical responses to Starnino included a blog post by Vancouver-based poet Brad Cran (2013) and CWILA member Erin Wunker's response on the CWILA blog (2013).

9. For an analysis of the role of translation in Canadian feminist poetics, see Elena Basile's dissertation (2013).

10. Several writers have built on the rich tradition of borderlands poetics established by writers like Gloria Anzaldua to develop a complex body of work that addresses the complexities of exchange between the United States and Mexico. Amy Sara Carroll's *Secession* (2012) is a key example of this work. Other Latinx writers who take up issues of language and identity in their poetry include Rosa Alcalá, Mónica de la Torre, and Carmen Giménez Smith.

11. This quotation is from a letter from Kathy Mezei to Barbara Godard, dated January 15, 1988.

12. The Canada Council for the Arts emerged as a result of the 1951 Massey-Levesque Commission Report, a government document that outlined policy recommendations for a federally funded series of grants to support arts patronage designed in part as a protectionist measure against American cultural dominance (Sheffield 2009, 1). The commission argued that "a national Canadian literature (and culture more generally) can only survive in a country as fragmented as Canada if it and its production are directly funded by the federal government" (Milz 2007, 87). Motivated in large part by a desire to define and preserve Canadian cultural production in the face of persistent American cultural influence, the report led to the creation of the Canada Council for the Arts, a federal granting agency that continues to provide funding to writers and publishers in Canada.

13. In an interview with Kit Dobson, Canadian poet Christian Bök argues: "If a work is . . . couched within stereotypical notions of what constitutes Canadian models of identity, then I think the work stands a greater chance of success than work by someone who actually produces a formally investigative project. I think that there's still a xenophobic attitude toward the avant-garde on the assumption that it's not a homegrown aesthetic" (Dobson 2013, 13). While Bök's position is polemical, there is some truth to his assertion that formally innovative work has not been funded as robustly as more conventional work in Canada. However, since the jury changes from year to year, the Canada Council's receptivity to avant-garde work undoubtedly varies depending on who is adjudicating the applicants.

14. In 1995, Quebec held its second referendum to ask voters in the province whether they wanted to separate from Canada. The "no" side won a very nar-

row victory with 50.58 percent of the vote, and Quebec remained a Canadian province.

15. Ann Vickery claims that the Kootenay School of Writing poets generated "one of the most innovative and strongly feminist of poetic communities existing in Canada today" (2000, 133). Indeed, this is true of KSW in the early 1990s when Nancy Shaw, Catriona Strang, Kathryn McLeod, Susan Clark, Julia Steele, and Lisa Robertson were on the collective. Susan Clark edited *Raddle Moon*, a journal that maintained a strong focus on feminist poetics, although it was not exclusively a journal of feminist poetics. However, KSW has not been consistent in its fostering of work by women, and its relationship to feminist poetics is somewhat fraught. Catriona Strang addresses the marginalization of women from KSW in her interview in *Prismatic Publics*:

> It seemed that women who didn't want to write just like men were writing had to push and create the space themselves. . . . There were women on the collective when I joined. In fact, Lisa Robertson and I joined at the same time, but as I said, at times it was a battle. In lots of ways KSW could be a very supportive space, and I certainly don't regret the time I spent on the collective. But for me it was not without difficulties. Part of what Nancy Shaw and I did later on was spend a lot of time deprogramming. We talked a lot about this. (Strang 2009, 274)

In many ways, the conflicted relationship many Canadian feminist writers had to the KSW mirrors the ambivalent relationship that many American feminist writers had to language writing, suggesting that in both countries, women struggled to create space for a feminist avant-garde within male-dominated movements.

PART 1

1. Strategic embodiment should not be confused with Gayatri Chakravorty Spivak's notion of "strategic essentialism" (1987). Strategic essentialism involves a minority group strategically setting aside its differences to forge a provisional, strategic collective. Strategic embodiment is not the deployment of a collective or group identity, bur rather the recognition that bodily experience is always mediated by the social (Scappettone 2007, 182). Strategic embodiment entails an acknowledgment of the necessity of thinking and writing about the body, and an acknowledgment that to do so does not necessarily mean that one is automatically positing that body as somehow primordial or outside of social and political considerations.

2. For an analysis of the debates regarding essentialism and social constructionism, as well as the ways in which anti-essentialist critique remains curiously

dependent upon and linked to essentialist positions, see Diana Fuss's *Essentially Speaking: Feminism, Nature, Difference* (1989).

3. This quotation comes from a review of Laura Elrick's *sKincerity* (2003). Prevallet's description of Elrick's poetry as "writing the body politic" could be more generally applied to a range of early twentieth-century texts that conjure and mobilize the body.

1. Much of Christakos's oeuvre is devoted to the development of procedural poetics and an exploration of maternal subjectivity. *What Stirs* follows in this respect from some of her previously published collections, including *Wipe Under a Love* and *Excessive Love Prostheses*.

2. As Wendy Brown has argued, in the context of neoliberalism

all dimensions of human life are cast in terms of a market rationality. While this entails submitting every action and policy to considerations of profitability, equally important is the production of all human and institutional action as rational entrepreneurial action, conducted according to a calculus of utility, benefit, or satisfaction against a microeconomic grid of scarcity, supply and demand, and moral-value neutrality. Neoliberalism does not simply assume that all aspects of social, cultural, and political life can be reduced to such a calculus; rather, it develops institutional practices and rewards for enacting this vision. (2005, 40)

3. The language poets actively resisted the widely held assumption that a poem functions as a kind of consumable product, and they often produced intentionally unreadable and unconsumable texts. As Clint Burnham argues,

By foregoing the syntactical crutch of conventional poetry—the stable, albeit ironical "I," and the grammatically regular sentence—language poetry makes evident how language itself is commodified: not simply, in a Naomi Klein sense, as a brand name or logo but, more profoundly, as a discourse. This is the most important meaning of the equal signs in the title of the journal L=A=N=G=U=A=G=E. (2011, 35)

For an extended analysis of the politics and aesthetics of unreadable or "anti-absorptive" texts, see Charles Bernstein's essay "Artifice or Absorption" in *Artifice and Indeterminacy: An Anthology of New Poetics* (1998).

4. I borrow this notion from Clint Burnham, who identifies an aspect of *jouissance* as inherent to the experience of reading poetry produced by members of the Kootenay School of Writing. Burnham argues that highly experimental texts

in which "meaning itself always eludes the reader . . . can become pleasurable (and perhaps even a matter of *jouissance*)" precisely through their unreadability (2011, 33).

5. As a collaboratively authored, political, "queer" poem, *sibyl unrest* bears some similarities to Daphne Marlatt and Betsy Warland's *Double Negative* (1988), which Deborah Mix argues is inherently political in and through its collaborative compositional structure. Collaboration "refus[es] the myth of the divinely inspired, independently creative author" and "subverts other constructs of self and other, inside and outside" (Mix 2007, 73). In its occupation of an "in between space, collaborative writing is inherently political, calling attention to processes of marginalization, identity construction, and readership" (73). Indeed, there are striking structural and compositional similarities between *Double Negative* and *sibyl unrest* specifically with regard to the politics and aesthetics of collaboration. Both texts address the geopolitics of the "now" in which they were written and both inscribe an embodied queerness. However, unlike *Double Negative*, *sibyl unrest* is not a love lyric; Lai and Wong are not sexually or romantically involved, even though the book is, at times, erotically charged.

6. Anti-Asian sentiment intensified in Canada after the completion of the Canadian Pacific Railroad when the need for Asian laborers became less urgent. Canada passed the Chinese Immigration Act in 1885, which required all Chinese immigrants to pay the government a "head tax" of $50. By 1903, this fee had increased to $500 per person.

CHAPTER 2

1. As of January 2016, Vancouver had the third most unaffordable housing market in the world, behind only Hong Kong and Sydney (Mathesen 2016).

2. Robert William Pickton was convicted in the deaths of six women and charged with the deaths of twenty more. He confessed to an undercover police officer posing as a cellmate to the deaths of forty-nine women. His victims were mostly sex workers, many of them Indigenous, from Vancouver's Downtown Eastside neighborhood. He is currently serving a life sentence for murder.

3. The Gardasil shot protects against the sexually transmitted human papillomavirus, which has been linked to cervical cancer.

4. In addition to writing overtly of the inability of her speaker to enter the gift economy, Zolf draws a direct connection between money and feces, a connection that is further emphasized by the book's cover image, an extreme close-up photograph of a shit-colored American penny by the artist Moyra Davey. This photograph is part of Davey's Copperhead Series, which features 100 extreme close-up images of American pennies.

PART 2

1. Sara Ahmed and Clare Hemmings have both questioned the ways in which new materialist feminist thinkers have cast post-structuralist feminism as anti-materialist. In *Why Stories Matter: The Political Grammar of Feminist Theory*, Hemmings frames the call for a "return" to materialism as a "story" Western feminism tells in which the linguistic turn that characterized post-structuralist feminism is cast as sterile rather than generative and as belonging to a bygone era. For Hemmings, the argument for a return to materiality utilizes "affects of neglect and disenchantment to secure a theoretical teleology in which the abandoned is cast as the abandoner" (2011, 109). Sara Ahmed similarly objects to what she sees as a wholesale rejection of post-structuralist feminism by theorists of new materialism. For Ahmed, such a rhetorical move has "problematic consequences for a genealogy of feminist thought" (2008, 24). Specifically, Ahmed questions the ways in which post-structuralist feminism's anti-biologism is taken for granted in the narratives and genealogies of feminism constructed under the banner of new materialism. Ahmed argues: "In claiming to return to matter, we might then be losing sight of how matter matters in different ways, for different feminisms over time," and she argues for a more rigorous, ethical, and careful engagement with the "feminist work that comes before us in all its complexity" (36). I wish to register these objections to the ways in which some strands of new materialist thinking situate themselves as constituting a break from earlier iterations of feminism that they see as being ill-equipped to deal with the material. My aim in this chapter is not to affirm or refute new materialism's critiques of post-structuralist feminism; post-structuralist thinking is varied and diverse, as is new materialist thinking. Rather, my aim is to place new materialist criticism and contemporary ecopoetics in dialogue to show how ecopoetics enacts and embraces matter in ways that intersect productively with strands of new materialist thought.

2. Bennett's theory of vital materialism differs from a conventional theory of environmentalism in significant ways. For Bennett, vital materialism understands its public to be comprised not just of humans but also of animals, vegetables, and minerals. In other words, environmentalism understands nonhuman actants as dimensions of a passive environment while a vital materialist approach "would need to include more earthlings in the swarm of actants. If environmentalists are selves who live on earth, vital materialists are selves who live as earth, who are more alert to the capacities and limitations—the 'jizz'—of the various materials that they are. If environmentalism leads to the call for the protection and wise management of an ecosystem that surrounds us, a vital materialism suggests that the task is to engage more strategically with a trenchant materiality that is us as it vies with us in agentic assemblages" (Bennett 2010, 111).

CHAPTER 3

1. Other recent poetic texts have deployed similar strategies of erasure in order to enact literary or textual decolonizations. For example, Jordan Abel's *Un/Inhabited* (2014) systematically erases references to the social and political aspects of land ownership in ninety-one Western novels.

2. *Darkness* is Morrison's third book of poetry. *Crop* (2003) and *Girl Scout Nation* (2008) establish Morrison's interest in the intersections between environmental destruction, capitalism, and the exploitation of those marginalized on the grounds of gender, race, and class, themes that are further explored in *Darkness*.

3. Morrison has a dual career as a poet and a visual artist, and *Darkness* functions as a piece of visual art as much as it does a work of text-based poetry. A note at the beginning of *Darkness* informs the reader that pages 3–10 were enacted as a 30-foot wall painting included in the Not Content event curated by Vanessa Place and Teresa Carmody at the Los Angeles Contemporary Exhibitions in 2010.

4. Morrison actively works to undo much of the excessively anthropomorphizing language of *Heart of Darkness*, a novel in which "vegetation rioted on the earth and the big trees were kings" (Conrad 1987, 66) and the "forest stepped leisurely across the water" (68).

5. One might also read the re-centering of the poet's agency as a kind of taking-up of a position of ethical and political responsibility. In this regard, Morrison's text stands in contrast to recent controversial works of conceptual poetry that take up the matter of race but elide issues of authorial intention, the politics of appropriation, and the ethical responsibility of the poet (see my discussion of Kenneth Goldsmith, Vanessa Place, and accusations of racism in conceptual poetry in the introduction to this volume).

6. For an extensive account of the environmental risks of tar sands development in Utah, see the Utah Chapter of the Sierra Club's website: https://utah.sierraclub.org/content/utah-oil-shale-and-tar-sands-development.

7. As Wendy Brown notes, the year after Saddam Hussein was killed, Paul Bremer, the America-appointed head of the Coalition Provisional Authority, mandated the sale of several state-run enterprises in Iraq and permitted foreign ownership of Iraqi companies and banks even though many of these orders were "in violation of the Geneva and Hague Conventions concerning war, occupation, and international relations" (Brown 2015, 142). To avoid violating these conventions, the U.S. government appointed an interim government in Iraq, which it then "pressed to ratify the orders when it was pronounced 'sovereign' in 2004" (142).

CHAPTER 4

1. Stacy Alaimo describes the "great garbage patch" as 3.5 million tons of garbage occupying a space in the Pacific Ocean roughly the size of Texas and comprised of "shoes, toys, bags, pacifiers, wrappers, toothbrushes, and bottles too numerous to count. . . . Everyday, ostensibly benign, human stuff becomes nightmarish as it floats forever in the sea. The recognition that these banal objects, intended for momentary human use, pollute for eternity, renders them surreally malevolent" (2012, 487). "Albatross" in this context is an intertextual reference to Coleridge's poem "The Rime of the Ancient Mariner." Following Coleridge's deployment of the symbol of the albatross, the term has come to function as a kind of cultural shorthand for a burden that weighs on one's conscience. Evelyn Reilly also works extensively with the symbol of the albatross, and I will explore her use of this symbol later in this chapter.

2. She also links "fossil fuels" to their geological and biological prehistoric sources in "motherboard," a poem in which "tractor with gas pedal for brake" sifts through the "earth torn hole" where it excavates "DDT remnants / tree roots tree corpse petrified / beetle decomposed dinosaur / layers of ancestor bird bones / wolf scat slow water transform / old meat dead petals scattered / pollen bee legs pine memory rich" (Wong 2015, 48). This defamiliarization prompts the reader to think about oil not just as a source of fuel for human consumption.

3. Reilly also claims that *Styrofoam* is "haunted" by D. H. Lawrence's "The Ship of Death" and Herman Melville's *Moby Dick* (specifically chapter 42, "The Whiteness of the Whale") (2009, 68).

4. References to birds occur frequently in the text; the poem "Wing/Span/Screw/Cluster (Aves)" contains the names of endangered hummingbird species and references to human activities that are contributing to the threat of extinction. *Styrofoam* also contains an image of a decomposing bird, with the accompanying caption "One of about 51,900 Google images search results for 'roadkill + bird'" (Reilly 2009, 25), as well as a picture of birds foraging in a garbage dump (13).

PART 3

CHAPTER 5

1. Jeff Derksen's *Annihilated Time* (2009) and Nicky Marsh's *Democracy in Contemporary US Women's Poetry* (2007a) both offer detailed overviews of anthologies of antiwar poetry published in the context of the aftermath of 9/11 and the military invasions and occupations of Afghanistan and Iraq.

2. Brand, a Canadian citizen of Trinidadian descent, explicitly rejects an alignment with nation or national belonging in her work.

3. I borrow the term "global intimacy" from Diana Brydon (2015), who in turn borrows and adapts Michael Herzfeld's (1997) concept of "cultural intimacy" in her reading of Dionne Brand's *Inventory*.

4. This examination of place must be read in relation to Spahr's ongoing project of utilizing experimental literary forms to critically examine the politics of location. Her persistent interest in the history and politics of place are evident in her earlier collection of poems, *Fuck You – Aloha – I Love You* (2001b), in which she critically examines her place as a white outsider living on an island with a long history of colonial occupation by white outsiders. Her poetic memoir/essay *The Transformation* (2007), written at around the same time as *This Connection of Everyone with Lungs*, also addresses the themes of connectivity and complicity in the aftermath of 9/11 and the invasion of Iraq, but weaves these concerns into a broader reflection of the ongoing U.S. occupation of Hawaii. *Well Then There Now* (2011) further extends her poetic inquiry into the political, natural, and social history of place. As in her previous work, she probes the political and ethical implications of the colonial occupation of Hawaii, but she also writes of her own childhood in Appalachia. Each poem in this collection is preceded by a map indicating Spahr's geographic location at the time of the work's composition (Hawaii, New York City, Berkeley). Her most recent collection of poems, *That Winter the Wolf Came* (2015b), explores the relationship between financial and economic crisis against the historical backdrop of the Occupy Oakland movement and the gentrification of the Bay Area. Her interest in the social history of place is also linked to the ecopoetic strain that runs through all of her work; Spahr incorporates aspects of ethnobotany and the flight paths of migratory birds into her poetry to consider the ways in which commercial trade, industry, and human activity have molded and shaped what we have come to understand as "nature."

5. Rankine's more recent and more widely discussed text, *Citizen: An American Lyric* (2014), takes a similar form and achieves a similar effect. *Citizen*, which can be read as a sequel to *Don't Let Me Be Lonely*, explores the micro- and macro-aggressions of racism in American culture.

6. The mobilization of affect through discourses of nationalism has intensified in recent months in the context of Donald Trump's presidency. The call to "Make American great again" relies on the mobilization of both affect and nostalgia to justify the vilification of undocumented workers, migrants, and refugees.

7. Brand's entire oeuvre is characterized by complex reflections on the question of identity and belonging in relation to race, nation, sexuality, place, and memory. See, for example, her novels *In Another Place, Not Here* (1996), *At the Full and Change of the Moon* (1999), *What We All Long For* (2005), *Love Enough* (2014); her essay *A Map to the Door of No Return* (2001); and her poetry collections *No Language Is Neutral* (1990), *Thirsty* (2002), and *Ossuaries* (2010).

8. Throughout the book, the speaker shifts from the first person to the third person, and is occasionally a collective "we," implying that the poet-witness is multiple and mutable. Leslie Sanders, who writes about the evolution of a poetics of witness across four of Brand's collections of poetry, sees the shifts between "I," "we," and "she" in this book as a manifestation of the speaker's grief: "In this poem, readers regard the poet witnessing, and we are addressed—both by the speaker and 'she': a she who is distraught, almost feverish, paranoid, undone by the act of witness. So wrenching is this act that the poet splits and the reader is pulled into the splitting" (Sanders 2015, 23).

9. Rankine similarly identifies the western as a manifestation of an American nationalist fantasy that implicitly informs the nation's imperialist geopolitical leanings (2004, 25).

CHAPTER 6

1. Zolf's project in *Janey's Arcadia* shares much in common with the poetics of Susan Howe. Like Howe, Zolf posits poetry as a mode of historical inquiry and challenges the selective framing and foreclosures of conventional historiography and national narratives.

2. In 2016, the newly elected Liberal government launched an inquiry into the crisis of missing and murdered Indigenous women; the inquiry is run at arm's length from the government and is overseen by five Indigenous commissioners. Prime Minister Justin Trudeau appointed Jody Wilson-Raybould, an Indigenous woman, as minister of justice and seems much more receptive to acknowledging the ongoing legacy of settler colonialism in Canada than was his predecessor, Stephen Harper. However, even a government with the best of intentions will not be able to reverse and undo the violent legacy of colonization. Furthermore, at this stage it remains to be seen whether a formal inquiry into the crisis of missing and murdered Indigenous women will be effective or what kinds of positive changes it might bring about.

3. The residential school system in Canada saw children forcibly removed from their families and communities and sent away to church-run boarding schools where many suffered physical and sexual abuse at the hands of priests and nuns. In 2008, the federal government issued a formal apology for its role in the operation of residential schools and launched the Truth and Reconciliation Commission, but refused to acknowledge the government's treatment of Indigenous people as a cultural genocide.

4. The Canadian Pacific Railway (CPR), completed in November 1885, was the first Canadian transcontinental railroad. For the first time in history, it was possible to travel from cities like Toronto and Montreal across the prairies and the Rocky Mountains to the west coast in relative comfort and speed. The comple-

tion of the CPR facilitated tourism and settlement in western Canada. The building of the CPR also coincided politically and historically with the creation of the reservation system across the Canadian prairies. The Indian Act was passed in 1876, around the time the CPR was being built. Louis Riel, Métis leader of the Red River Uprising in 1885, was executed for treason the same month the CPR was completed.

5. Until 1985, Indigenous women who married non-Indigenous men lost their status. Without status, women could not live on reserves, inherit family property, be buried on reserves, or have access to treaty rights. This law alienated Indigenous women from their traditional culture and destroyed Indigenous families. Bill C-31, introduced in 1985, amended the Indian Act and allowed women to apply to have their status restored.

6. The Indian Act was introduced in the House of Commons in 1876 as acts relating to the enfranchisement of Indians and the management of Indian affairs. As Janine Brodie points out, the reference to enfranchisement refers specifically to section C-18 of the act which enabled "Indians to acquire full legal status as British subjects only by surrendering their ties to Indigenous history and treaty rights" (2012, 105). Those who refused the invitation to become British subjects and to opt instead for their treaty rights "were defined by law as non-persons and therefore ineligible to make claims to the status and rights of legal personhood" (105). The act explicitly understood the term "person" to mean "an individual other than an Indian" (105) and was designed to facilitate cultural genocide. Brodie refers to the legal construction of Indigenous peoples as "non-persons" as "exemplars of the biopolitics of state racism" that "remained as provisions of the Indian act until 1951" (105).

7. Idle No More, the grassroots movement for Indigenous sovereignty that began in 2012, was prompted in part as a show of support and solidarity with Chief Spence. Participants in Idle No More protests held round dances in public spaces such as shopping malls and streets in order to draw attention to the issues facing Indigenous people today and to oppose the continued exploitation of land and resources by colonial governments.

8. These polyvocal actions were filmed and are archived on Zolf's PennSound authors page (2015).

9. The U.S. Constitution consists of seven articles and twenty-seven amendments that articulate the principles of American democracy and the operational structure of the government. As a document that dates back to the founding of the nation, the Constitution is vital to the operation of the American legal and political systems and is crucial for understandings of individual freedom, equality, and legal rights. It is the legal responsibility of the Supreme Court to interpret the Constitution and guarantee the constitutional rights of American citizens.

10. For Brown, this legal ruling "submits politics, rights, representation, and speech to economization, it subverts key components of liberal democracy—popular sovereignty, free elections, political freedom, and equality. Casting every actor and activity in market terms, it vanquishes the political meaning of citizenship and erases the crucial distinction between economic and political orders essential to the most modest version of popular sovereignty. . . . It supplants democratic political deliberation and voices with a formulation of speech as capital and free speech as unhindered capital right" (Brown 2015, 173).

11. Brown's central argument in *Undoing the Demos: Neoliberalism's Stealth Revolution* is that the ascension of neoliberalism has coincided with, and contributed to, the decline of democracy.

12. Descartes saw animal and human bodies as mere machines and understood the conceptual abilities of the human mind as that which set humans apart. As Bruce Grenville observes, the "human and animal automata produced from the seventeenth century onward were in part influenced by those philosophical traditions that viewed the function of the human and animal body in mechanical terms" (2002, 14).

13. The human microphone is a strategy for conveying the words of a speaker to a large crowd of listeners without the aid of an actual microphone. People standing close to the speaker repeat the speaker's words for the crowd, thus amplifying them and allowing them to be heard by a large group of listeners.

14. Benka's poem echoes the lines of Emma Lazarus's "The New Colossus": "Give me your tired, your poor, your huddled masses yearning to breathe free." The speaker of Lazarus's poem is the Statue of Liberty welcoming new immigrants to America as they sail past the statue on their way to Ellis Island.

15. The Defense of Marriage Act was passed into law in 1996 (and was in effect when Benka's book was written and published) and was eventually ruled unconstitutional in 2013. DOMA limited federal rights, benefits, and privileges to those married under the law, effectively denying benefits to same-sex couples.

CODA

1. Some of the most exciting poetry published in Canada in the past two years is by Indigenous authors like Liz Howard and Jordan Abel, and directly addresses issues of indigeneity and colonialism.

BIBLIOGRAPHY

Abel, Jordan. 2013. *The Place of Scraps*. Vancouver, BC: Talon.
———. 2014. *Un/Inhabited*. Vancouver, BC: Project Space Press and Talon Books.
———. *Injun*. 2016. Vancouver, BC: Talon Books.
Ahmed, Sara. 2004. *The Cultural Politics of Emotion*. Durham, NC: Duke University Press.
———. 2006. *Queer Phenomenology: Orientations, Objects, Others*. Durham, NC: Duke University Press.
———. 2008. "Imaginary Prohibitions: Some Preliminary Remarks on the Founding Gestures of the 'New Materialism.'" *European Journal of Women's Studies* 15, no. 1: 23–29.
———. 2010. *The Promise of Happiness*. Durham, NC: Duke University Press.
Ahmed, Sara, and Jackie Stacey. 2001. *Thinking Through the Skin*. New York: Routledge.
Alaimo, Stacey. 2009. "Trans-Corporeal Feminisms and the Ethical Space of Nature." In *Material Feminism*, edited by Stacy Alaimo and Susan Heckman, 237–64. Bloomington: Indiana University Press.
———. 2010. *Bodily Natures: Science, Environment, and the Material Self*. Bloomington: Indiana University Press.
———. 2012. "States of Suspension: Trans-Corporeality at Sea." *Interdisciplinary Studies in Literature and Environment* 19, no. 3: 476–93.
———. 2014. "Oceanic Origins, Plastic Activism, and New Materialism at Sea." In *Material Ecocriticism*, edited by Serenella Iovino and Serpil Oppermann, 186–203. Bloomington: Indiana University Press.
———. 2016. *Exposed: Environmental Politics and Pleasures in Posthuman Times*. Minneapolis: University of Minnesota Press.
Amnesty International. 2015. "No More Stolen Sisters." http://www.amnesty .ca/our-work/campaigns/no-more-stolen-sisters.
Ashton, Jennifer. 2007. "Our Bodies, Our Poems." *American Literary History* 19, no. 1: 211–31.
Athanasiou, Athena, and Judith Butler. 2013. *Dispossession: The Performative in the Political*. London: Polity.
Barad, Karen. 2007. *Meeting the Universe Halfway: Quantum Physics and the Entanglement of Meaning*. Durham, NC: Duke University Press.
Basile, Elena. 2013. "Affect in Translation: *Tessera* and the Politics of Feminist

Experimental Poetics in Canada (1984–2005)." Dissertation. Toronto: York University Press.

Bellamy, Dodie. 1983. "postcards." *HOW(ever)* 1, no. 2.

Benka, Jen. 2005. *A Box of Longing with Fifty Drawers*. Brooklyn, NY: Soft Skull.

Benka, Jen, and Carol Mirakove. 2007. *1,138*. New York: Belladonna*.

Bennett, Jane. 2010. *Vibrant Matter: A Political Ecology of Things*. Durham, NC: Duke University Press.

Berlant, Lauren. 1998. "Intimacy: A Special Issue." *Critical Inquiry* 24, no. 2: 281–88.

———. 2008. *The Female Complaint*. Durham, NC: Duke University Press.

———. 2011. *Cruel Optimism*. Durham, NC: Duke University Press.

———. 2015. "Living in Ellipsis: Biopolitics and the Attachment to Life." Unpublished keynote address presented at "The Affect Project: Memory, Aesthetics, and Ethics." Winnipeg, Manitoba.

Bernstein, Charles. 1998. "Artifice or Absorption." In *Artifice and Indeterminacy: An Anthology of New Poetics*, edited by Christopher Beach, 3–23. Tuscaloosa: University of Alabama Press.

Bettridge, Joel. 2005. "A Conversation with Juliana Spahr." *How2* 2, no. 3.

Boutilier, Alex. 2014. "Native Teen's Slaying a 'Crime,' Not a 'Sociological Phenomenon.'" *The Star*, August 21. https://www.thestar.com/news/canada/2014/08/21/native_teens_slaying_a_crime_not_a_sociological_phenomenon_stephen_harper_says.html.

Bowling, Tim. 2013. "An Interview with Carmine Starnino." *Contemporary Verse 2*, October 28. http://www.contemporaryverse2.ca/en/interviews/excerpt/an-interview-with-carmine-starnino.

Braidotti, Rosi. 2002. *Metamorphoses: Towards a Materialist Theory of Becoming*. London: Polity.

———. 2006. *Transpositions: On Nomadic Ethics*. London: Polity.

———. 2013. *The Posthuman*. London: Polity.

Brand, Dionne. 1990. *No Language Is Neutral*. Toronto: Coach House.

———. 1996. *In Another Place, Not Here*. Toronto: Knopf Canada.

———. 1999. *At the Full and Change of the Moon*. Toronto: Knopf.

———. 2001. *A Map to the Door of No Return: Notes to Belonging*. Toronto: Random House.

———. 2002. *Thirsty*. Toronto: McClelland and Stewart.

———. 2005. *What We All Long For*. Toronto: Knopf Canada.

———. 2006. *Inventory*. Toronto: McClelland and Stewart.

———. 2010. *Ossuaries*. Toronto: McClelland and Stewart.

———. 2014. *Love Enough*. Toronto: Knopf Canada.

Brodie, Janine. 2012. "White Settlers and the Biopolitics of State Building in

Canada." In *Shifting the Grounds of Canadian Literary Studies*, edited by Smaro Kamboureli and Robert Zacharias, 87–108. Waterloo, ON: Wilfred Laurier University Press.

Brown, Wendy. 2005. *Edgework: Critical Essays on Knowledge and Politics.* Princeton, NJ: Princeton University Press.

———. 2015. *Undoing the Demos: Neoliberalism's Stealth Revolution.* Cambridge, MA: Zone Books.

Brydon, Diana. 2015. "Dionne Brand's Global Intimacies: Practicing Affective Citizenship." *University of Toronto Quarterly* 77, no. 3: 990–1006.

Burnham, Clint. 2011. *The Only Poetry That Matters: Reading the Kootenay School of Writing.* Vancouver, BC: Arsenal Pulp.

Butler, Judith. 1993. *Bodies That Matter: On the Discursive Limits of Sex.* New York: Routledge.

———. 2004. *Precarious Life: The Powers of Mourning and Violence.* New York: Verso.

———. 2009. *Frames of War: When Is Life Grievable.* New York: Verso.

———. 2015. *Notes Toward a Performative Theory of Assembly.* Boston: Harvard University Press.

Canadian Pacific Railway. 1886. *What Women Say of the Canadian Northwest: A Simple Statement of the Experiences of Women Settled in All Parts of Manitoba and the Northwest Territories.* London: M. Blacklock. http://eco.canadiana.ca/view/oocihm.16869/1?r=0&s=1.

Carroll, Amy Sara. 2012. *Secession.* San Diego, CA: Hyperbole Books.

Chandler, Mielle, and Astrida Neimanis. 2013. "Water and Gestationality: What Flows beneath Ethics." In *Thinking with Water*, edited by Cecelia Chen, Janine MacLeod, and Astrida Neimanis, 61–83. Montreal: McGill-Queens University Press.

Chen, Mel Y. 2012. *Animacies: Biopolitics, Racial Mattering, and Queer Affect.* Durham, NC: Duke University Press.

Christakos, Margaret. 2008. *What Stirs.* Toronto: Coach House.

———. 2009. "Interview." In *Prismatic Publics: Innovative Canadian Women's Poetry and Poetics*, edited by Kate Eichhorn and Heather Milne, 112–23. Toronto: Coach House.

Chung, Emily. 2013. "Muzzling of Federal Scientists Widespread, Survey Suggests." *CBC News*, October 21. http://www.cbc.ca/news/technology/muzzling-of-federal-scientists-widespread-survey-suggests-1.2128859.

Cixous, Hélène. 1976. "The Laugh of the Medusa." Translated by Keith Cohen and Paula Cohen. *Signs* 1, no. 4: 875–93.

Conrad, Joseph. (1902) 1987. *Heart of Darkness.* New York: Penguin.

Coole, Diana, and Samantha Frost. 2010. "Introducing New Materialisms." In *New Materialisms: Ontology, Agency, Politics*, edited by Diana Coole and Samantha Frost, 1–46. Durham, NC: Duke University Press.

Cotnoir, Louise, Barbara Godard, Susan Knutson, Daphne Marlatt, Kathy Mezei, and Gail Scott. 1994. "Introduction: Women of Letters." In *Collaboration in the Feminine: Writings on Women and Culture from Tessera*, edited by Barbara Godard. Toronto: Second Story.

Cran, Brad. 2013. "Lazy Jerkism: An Open Letter to Carmine Starnino." *Brad Cran*, December 12. http://bradcran.com/vancouver_verse/an-open-letter -to-carmine-starnino/.

Cross, Michael. 2014. "Review of *From Dame Quickly*." *ON: Contemporary Practice* 2.

Currin, Jen, et al. (The Enpipe Line Contributors). 2012. *The Enpipe Line: 70,000 Km of Poetry Written in Resistance to the Enbridge Northern Gateway Pipeline Proposal*. Smithers, BC: Creekstone.

Cvetkovich, Ann. 2012. *Depression: A Public Feeling*. Durham, NC: Duke University Press.

Dangerfield, Katie. 2017. "White Nationalist Groups on the Rise in Canada, Planning More Rallies." *Global News*. August 15. https://globalnews.ca /news/3670776/white-nationalist-groups-canada-on-the-rise/.

Dean, Jodi. 2010. *Democracy and Other Neoliberal Fantasies: Communicative Capitalism and Left Politics*. Durham, NC: Duke University Press.

———. 2011a. *Blog Theory: Feedback and Capture in the Circuits of Drive*. London: Polity.

———. 2011b. *The Communist Horizon*. New York: Verso.

———. 2016. *Crowds and Party*. New York: Verso.

De Jesus, Joey. 2015. "Goldsmith, Conceptualism & the Half-Baked Rationalization of White Idiocy." *Apogee*, March 18. http://apogeejournal .org/2015/03/18/goldsmith-conceptualism-the-half-baked-rationalization -of-white-idiocy/.

Deleuze, Gilles, and Felix Guattari. 1987. *A Thousand Plateaus: Capitalism and Schizophrenia*. Translated by Brian Massumi. Minneapolis: University of Minnesota Press.

Derksen, Jeff. 2003. "Where Have All the Equal Signs Gone? Inside/Outside the L=A=N=G=U=A=G=E Site." In *Assembling Alternatives: Reading Postmodern Poetries Transnationally*, edited by Romana Huk, 41–65. Middletown, CT: Wesleyan University Press.

———. 2009. *Annihilated Time: Poetry and Other Politics*. Vancouver, BC: Talon Books.

———. 2012. "National Literatures in the Shadow of Neoliberalism." In *Shifting the Ground of Canadian Literary Studies*, edited by Smaro Kamboureli and Robert Zacharias, 37–63. Waterloo, ON: Wilfrid Laurier University Press.

———. 2013. *After Euphoria*. Zurich: JRP/Ringier.

Derrida, Jacques. 1994. *Specters of Marx: The State of Debt, the Work of Mourning, and the New International*. Translated by Peggy Kamuf. New York: Routledge.

Dobson, Kit. 2013. "Too Bloody Minded to Give Up: Interview with Christian Bok." In *Producing Canadian Literature: Authors Speak on the Literary Marketplace*, edited by Kit Dobson and Smaro Kamboureli, 11–27. Waterloo, ON: Wilfrid Laurier University Press.

DuPlessis, Rachel Blau. 2001. "A Few Words about *HOW(ever)*." *HOW2*, no. 5.

———. 2006. *Blue Studios: Poetry and Its Cultural Work*. Tuscaloosa: University of Alabama Press.

Durand, Marcella. 2008. "The Anatomy of Oil." In *Area*, 61–79. Brooklyn, NY: Belladonna*.

———. 2010. "The Ecology of Poetry." In *)((Eco(Lang)(Uage(Reader))*, edited by Brenda Ijima, 114–24. Brooklyn, NY: Portable Press at Yo-Yo Labs.

Eichhorn, Kate, and Barbara Godard, eds. 2009. "Beyond Stasis: Poetics and Feminism Today." Special issue of *Open Letter* 13, no. 9.

Eichhorn, Kate, and Heather Milne. 2009. *Prismatic Publics: Innovative Canadian Women's Poetry and Poetics*. Toronto: Coach House.

Elrick, Laura. 2003. *sKincerity*. Berkeley, CA: Krupskaya.

———. 2005. *Fantasies in Permeable Structures*. New York: Factory School.

———. 2010. "Poetry, Ecology, and the Production of Lived Space." In *) ((Eco(Lang)(Uage(Reader))*, edited by Brenda Ijima, 186–99. Brooklyn, NY: Portable Press at Yo-Yo Labs.

Enpipe Collective. 2012. *The Enpipe Line: 70,000 Km of Poetry Written in Resistance to the Northern Gateway Pipeline*. Smithers, BC: Creekstone.

Fagin, Betsy. 2015. *All Is Not Yet Lost*. New York: Belladonna*.

Felman, Shoshana, and Dori Laub. 1992. *Testimony: Crisis of Witnessing in Literature, Psychoanalysis, and History*. New York: Routledge.

Felski, Rita. 2009. *Beyond Feminist Aesthetics: Feminist Literature and Social Change*. Cambridge, MA: Harvard University Press.

Flood, Alison. 2015. "US Poet Defends Reading Michael Brown Autopsy Report as a Poem." *The Guardian*, March 17. https://www.theguardian.com/books/2015/mar/17/michael-brown-autopsy-report-poem-kenneth-goldsmith.

Forché, Carolyn. 1993. *Against Forgetting: Twentieth Century Poetry of Witness*. New York: W.W. Norton.

Fraser, Kathleen. 1994. "The Jump: Editing *HOW(ever)*." *Chain* 1 (Spring/Summer).

———. 2000. *Translating the Unspeakable: Poetry and the Innovative Necessity*. Tuscaloosa: University of Alabama Press.

Freud, Sigmund. (1962) 1991a. "Character and Anal Eroticism." In *Three*

Essays on the Theory of Sexuality and Other Works, edited by Angela Richards, translated by James Strachey, 209–15. Toronto: Penguin.

———. (1962) 1991b. "Infantile Sexuality." In *Three Essays on the Theory of Sexuality and Other Works*, edited by Angela Richards, translated by James Strachey, 88–126. Toronto: Penguin.

Frost, Elizabeth. 2002. "Introduction – Poetry Post 9-11: Witnessing Dissent." *How2* 1, no. 7.

———. 2003. *The Feminist Avant-Garde in American Poetry*. Iowa City: University of Iowa Press.

Frye, Northrop. (1971) 1995. *The Bush Garden: Essays on the Canadian Imagination*. Toronto: House of Anansi.

Fuss, Diana. 1989. *Essentially Speaking: Feminism, Nature, Difference*. New York: Routledge.

Giroux, Henry A. 2017. *America at War with Itself*. San Francisco: City Lights.

Godard, Barbara. 1994. *Collaboration in the Feminine: Writings on Women and Culture from Tessera*. Toronto: Second Story.

Godard, Barbara, and Smaro Kamboureli. 2008. "The Critic, Institutional Culture, and Canadian Literature: Barbara Godard in Conversation with Smaro Kamboureli." In *Canadian Literature at the Crossroads of Language and Culture: Selected Essays by Barbara Godard*, edited by Smaro Kamboureli, 17–52. Edmonton, AL: NeWest.

Goldsmith, Kenneth. 2011. *Uncreative Writing*. New York: Columbia University Press.

Gomez, Elena. 2015. "When Poetry Is White Supremacist." *Overland*, April 17. https://overland.org.au/2015/04/when-poetry-is-white-supremacist/.

Greenburg, David Micah. 2017. "Poetry and Agency under Trump." *The Boston Review*. April 5, 2017. http://bostonreview.net/poetry/david-micah-greenberg-poetry-and-agency-under-trump.

Greer, Michael. 1989. "Ideology and Theory in Recent Experimental Writing or, the Naming of 'Language Poetry.'" *Boundary 2* 16, no. 2/3: 335–55.

Grenville, Bruce. 2002. *The Uncanny: Experiments in Cyborg Culture*. Vancouver, BC: Arsenal Pulp.

Grewal, Inderpal. 2005. *Transnational America: Feminisms, Diasporas, Neoliberalisms*. Durham, NC: Duke University Press.

Grewal, Inderpal, and Caren Kaplan. 2004. "Transnational Feminist Practices and Questions of Postmodernity." In *Scattered Hegemonies: Postmodernity and Transnational Feminist Practices*, edited by Inderpal Grewal and Caren Kaplan. Minneapolis: University of Minnesota Press.

Grosz, Elizabeth. 2005. *Time Travels: Feminism, Nature, Power*. Durham, NC: Duke University Press.

———. 2011. *Becoming Undone: Darwinian Reflections on Life, Politics, and Art*. Durham, NC: Duke University Press.

Hall, Elaine J., and Marnie Salupo Rodriguez. 2003. "The Myth of Postfeminism." *Gender and Society* 17, no. 6: 878–902.

Haraway, Donna J. 1991. *Simians, Cyborgs, and Women: The Reinvention of Nature*. New York: Routledge.

Helmore, Edward. 2015. "Gone with the Wind Tweeter Says She Is Being Shunned by US Art Institutions." *The Guardian*, June 25. https://www.theguardian.com/books/2015/jun/25/gone-with-the-wind-tweeter-shunned-arts-institutions-vanessa-place.

Hemmings, Clare. 2011. *Why Stories Matter: The Political Grammar of Feminist Theory*. Durham, NC: Duke University Press.

Henderson, Jennifer. 2003. *Settler Feminism and Race Making in Canada*. Toronto: University of Toronto Press.

Herzfeld, Michael. 1997. *Cultural Intimacy: Social Poetics in the Nation-State*. Abingdon, UK: Psychology.

Howard, Liz. 2015. *Infinite Citizen of the Shaking Tent*. Toronto: McClelland and Stewart.

Huggan, Graham, and Helen Tiffin. 2010. *Postcolonial Ecocriticism: Literature, Animals, Environment*. New York: Routledge.

Iovino, Serenella, and Serpil Oppermann. 2014. "Introduction: Stories Come to Matter." In *Material Ecocriticism*, edited by Serenella Iovino and Serpil Oppermann, 1–20. Bloomington: Indiana University Press.

Irigaray, Luce. 1985. *This Sex Which Is Not One*. Translated by Catherine Porter. Ithaca, NY: Cornell University Press.

Jameson, Fredric. 1999. "Marx's Purloined Letter." In *Ghostly Demarcations: A Symposium on Jacques Derrida's Specters of Marx*, edited by Michael Sprinker, 26–67. London: Verso.

———. 2001. "Postmodernism, or, the Cultural Logic of Late Capitalism." In *Media and Cultural Studies: Key Works*, edited by Meenakshi Gigi Durham and Douglas Kellner, 550–87. London: Blackwell.

Johnson, A. James M. 1997. "Victorian Anthropology, Racism, and 'Heart of Darkness.'" *ARIEL: A Review of International English Literature* 28, no. 4: 111–31.

Kamboureli, Smaro. 2012. "Introduction Shifting the Ground of a Discipline: Emergence and Canadian Literary Studies in English." In *Shifting the Ground of Canadian Literary Studies*, edited by Smaro Kamboureli and Robert Zacharias, 1–36. Waterloo, ON: Wilfrid Laurier University Press.

Kaplan. E. Ann. 2005. *Trauma Culture: The Politics of Terror and Loss in Media and Literature*. New Brunswick, NJ: Rutgers University Press.

Keller, Lynn. 2010. *Thinking Poetry: Readings in Contemporary Women's Exploratory Poetics*. Iowa City: University of Iowa Press.

King, Amy, and Heidi Lynn Staples. 2010. *Poets of Living Waters*. https://poetsgulfcoast.wordpress.com.

Kinnahan, Linda. 2002. "Introduction: Innovative Writing, Public Discourse, and Social Action." *How2* 1, no. 7.

———. 2004. *Lyric Interventions: Feminism, Experimental Poetry and Contemporary Discourse.* Iowa City: University of Iowa Press.

Knutson, Susan. 2000. *Narrative in the Feminine: Daphne Marlatt and Nicole Brossard.* Waterloo, ON: Wilfrid Laurier University Press.

Kristeva, Julia. (1941) 1982. *Powers of Horror: An Essay on Abjection.* Translated by Leon S. Roudiez. New York: Columbia University Press.

———. (1977) 1985. "Stabat Mater." Translated by Arthur Goldhammer. *Poetics Today* 6, no. 1-2: 133–52.

L'Abbé, Sonnet. 2011. "Infiltrate as Cells: The Biopolitically Ethical Subject of *sybil unrest.*" *Canadian Literature* 210-211 (Autumn/Winter): 169–89, 267.

Lacan, Jacques. 1982. *Feminine Sexuality,* edited by Juliet Mitchell and Jacqueline Rose, translated by Jacqueline Rose. New York: Norton.

Lai, Larissa. 2002. *Salt Fish Girl.* Toronto: Dundurn.

———. 2009. *Automaton Biographies.* Vancouver, BC: Arsenal Pulp.

Lai, Larissa, and Rita Wong. (2008) 2013. *sybil unrest.* Vancouver, BC: New Star Books.

Little, Mark. 2015. "Facts about Landfill and Styrofoam." *Livestrong.com,* October 5. http://www.livestrong.com/article/159954-facts-about-landfill-styrofoam/.

Livingston, Julie, and Jasbir K. Puar. 2011. "Interspecies." *Social Text* 29, no. 1: 3–14.

Maddison, Steve. 2013. "Beyond the Entrepreneurial Voyeur? Sex, Porn, and Cultural Politics." *New Formations* 80–81: 102–18.

Marlatt, Daphne. 1989. "Why?" *HOW(ever)* 5, no. 2.

———. 1990. "Re-Belle at the Writing Table." *HOW(ever)* 6, no. 2.

Marlatt, Daphne, and Betsy Warland. 1988. *Double Negative.* Charlottetown, PEI: Gynergy Books.

Marsh, Nicky. 2007a. *Democracy in Contemporary US Women's Poetry.* New York: Palgrave.

———. 2007b. "Going 'Glocal': The Local and the Global in Recent Experimental Women's Poetry." *Contemporary Women's Writing* 1, no. 1/2: 192–202.

Mas, Susanna. 2015. "Trudeau Lays Out Plan for New Relationship with Indigenous People." *CBC News,* December 8. http://www.cbc.ca/news/politics/justin-trudeau-afn-indigenous-aboriginal-people-1.3354747.

Mathesen, Darcy. 2016. "Vancouver Ranked World's 3rd Most Unaffordable Housing Market." *CTV News Vancouver,* January 26. http://bc.ctvnews.ca/vancouver-ranked-world-s-3rd-most-unaffordable-housing-market-1.2751319.

Mau, Bruce, and the Institute without Boundaries. 2004. *Massive Change*. London: Phaidon.

Mayer, Sophie. 2009a. "Aggregators: RSS (Radically Subversive Syndication Poetics)." *SubStance*, 38, no. 2 (issue 119): 43–62.

———. 2009b. "Review: *sybil unrest* by Larissa Lai and Rita Wong." *Chroma*, January 21. http://chromajournal.blogspot.ca/2009/01/review-sybil-unrest -by-larissa-lai-and.html.

McCaffery, Steve. 1998. "Writing as a General Economy." In *Artifice and Indeterminacy: An Anthology of New Poetics*, edited by Christopher Beach, 201–21. Tuscaloosa: University of Alabama Press.

McCarthy, Jeffrey Mathes. 2009. "'A Choice of Nightmares': The Ecology of *Heart of Darkness*." *MFS: Modern Fiction Studies* 55, no. 3: 620–48.

McRobbie, Angela. 2009. *The Aftermath of Feminism: Gender, Culture and Social Change*. London: Sage.

Miller, Nancy K. 2003. "Reporting the Disaster." In *Trauma at Home: After 9/11*, edited by Judith Greenberg, 39–47. Lincoln: University of Nebraska Press.

Milz, Sabine. 2007. "Canadian Cultural Policy-Making at a Time of Neoliberal Globalization." *ESC: English Studies in Canada* 33, no. 1–2: 85–107.

Mirakove, Carol. 2004. *Occupied*. San Francisco: Kelsey Street.

———. 2006. *Mediated*. New York: Factory School.

Mix, Deborah. 2007. *A Vocabulary of Thinking: Gertrude Stein and Contemporary North American Innovative Women's Writing*. Iowa City: University of Iowa Press.

Mohanty, Chandra Talpade. 2006. "US Empire and the Project of Women's Studies: Stories of Citizenship, Complicity and Dissent." *Gender, Place and Culture* 13, no. 1: 7–20.

Morrison, Yedda. 2003. *Crop*. Berkeley, CA: Kelsey Street.

———. 2008. *Girl Scout Nation*. Chicago: Displaced.

———. 2012a. *Darkness*. Los Angeles: Make Now.

———. 2012b. "This Conceptual Writing Is." In *I'll Drown My Book: Conceptual Writing by Women*, edited by Caroline Bergvall, Laynie Browne, Teresa Carmody, and Vanessa Place, 177–78. Los Angeles: Les Figues.

Morton, Timothy. 2010. *The Ecological Thought*. Cambridge, MA: Harvard University Press.

———. 2012. "An Object-Oriented Defense of Poetry." *New Literary History* 43, no. 2: 205–24.

———. 2013. *Hyperobjects: Philosophy and Ecology at the End of the World*. Minneapolis: University of Minnesota Press.

———. 2014. "The Liminal Space between Things: Epiphany and the Physical." In *Material Ecocriticism*, edited by Serenella Iovino and Serpil Oppermann, 269–77. Bloomington: Indiana University Press.

Mullen, Harryette. 1991. *Trimmings*. New York: Tender Buttons.

———. 1992. *S*PeRM**K*T*. San Diego, CA: Singing Horse.

Ngai, Sianne. 2005. *Ugly Feelings*. Cambridge, MA: Harvard University Press.

O'Keefe, Derrick. 2009. "Harper in Denial at G20: 'Canada Has No History of Colonialism.'" *Rabble*, September 29. http://rabble.ca/blogs/bloggers /derrick/2009/09/harper-denial-g20-canada-has-no-history-colonialism.

Oneofthelibrarians. 2013. "Occupation Libraries: Gezi Parki Edition." The Occupy Wall Street People's Library, June 4. https://peopleslibrary.wordpress .com/2013/06/04/occupation-libraries-gezi-parki-edition/.

Osman, Jena. 1999. *The Character*. Boston: Beacon.

———. 2010. *The Network*. Albany, NY: Fence Books.

———. 2012. *Public Figures*. Middletown, CT: Wesleyan University Press.

———. 2014. *Corporate Relations*. Providence, RI: Burning Deck.

The People's Library. 2011–2015. Occupy Wall Street. https://peopleslibrary .wordpress.com.

Perloff, Marjorie. 1996. *Dance of the Intellect: Studies in the Poetry of the Pound Tradition*. Evanston, IL: Northwestern University Press.

———. 2010. *Unoriginal Genius: Poetry by Other Means in the New Century*. Chicago: University of Chicago Press.

Philip, M. NourbeSe. 2008. *Zong!* Middletown, CT: Wesleyan University Press.

Place, Vanessa, and Robert Fitterman. 2009. *Notes on Conceptualisms*. Berkeley: Ugly Duckling.

Povinelli, Elizabeth. 2006. *The Empire of Love: Toward a Theory of Intimacy, Genealogy, and Carnality*. Durham, NC: Duke University Press.

Power, Nina. 2009. *One Dimensional Woman*. London: Zero Books.

Pratt, Geraldine, and Victoria Rosner. 2012. "Introduction: The Global and the Intimate." In *The Global and the Intimate: Feminism in Our Time*, edited by Geraldine Pratt and Victoria Rosner, 1–27. New York: Columbia University Press.

Pratt, Mary Louise. 1992. *Imperial Eyes: Travel Writing and Transculturation*. New York: Routledge.

Prevallet, Kristin. 2012. "Review of Laura Elrick's *sKincerity*." http://kayvallet .com/?page_id=171.

Rankine, Claudia. 2004. *Don't Let Me Be Lonely: An American Lyric*. Saint Paul, MN: Graywolf.

———. 2014. *Citizen: An American Lyric*. London: Penguin Books.

Reed, Brian. 2011. "In Other Words: Postmillennial Poetry and Redirected Language." *Contemporary Literature* 52, no. 4: 756–90.

———. 2013. *Nobody's Business: Twenty-First Century Avant-Garde Poetics*. Ithaca, NY: Cornell University Press.

Reilly, Evelyn. 2009. *Styrofoam*. New York: Roof Books.

———. 2010. "Eco-Noise and the Flux of Lux." In *)((Eco(Lang) (Uage(Reader))*, edited by Brenda Ijima, 255–74. Brooklyn, NY: Portable Press at Yo-Yo Labs.

Reimer, Nikki. 2010. *[sic]*. Calgary, AB: Frontenac House.

———. 2014. *Downverse*. Vancouver, BC: Talon.

Retallack, Joan. 2003. *The Poethical Wager*. Berkeley: University of California Press.

Robertson, Lisa. 2002. "How Pastoral: A Manifesto." In *Telling It Slant: Avant-Garde Poetics of the 1990s*, 21–26. Tuscaloosa: University of Alabama Press.

Royal Canadian Mounted Police. 2014. "Missing and Murdered Aboriginal Women: A National Operational Overview." *Royal Canadian Mounted Police*. http://www.rcmp-grc.gc.ca/en/missing-and-murdered-aboriginal -women-national-operational-overview.

Sanders, Leslie. 2015. "What the Poet Does for Us." *Topia: Canadian Journal of Cultural Studies* 24: 13–26.

Scappettone, Jennifer. 2007. "Bachelorettes, Even: Strategic Embodiment in Contemporary Experimentalism by Women." *Modern Philology* 105, no. 1: 178–84.

———. 2009a. "Conversation with Al Filreis at the Kelly Writers House." *Pennsound*, April 14. http://writing.upenn.edu/pennsound/x/Scappettone .php.

———. 2009b. *From Dame Quickly*. Brooklyn, NY: Litmus.

Scarry, Elaine. 1985. *The Body in Pain: The Making and Unmaking of the World*. London: Oxford University Press.

Shaw, Kent. 2014. "Review of *Corporate Relations*." *The Rumpus*, October 4. http://therumpus.net/2014/10/corporate-relations-by-jena-osman/.

Sheffield, Rebecca. 2009. "We'd Lose Our Shirt!: How Canadian Cultural Policy Has Shaped the Canadian Literary Canon." *Faculty of Information Quarterly: Housing Memory Conference Proceedings* 1, no. 3: 1–15.

Shiva, Vandana. 1997. *Biopiracy: The Plunder of Nature and Knowledge*. Boston: South End.

Shockley, Evie. 2013. "Is 'Zong!' Conceptual Poetry? Yes It Isn't." *Jacket2*, September 17. http://jacket2.org/article/zong-conceptual-poetry-yes-it-isn't.

Siklosi, Kate. 2017. "Hot and Bothered: Or How I Fell In and Out of Love with Conceptualism." *The Town Crier*, May 9. http://towncrier.puritan-magazine .com/ephemera/poetic-terrorism/.

Simpson, Audra. 2016. "The State Is a Man: Theresa Spence, Loretta Saunders and the Gender of Settler Sovereignty." *Theory & Event* 19, no. 4.

Simpson, Megan. 2000. *Poetic Epistemologies: Gender and Knowing in Women's Language-Oriented Writing*. Abany: State University of New York Press.

Skloot, Rebecca. 2010. *The Immortal Life of Henrietta Lacks*. New York: Broadway Books.

Spahr, Juliana. 2001a. *Everybody's Autonomy: Connective Reading and Collective Identity*. Tuscaloosa: University of Alabama Press.

———. 2001b. *Fuck You – Aloha – I Love You*. Middletown, CT: Wesleyan University Press.

———. 2004. "Poetry in a Time of Crisis." Readings from the Event at UC Santa Cruz. http://viz.ucsc.edu/wp/vizArchive/vizEventPp129-133.pdf.

———. 2005. *This Connection of Everyone with Lungs*. Berkeley: University of California Press.

———. 2007. *The Transformation*. Berkeley, CA: Atelos.

———. 2011. *Well Then There Now*. Boston: Black Sparrow.

———. 2015a. "Politics in a Poem." *Vimeo*, June 23. https://vimeo.com /131520019.

———. 2015b. *That Winter the Wolf Came*. Oakland, CA: Commune Editions.

Spahr, Juliana, and Stephanie Young, eds. 2011. *A Megaphone: Some Enactments, Some Numbers, and Some Essays about the Continued Usefulness of Crotchless Pants and a Machine-Gun Feminism*. Oakland, CA: Chain Links Books.

Spivak, Gayatri Chakravorty. 1987. *In Other Worlds: Essays in Cultural Politics*. New York: Routledge.

Sprinkler, Michael. 1999. *Ghostly Demarcations: A Symposium on Jacques Derrida's "Specters of Marx."* London: Verso.

Stewart, Kathleen. 2007. *Ordinary Affects*. Durham, NC: Duke University Press.

Strang, Catriona. 2009. "Interview." In *Prismatic Publics: Innovative Canadian Women's Poetry and Poetics*, edited by Kate Eichhorn and Heather Milne, 268–77. Toronto: Coach House.

Tasker, John Paul. 2016. "Confusion Reigns over Number of Missing, Murdered Indigenous Women." CBC News. February 17. http://www.cbc.ca/news /politics/mmiw-4000-hajdu-1.3450237.

Vickery, Ann. 2000. *Leaving Lines of Gender: A Feminist Genealogy of Language Writing*. Hanover, NH: Wesleyan University Press.

———. 2002. "Editor's Notes on How2/7." *How2* 1, no. 7.

Wald, Priscilla. 2012. "Cells, Genes, and Stories: HeLa's Journey from Labs to Literature." In *Genetics and the Unsettled Past: The Collision of DNA, Race and History*, edited by Catherine Lee, Alondra Nelson, and Keith Wailoo, 247–65. New Jersey: Rutgers University Press.

Williams, Tyrone. 2008. "Review of *The Anatomy of Oil* by Marcella Durand." *Galatea Resurrects (A Poetry Engagement)* 10. http://galatearesurrection10 .blogspot.ca/2008/07/anatomy-of-oil-by-marcella-durand.html.

Wong, Rita. 1999. *monkeypuzzle*. Vancouver, BC: Press Gang.

———. 2007. *forage*. Gibsons, BC: Nightwood Editions.

———. 2009. "Interview." In *Prismatic Publics: Innovative Canadian Women's Poetry and Poetics*, edited by Kate Eichhorn and Heather Milne, 344–53. Toronto: Coach House.

———. 2015. *undercurrent*. Vancouver, BC: Nightwood Editions.

Wunker, Erin. 2013. "Reflections on Risk and 'Running with the Pack.'" *CWILA: Canadian Women in the Literary Arts*, December 16. http://cwila .com/reflections-on-risk-and-running-with-the-pack/.

Young, Iris Marion. 1989. "Polity and Group Difference: A Critique of the Ideal of Universal Citizenship." *Ethics* 99, no. 2: 250–74.

Youth For Christ. 2017. "Home." http://yfcwinnipeg.com.

Žižek, Slavoj. 2009. "Troubles with the Real: Lacan as a Viewer of Alien." *Lacan.com.* http://www.lacan.com/essays/?p=180.

Zolf, Rachel. 2007. *Human Resources*. Toronto: Coach House.

———. 2009. "Interview." In *Prismatic Publics: Innovative Canadian Women's Poetry and Poetics*, edited by Kate Eichhorn, 186–96. Toronto: Coach House.

———. 2010. *Neighbour Procedure*. Toronto: Coach House.

———. 2012. "untitled note." In *I'll Drown My Book: Conceptual Writing by Women*, edited by Caroline Bergvall, Laynie Browne, Teresa Carmody, and Vanessa Place, 440. Los Angeles: Les Figues.

———. 2014. *Janey's Arcadia*. Toronto: Coach House.

———. 2015. PennSound Centre for Programs in Contemporary Writing. http://writing.upenn.edu/pennsound/x/Zolf.php.

———. 2016. "Avant Canada Talk." In *Avant Canada: On the Canadian Avant Garde*, edited by Gregory Betts and Katie Price. https://media.sas.upenn.edu /app/public/watch.php?file_id=202724.

INDEX

Abel, Jordan, 243n3, 249n1, 254n1
abjection, 77
Achebe, Chinua, 106
Acker, Kathy, 206–07
affect: and critique of geopolitics,
   31, 153, 158–60, 161, 175–76, 187,
   195; in *Don't Let Me Be Lonely*
   (Rankine), 175–84; in *Inventory*
   (Brand), 185–89, 192, 193; and
   poetry, 2, 29, 30, 237, 239, 251n6;
   and technology, 48–50, 153; in
   This Connection of Everyone
   With Lungs (Spahr), 162, 163,
   165, 166, 169, 173; in *What Stirs*
   (Christakos), 47–60. *See also* affect
   alien; affect theory; disgust
affect alien, 177, 178, 180, 183
affect theory: and feminist poetics, 2,
   10, 12, 29, 31, 35, 91, 155, 157–60,
   195; and 9/11, 155–57. *See also*
   affect
agency: body as site of, 68–70, 76; and
   matter, 38, 94, 95; and nonhuman
   actants, 97, 98, 101–04, 106, 107,
   110, 111, 126, 129, 145; and poetry,
   239, 240. *See also* nonhuman
   agency
agential realism, 94, 97, 102, 103
Ahmed, Sara: on affect and emotion,
   10, 31, 79, 81, 156, 175, 177–78,
   188, 194–95; on new materialisms,
   248n1; on phenomenology, 163; on
   skin, 172
Alaimo, Stacy, 10, 93, 95, 100, 121,
   125, 129, 134, 250n1. *See also*
   trans-corporeality

Alcalá, Rosa, 244n10
"The Anatomy of Oil" (Durand): and
   anthropomorphism, 115, 120; and
   ecopoetics, 7, 30, 99, 100, 111–20;
   and limitations of human frames of
   reference, 113–14, 117–18; and the
   posthuman, 118–19, 120
Andrews, Bruce, 25, 78, 84
anthropocentrism, 94, 95, 110, 120.
   See also non-anthropocentrism
anthropomorphism, 99, 104, 115
anti-absorptive writing, 78, 85, 246n3
anti-austerity protests, 5
antiwar poetry, 3, 6, 31, 153, 157–60,
   195, 250n1. *See also* protest poetry
Anzaldua, Gloria, 244n10
Arab Spring, 3, 230
Ashton, Jennifer, 33
At the Full and Change of the Moon
   (Brand), 251n7
Athanasiou, Athena, 2
Aufgabe, 27
Automaton Biographies (Lai), 61

Barad, Karen, 10, 94, 95, 96, 97, 102–
   03, 110. *See also* agential realism
Basile, Elena, 18, 19, 24, 244n9
Bataille, Georges, 89
Belladonna*, 26–27. *See also* Levit-
   sky, Rachel
Benka, Jen, 31, 32, 153, 196–200,
   230–34, 235. See also *Box of Long-
   ing with Fifty Drawers*
Bennett, Jane, 10, 94–95, 101, 104,
   110, 115, 126, 128, 248n2. *See also*
   vital materialism

Mezei, Kathy, 18, 244n11
military invasion and occupation
   of Afghanistan and Iraq, 11, 153,
   249n7; poetic engagements with,
   3, 6, 31, 47, 60, 111, 119, 155–60,
   250n1; in *This Connection of
   Everyone with Lungs* (Spahr),
   160–74; in *Inventory* (Brand),
   185–95
MillAr, Jay, 27. *See also* BookThug;
   Toronto New School of Writing
mimicry: as feminist tactic, 86–87
Mirakove, Carol, 32, 232
missing and murdered Indigenous
   women in Canada, 7, 31, 197, 201,
   202–03, 210; and government
   inquiry into, 202–03, 252n2; in
   Janey's Arcadia (Zolf), 202, 209–11
Mix, Deborah, 16, 63, 247n5
Mohanty, Chandra Talpade, 9
Mongrel Coalition Against Gringpo, 8
Monkeypuzzle (Wong), 61
Morrison, Yedda, 7, 9, 30, 99, 101–11,
   151. See also *Darkness*
Morton, Timothy, 65, 219; on ecologi-
   cal thought, 139; on hyperobjects,
   136–37, 144, 145; on the mate-
   riality of poetry, 98, 151; on the
   strange stranger, 128. *See also*
   ecological thought; hyperobjects
Moure, Erín, 13, 19, 32
Mullen, Harryette, 9, 13, 63, 243n3
Murakami, Sachiko, 32
Murphy, Emily, 206, 211

Nathanaël, 32
nation: as agent of violence, 153–54,
   158–59, 196–200, 234; as site of
   destabilization and target of cri-
   tique in poetry, 28, 31–32, 153–54,
   158–59, 196–234

nationalism, 28, 62, 70, 153, 175, 183,
   196, 198, 233, 237, 240
Neighbour Procedure (Zolf), 82, 201
Neimanis, Astrida, 123, 124
neoliberalism, 2, 3, 9, 176, 182,
   193, 222–23, 238, 246n2; and art,
   199–200; and decline of democracy,
   182, 254n11; and depression, 156,
   180; and feminism, 10, 12, 33–36;
   in feminist poetics, 2, 12, 29, 30,
   48–59, 60–70, 71–73, 75, 77–78,
   90–91; and history, 199–200; and
   individualism, 227; and poetry, 11,
   28, 162; and technology, 48–60
Network (Osman), 217
new materialisms, 10, 93–100; and
   ecopoetics, 93, 97–99, 120; and
   feminism, 100; and feminist poetics,
   2. *See also* agential realism; matter;
   posthuman; trans-corporeality;
   vital materialism
New Poetics Colloquium, 25
news media, 47, 157–58, 159, 160,
   165, 167, 168, 188, 192, 193, 196
Ngai, Sianne, 12–13, 73–74, 77, 78,
   82, 84–85
No Language is Neutral (Brand),
   251n7
non-anthropocentrism, 94, 96
nonhuman agency, 101, 102, 145. *See
   also* agential realism
*Notes Toward a Performative Theory
   of Assembly* (Butler), 197, 227–28,
   231
Nowak, Mark, 243n3
"Numbers Trouble" (Spahr and
   Young), 15

Occupy Wall Street, 3, 4, 227, 228,
   230, 231; and human microphone,
   227, 254n13; and lending libraries,

queerness, queer identity, 9, 10, 30, 240
Queyras, Sina, 32

Raddle Moon, 24
Rankine, Claudia, 29, 31, 153, 157, 158, 159, 174–85, 195, 251n5. See also *Don't Let Me Be Lonely*
rawlings, a., 32
redirected language, 6. *See also* found text
Reed, Brian, 6, 85
Reilly, Evelyn, 7, 30, 100, 111, 120, 121, 133–50, 151, 250n1. See also *Styrofoam*
Reimer, Nikki, 30, 35, 71–81, 90, 91. See also *[sic]*
residential schools, 206, 211, 214, 215, 252n3
Retallack, Joan, 9, 96, 234
Rhodes, Shane, 243n3
Rich, Adrienne, 14
"Rime of the Ancient Mariner" (Coleridge), 138–39, 250n1
Robertson, Lisa, 32, 245n15; and pastoral poetry, 99, 116, 201
Rodriguez, Marnie Salupo, 2
Rosner, Geraldine, 31, 63, 166, 168, 171, 186

Salah, Trish, 32, 243n4
Salt Fish Girl (Lai), 61
Samprisi, Jenny, 27
Sanders, Leslie, 186, 187, 252n8
Scalapino, Leslie, 13
Scappettone, Jennifer, 30, 33–34, 37–47, 91. See also *From Dame Quickly*
Scarry, Elaine, 143
Scott, Gail, 18, 19, 25, 27
September 11, 2001, 10, 11, 190–91,

237; and deployment of nationalism, 175–76, 183; in *Don't Let Me Be Lonely* (Rankine), 179, 182–84; in *Inventory* (Brand), 190–91; poetic responses to, 28, 31; in *This Connection of Everyone With Lungs* (Spahr), 155–59, 160–65
settler colonialism: in *Janey's Arcadia* (Zolf), 12, 29, 82, 200, 202, 211, 212, 216
sexuality, 60, 69; and capitalism, 36, 60–63, 68–70, 71–81; and queerness, 62; and race, 68–70
Shakespeare, William: and Dame Quickly, 38–41, 46; and "Henry IV," 38
Shaw, Kent, 220–21
Shaw, Nancy, 32, 245n15
Shiva, Vandana, 66
Shockley, Evie, 243n2
[sic] (Reimer), 30, 35, 71–81, 91; the body and sexuality in, 71–72, 74–80; and disgust, 77–80, 90, 91; and feminism, 71–81; and neoliberalism, 71–81
Siklosi, Kate, 243n3
Silliman, Ron, 25
Simpson, Audra, 210, 213
Simpson, Megan, 8, 11, 16, 35
slavery, 28, 198, 232
Smith, Carmen Giménez, 244n10
Spahr, Juliana, 4, 5, 6, 12, 31, 153, 157, 160–74, 191, 192, 195, 235; and "Foulipo," 44–45; and "Numbers Trouble," 15; and "Tell U.S. Feminists," 27. See also *This Connection of Everyone With Lungs*
Spence, Teresa, 213, 253n7
Spinoza, Baruch, 156
Spivak, Gayatri Chakravorty, 245n1
Stacey, Jackie, 172

United States Constitution (*continued*)
31, 197, 198, 217, 219, 220, 221,
227, 234, 235. *See also* democracy

Vallejo, César, 181
Vickery, Ann, 14, 16, 21, 28, 25, 155,
243n5, 245n15
Vicuña, Cecilia, 9
VIDA: Women in Literary Arts, 16,
243n6
vital materialism, 95, 248n2

Wald, Priscilla, 148, 149
Walker, Alice, 14
Warland, Betsy, 13, 19, 21, 247n5
water: in *undercurrent* (Wong), 100,
121, 122–33
Watten, Barrett, 25
"we the people," 197, 227–28, 230–32.
See also United States Constitution
Well Then There Now (Spahr), 251n4
What Stirs (Christakos), 6, 30, 34,
47–60, 91; and attachment, 48–57;
and breast-feeding latch as meta-
phor, 48–49, 50–52; and commu-
nicative capitalism, 49–60; and the
maternal, 48–60, 246n1
What We All Long For (Brand),
251n7

What Women Say of the Northwest,
206, 208–09
Williams, William Carlos, 80, 98
Wipe Under a Love (Christakos),
261n1
witness. *See* mediatized witness;
poetry of witness
Wittig, Monique, 87–88
Women and Words Conference, 18,
25
Wong, Rita, 4, 7, 9, 30, 34, 35,
60–70, 91, 92, 100, 111, 120, 121,
122–33, 151. See also *sibyl unrest;
undercurrent*
Wunker, Erin, 244n8

Young, Iris Marion, 199
Young, Stephanie: and "Foulipo,"
44–45; and "Numbers Trouble," 15;
and "Tell U.S. Feminists," 27

Žižek, Slavoj, 146
Zolf, Rachel, 6, 7, 8, 9, 12, 29, 30,
31, 35, 80, 81–91, 153, 196–200,
200–16, 235, 243n3, 252n1. See also
Human Resources; Janey's Arcadia
Zong! (Philip), 243nn2–3